RELIGIOUS FREEDOM IN AN EGALITARIAN AGE

RELIGIOUS FREEDOM IN AN EGALITARIAN AGE

Nelson Tebbe

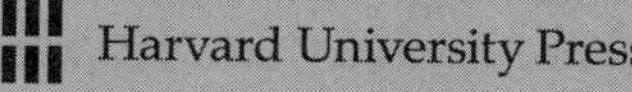

Cambridge, Massachusetts
London, England
2017

Printed in the United States of America

First printing

Library of Congress Cataloging-in-Publication Data

Names: Tebbe, Nelson, author.

Title: Religious freedom in an egalitarian age / Nelson Tebbe.

Description: Cambridge, Massachusetts : Harvard University Press, 2017. | Includes bibliographical references and index.

Identifiers: LCCN 2016013961 | ISBN 9780674971431 (alk. paper)

Subjects: LCSH: Freedom of religion—United States. | Equality before the law—United States. | Discrimination—Law and legislation—United States. | Discrimination—Religious aspects. | Civil rights—United States. | Civil rights—Religious aspects. | Sexual minorities—Civil rights—Religious aspects. | Law—Methodology.

Classification: LCC KF4783 .T43 2017 | DDC 342.7308/52—dc23

LC record available at https://lccn.loc.gov/2016013961

For Diana

CONTENTS

PREFACE

For extraordinary generosity in reading the manuscript and offering thoughtful advice, I am grateful to Carlos Ball, Corey Brettschneider, Alan Brownstein, Mary Anne Case, James Childress, Marc DeGirolami, Chad Flanders, Katherine Franke, Kent Greenawalt, Abner Greene, Jeremy Kessler, Andrew Koppelman, Cécile Laborde, Kara Loewentheil, Stephen Macedo, Patricia Marino, Charles Mathewes, Mark Movsesian, James Nelson, Elizabeth Platt, Lawrence Sager, Richard Schragger, Micah Schwartzman, Elizabeth Sepper, Steven Shiffrin, and two anonymous reviewers. Extraordinarily valuable research assistance was provided by Steven Bovino, Alex Goldman, John Moore, and Alana Siegel. The work also benefited from workshops at the Annual Law and Religion Roundtable, the American Association of Law Schools' Section on Sexual Orientation and Gender Identity Issues, Brigham Young University School of Law, Brooklyn Law School, Cornell Law School, Saint John's University School of Law, Temple University Beasley School of Law, University of Detroit Mercy School of Law (McElroy Lecture on Law and Religion), University of Texas School of Law, University of Virginia School of Law, and Washington University in Saint Louis School of Law. Generous financial support came from Cornell Law School and the Dean's Summer Research Program at Brooklyn Law School.

Although all the writing is new, and although many of the arguments have been revisited, the first two chapters further explore themes discussed in "Religion and Social Coherentism," *Notre Dame Law Review* 91 (2015): 363–403. Chapter 3 is indebted to various pieces written with

Richard Schragger and Micah Schwartzman, including "When Do Religious Accommodations Burden Others?," in *The Conscience Wars: Rethinking the Balance between Religion, Identity, and Equality*, edited by Susanna Mancini and Michel Rosenfeld (Cambridge: Cambridge University Press, forthcoming), and "How Much May Religious Accommodations Burden Others?," in *Law, Religion, and Health in the United States*, edited by Elizabeth Sepper, Holly Fernandez Lynch, and I. Glenn Cohen (Cambridge: Cambridge University Press, forthcoming). Chapter 6 builds on "Government Nonendorsement," *Minnesota Law Review* 98 (2013): 648–712, and Chapter 10 owes some of its ideas to "Excluding Religion," *University of Pennsylvania Law Review* 156 (2008): 1263–1339.

Finally, I would like to offer warm thanks to my editor, Thomas LeBien, for his wisdom, vision, and unfailing patience.

RELIGIOUS FREEDOM IN AN EGALITARIAN AGE

INTRODUCTION

MANY AMERICANS sense that they are living through a period of intense conflict between religious freedom and equality law. On the one hand, people see that a widening variety of individuals require protection from discrimination if they are to enjoy full and equal citizenship and, on the other hand, Americans share a basic and long-standing commitment to religious freedom, including for those who dissent from aspects of egalitarianism. How should conflicts between these two values be resolved, as a matter of law? That is the question that this book sets out to answer.

Complex factors are contributing to the perception of conflict between religious freedom and equality law today but, among these, two are prominent. First, there is the social and political mobilization by lesbian, gay, bisexual, transgender, queer, and gender-fluid citizens—what is commonly known as the movement for LGBT rights. Over a relatively short period of time, LGBT advocates have seen significant successes. A signal moment came when the Supreme Court guaranteed marriage equality in *Obergefell v. Hodges*.[1]

Although the campaign for LGBT rights is ongoing—the federal government and about half the states still do not provide comprehensive civil rights protections, for instance—its achievements to date have affected the relationship between the government and those who adhere to certain traditional theologies on questions of sexuality. Expansion of equality law has contributed to a sense among some religious traditionalists that there has been an inversion. They feel they now are the minorities who require protection from an overweening liberal orthodoxy.

A second factor has been the Obama administration's policy making in the area of women's equality, including rights to reproductive freedom and adequate health care. Although tension between feminism and religious traditionalism is nothing new, it is thought to have entered a distinct phase. The Patient Protection and Affordable Care Act, more commonly known as Obamacare or the ACA, implemented a number of reforms in these areas. Although many of the changes had precursors in state law, their enactment as federal law has been significant. For example, the ACA empowered the administration to implement what came to be known as the contraception mandate. That provision requires employers who provide health plans for their employees to include coverage for female contraception at no additional cost to workers. A conflict between the contraception mandate and religious employers led to the Supreme Court's landmark decision *Burwell v. Hobby Lobby Stores, Inc.* And federal courts currently are considering a second major case concerning the contraception mandate.[2]

So struggles between religious traditionalists and egalitarians have become salient for reasons that are plural and intricate. Whatever the explanations, however, the fact of heightened visibility is widely appreciated. So is the debate's intense rhetoric. Political progressives have decried the campaign by religious actors to win a "right to discriminate," while conservatives have warned that the contemporary conflict could mean not just lessened protection for observance but "the end of religious freedom" itself.[3]

Consider two concrete examples. Vanessa Willock and Misti Collinsworth fell in love and decided to commit themselves to each other for life. They began to plan a ceremony. In the course of arranging the event, Willock e-mailed Elane Photography, a local wedding vendor, to ask about pricing and availability. Elaine Huguenin, an owner of the business and its lead photographer, responded that the company only served "traditional weddings" for religious reasons. After verifying that the company was refusing to serve them because they were both women, Willock and Collinsworth then brought a civil rights lawsuit. Like many other states, New Mexico prohibited discrimination in public accommodations, which included businesses held open to the public such as Huguenin's photography studio. Unlike many other states, however, New Mexico prohibited those accommodations from discriminating on the basis of LGBT status, in addition to characteristics such as race, religion, sex, and national origin. In response, Elane Photography argued that it was protected by laws guaranteeing freedom of religion and speech. The New Mexico Supreme Court ruled for the couple, but its decision remains controversial.[4]

Or think of Kim Davis, the Rowan County clerk in Kentucky. After the Supreme Court handed down *Obergefell,* Davis prohibited her office from issuing any marriage licenses, citing her religious opposition to marriage for same-sex couples. Several couples brought suit. Initially, Davis remained defiant and was briefly jailed by a federal judge. Eventually, however, she relented and allowed her deputies to issue the licenses, but only after they took steps to safeguard her religious convictions. Davis allegedly ordered them to remove any reference to her name or her office, she instructed them to include a disclaimer that the license was being issued by order of a federal court, and she told them to sign the licenses in their capacities as notaries rather than deputy clerks.[5]

Those cases, *Elane Photography v. Willock* and *Miller v. Davis,* are just two of many that have emerged. Although each implicates a different area of civil rights doctrine, they all pit religious freedom against equality law in some general sense:

- The Little Sisters of the Poor is an order of Roman Catholic nuns that provides care for the elderly. It offers health insurance for its workers, but it excludes coverage for contraception, abortifacients, and sterilization—all of which are prohibited by its theology. The government exempts religious nonprofits from the contraception mandate, and it arranges for their employees to receive coverage another way. That accommodation becomes effective once the employer notifies the government or the insurer. But the sisters argue that even submitting the form makes them complicit in their employees' violation of church teaching. After losing in a lower court, Sister Loraine Marie Maguire said, "We simply cannot choose between our care for the elderly poor and our faith. . . . All we ask is to be able to continue our religious vocation free from government intrusion." In 2016, the Supreme Court remanded the case, *Zubik v. Burwell,* sending it back to lower courts for additional proceedings. Presumably, it will be back in the Supreme Court before too long.[6]
- Indiana and Arkansas proposed laws that strengthened religious freedom protections. After an outcry that focused on the relationship between the laws and the impending *Obergefell* decision, Indiana made its provision inapplicable to most civil rights protections, while Arkansas scaled back its statute's language to match federal law.[7]
- A church-run primary school, Hosanna-Tabor Academy, fired a teacher after she complained to the government that she had been

disadvantaged at work because of a disability. The Supreme Court ruled in favor of the school, reasoning that it was protected by the Constitution from employment discrimination laws because the teacher was a minister. Now, Roman Catholic schools in San Francisco are invoking that precedent to defend a new policy that prohibits teachers from taking public positions against church doctrine. Apparently, teachers were supporting marriage equality on Facebook.[8]

- Also in California, a state-run law school required that groups be open to all students in order to be recognized as student organizations. The Christian Legal Society (CLS) could not comply with the policy because of its policy on sexual morality, which effectively excluded most LGBT students. The Supreme Court ruled that the school could decline to support speech that contravened its antidiscrimination policies.[9]

Consider the range of issues that these examples implicate: health law, employment discrimination, public accommodations, university policies, and public funding, among others. Nondiscrimination law seeks to protect against discrimination not just on the basis of sexual orientation and sex or gender but increasingly on the basis of gender identity as well. And its equality protections are pitted against both religious freedom and free speech—rights that are guaranteed not only in federal and state constitutions, but in statutes and administrative rules as well. Moreover, litigants involved in these cases can be as diverse as wedding vendors, restaurants, landlords, retail corporations, hospitals, schools, social service agencies, student groups, and public officials. So the issues facing lawyers and lawmakers are staggeringly diverse. What they share, again, is the tension between religious freedom and equality law. This book takes the entire subject as its topic, though it focuses on the questions that are most visible—particularly those concerning LGBT rights and women's equality, including the related right to reproductive freedom.

It is important not to oversimplify the perceived face-off between religious freedom and equality law. Many religious traditions place commitments of nondiscrimination at or near the center of their faith. Conversely, civil rights law safeguards believers alongside members of other protected groups. And it is no longer clear that constitutional law should treat religious belief as special, as compared to nonreligious beliefs or nonbelief. Doubt about the specialness of religion, a theme that runs through this book, raises another set of complications. A final caveat is that today's face-off is not entirely new; it reprises some but not all aspects of earlier conflicts, particularly concerning racial justice and women's equality. Yet despite these intricacies, it is impossible to miss the felt tension that characterizes this particular moment in the history of both religious freedom and civil rights protections.

How should we respond? Several of the situations mentioned above—and analyzed in the pages that follow—present genuinely difficult questions of constitutional law and political morality. Simple reactions, which have been all too common in media commentary among both progressives and conservatives, are often unsatisfying and inaccurate. A careful approach is needed, even if it stands scant chance of winning a consensus. Only a proposal that appreciates the power of arguments on both sides can provide a stable, defensible foundation for the future of both free exercise and antidiscrimination law.

Despite that difficulty, these questions of religion and equality law *can* be answered. Matters are not so complex that considerations of law and political morality cannot generate solutions that are defensible. Interests and ideologies will shape arguments, but not in ways that make the arguments irrelevant. And getting it right matters, not only because the disputes themselves are consequential but also because the solutions that are found during this period will form precedents that shape law and policy into the future. So we should insist *both* that current conflicts between religious freedom and equality law are intricate *and* that they are not intractable. Justified solutions can and must be found. That is important for the particular groups involved on both sides, and for everyone who shares an interest in the sustained health and vibrancy of American constitutionalism.

Skepticism

If that seems obvious or anodyne, consider that the very possibility of crafting solutions is being questioned at the moment by serious thinkers. Skeptics have been arguing not only that the jurisprudence on religious freedom is messy—a cliché among experts on the subject—but further that the law is *inherently* or *necessarily* patternless. These thinkers believe that deep forces within modern constitutionalism frustrate attempts to rationalize the First Amendment's religion provisions. And the skeptics have gained attention, at least among specialists.[10]

Notably, skeptics can be found across the political spectrum. Some scholars on the left argue that the category of religion is so difficult to define that it makes defending religious freedom virtually impossible. They draw on critical work in law, social science, and the humanities, and they are widely respected. It is fair to say, however, that the skeptical arguments that are having the most influence today are coming from political conservatives—meaning, in this context, people who generally support a greater role for religion in government policy making and greater protection for religion from government action. Generalizations are dangerous here, as elsewhere, but it is perhaps not completely inaccurate to say that skeptical arguments by religious traditionalists are the ones that are gaining greatest traction. And for good reason: their arguments have power.[11]

Some skeptics suggest further that the only satisfying justifications for religious freedom are themselves religious—that protecting free exercise only makes sense on theological grounds. When modern democracy separated itself from religious justifications, according to one historical narrative, it lost the ability to offer a cogent defense of either free exercise or the separation of church and state. And yet impulses from that earlier era persist in the form of durable doctrines, such as the notion that congregations should be able to choose their clergy without interference from the state, to take just one example. As a consequence of this tension, among others, legal decisions necessarily will devolve into conclusory thinking, irrationality, or ipsedixitism.[12]

Yet their conclusion is not usually that we should restore theological justifications for lawmaking. Instead, they think judges and lawmakers should continue to muddle through, seeking modus vivendi solutions without any hope of principled results. That may seem like capitulating to the status quo. But it sometimes has another possible component—a ramification for government design. On this account, because constitutional decision making on these matters is inherently unprincipled, it should be kept out of court. Decisions on such questions should be made instead by legislators or executive branch officials, who are better designed to generate outcomes under conditions of moral uncertainty and political struggle. Messiness is thought to be tolerable in those institutions because lawmakers are accountable to the voters in a way that judges are not. Therefore, questions about religious freedom and antidiscrimination law should be made outside of courts.[13]

Denying the possibility of principled decision making on questions of religious freedom may have a different and more profound practical implication as well. It may incline people to believe that constitutional arguments cannot be made in *any* forum. Not only judges but lawmakers and other officials should stop pretending that religious freedom disputes can be resolved in a manner that can be justified. Therefore, they should refrain from speaking in terms of constitutional principle at all.[14]

Of course, skeptics do not have controlling influence over such policies. Moreover, they are not the only ones seeking to keep religious freedom cases away from judges or even outside constitutional law; nonskeptics are pressing for those changes, too. (And some skeptics are not asking for them.) But the skeptics add a different and important argument. And the Supreme Court seems to be receptive to some mix of these concerns: it has made several changes that work to keep religious freedom cases out of court.[15]

Admittedly, skeptics on religious freedom jurisprudence have a point. Current law *is* complex and often contradictory. And no one has identified a single tenet or rubric that is capable of organizing all of First Amendment law. Instead, the doctrine is driven by multiple commitments. Perhaps for that reason, the law seems immune to systematization or meaningful simplification. Perhaps another consequence is that disagreement among constitutional actors is widespread. Critique of that situation can have force.[16]

And so far, there has been no satisfying response to the skeptics. Leading figures have responded only that at a certain point reasons run out; decisions can only be based on an intuitive sense that the arguments supporting one result seem stronger than the arguments supporting the alternative. Especially vulnerable to skeptical argument are pluralists, meaning those who embrace the idea that multiple values are needed to account for correct judgments across the entire range of religious freedom cases. Pluralists are right about that, but they then must face the criticism that reasons cannot be given for their ultimate choices in hard cases.[17]

A striking feature of this debate is that, actually, skeptics and pluralists have remarkably similar ways of working on ground-level conflicts. Members of both camps evaluate competing considerations; both incorporate arguments of principle and pragmatics; and both recommend outcomes based on all-things-considered judgments without pretending that theirs is the only reasonable position (except in easy cases). What separates them is their evaluation of this method: skeptics find it devoid of rationality, and necessarily so, whereas pluralists are more sanguine. Without a more satisfying methodology, however, their optimism could be seen as misplaced.[18]

Social Coherence

Skepticism is not the only available response to the current conflagration—and it should not be seen as the most attractive one. This book describes and defends an alternative method for thinking about religious freedom and civil rights. *Social coherence* provides a way of working through these problems that is capable of generating reasoned conclusions. Judgments can be reached without arbitrariness using the coherence method, whether by courts or by policy makers sitting in legislatures or executive branch offices. The approach therefore offers a convincing response to religious-freedom skeptics.

Social coherence has another benefit, however. It describes a method that is simply *useful* for thinking through new questions of law and political morality, including questions about the relationship between religion and equality. This second goal is constructive, rather than defensive, and it is independent of the first. The coherence approach is not only sound, in other words, but also handy. Notably, it does not pretend to determine unique answers to pressing substantive questions of religious freedom that are dividing the political community. But it does provide a manner of analyzing them that is clarifying. It therefore structures discussions throughout the chapters that follow.

So when this book asks its basic question—How should we respond to conflicts between religious freedom and equality law?—it suggests two ways to think about the answer. First, a method is needed for discussing complicated questions of constitutional law, about which there are strong convictions on both sides, in a reasoned way. Second, it is important to know how particular legal issues should be resolved. So there is a methodological component to the question, and there is a substantive component. The chapters that follow will speak to both.

How does the method work? Begin with the way that people reason through moral problems in everyday life. When people confront a new scenario, they compare it to familiar situations and to conclusions they have drawn about them after careful consideration. These could be judgments about concrete scenarios, in which case people will argue from them by making analogies (or by drawing distinctions). Or they could be principles, meaning tenets that they have abstracted from particular conflicts, in which case they will apply them to the new situation. Either way, they are likely to rely on commitments that they have come to trust.

Reflecting on the problem at hand, people then try to find a resolution that fits together with their existing judgments (about concrete cases) and principles (that abstract from them). Working back and forth, they test out solutions, looking for harmony. Nothing is foundational, in principle; even long-standing convictions can be revised in light of new evidence or new thinking. Yet when people come to a conclusion that resonates with their other judgments, they can claim that the solution is warranted—that is, backed by reasons. They may even be able to claim that the conclusion is demanded or determined by those reasons. Nothing more is needed to show that an outcome is not ad hoc or conclusory. Others may disagree with the conclusions they reach, but the mere fact of disagreement should not lead to skepticism.

Although the method owes much to liberal political theory, it does not require adherence to the thinking of John Rawls or any other thinker. Conceivably, it could be compared with certain forms of moral pragmatism and even some critical theory. That is because the approach is thin and ecumenical—it claims only as much as necessary to defend the possibility of moral reasoning on questions of constitutional significance.[19]

As much as any particular political theory, the coherence approach resembles common-law adjudication. Lawyers and judges argue over the correct interpretation and application of legal doctrines by reference to established precedents and principles, using something like a more formal and institutionalized version of the coherence method. Not surprisingly, then, the relevance of coherence approaches for legal thinking is widely recognized. And that resemblance bolsters the attractiveness of the methodology as an account of how justification works in law.[20]

(Incidentally, it is assumed here that normative thinking plays a role in legal interpretation. Interpreting ambiguous provisions involves considering how they *should* be understood. That is not something that can be established within the boundaries of this project, but it is amply defended in the legal literature. The point here is just that such reasoning can be justified.[21])

Even though the search for coherence resembles a certain kind of legal reasoning, however, it does not depend on a clean distinction between law and politics. On the contrary, it embraces the reality that our legal reasoning is shot through with political and social dynamics. This is the *social* aspect of the approach. Whether people realize it or not, they are influenced by movements and mobilizations that provide paradigm cases, that suggest principles, and that influence their judgments about how those principles apply to new problems. Interpreters also inevitably reason from the perspective of their own social location. But little about the inevitability of interests or ideologies means that the process of thinking through to a conclusion is completely unreasoned. It just tends to be *incompletely* reasoned. And in fact, the method is designed to stimulate interrogation of the unarticulated impulses that often accompany social interest and political identification. That is close to its main point. The critique of oneself and others matters, even if it will always remain unfinished.

To clarify, the inclusion of a social dimension does not mean that constitutional actors must deliberately take account of historical context. Instead, this aspect of the account just acknowledges an inevitable feature of our legal reasoning. And it insists that this inevitability is not a reason for skepticism. Social coherence therefore provides a complete and nuanced defense of constitutional argument on these matters.

It is important to recognize, too, that some people defend broad conceptions of free exercise *without* skepticism. And social coherence itself is not designed to answer them; only substantive arguments can support particular solutions against substantive opposition.

So, again, the book has two discrete goals, each of which aims to fill a worrisome gap in our understanding of religious freedom and antidiscrimination law. First, it offers an alternative to skepticism—a technique for resolving conflicts in a fashion that is rationally justifiable. That alone is important for the health of constitutional discourse at a moment when political bifurcation threatens to make reasonable debate impotent or even impossible. Nothing about the project promises agreement, however. On the contrary, it insists that disagreement, both reasonable and unreasonable, is a fixed feature of constitutional politics. But it does insist that warranted positions are attainable on questions of religious freedom, as elsewhere.

Second, the book provides a substantive vision of how conflicts between traditional believers and egalitarians ought to be resolved. It offers a set of principles to guide our understanding of the place of religious freedom in an age of expanding equality guarantees. It then applies those principles and makes concrete recommendations in the areas of legal contestation that are likely to express the conflict between religion and equality in the future. More about those proposals in a moment.

For now, the point is just that this book will succeed in its second objective if it can convince decision makers to adopt its solutions to conflicts between religious freedom and civil rights law. But it will succeed in its first objective if it can encourage antagonists to have the conversation itself, and to do so by offering explanations, without relying on raw power contests—or at least without relying on them alone. Arguments can also make a difference, however overdetermined they might be. Here it resists writers who believe that moral reasoning is useless in resolving legal disputes.[22]

Another tension runs throughout the account as well. On the one hand, the discussion comes at questions of law and politics from a particular perspective. No full response currently exists to scholarly arguments for broad religion exemptions in this historical moment. The chapters here seek to provide that account, and they do that from a viewpoint. That the book is argued from a particular perspective is inevitable and not something to regret.

On the other hand, however, the argument carries authority independent of any view of American law and politics. This commitment cannot be compromised. Points of wide agreement provide the starting places for the discussion, which builds on them using recognized techniques of interpretive argument. Conclusions drawn in this manner carry authority for all lawyers and lawmakers, and they must be confronted on their own terms.

Again, social coherence claims as a central virtue that it forces interpreters to interrogate their unreflective impulses, asking whether their assumptions really fit together with fixed points of legal and moral authority, including constitutional text, history, structure, and precedent. That the book regularly generates outcomes that will surprise progressives is some evidence of integrity in that endeavor. More evidence will follow if those outcomes can be defended using reasons that its critics will recognize as persuasive, even if they are not ultimately persuaded.

Throughout, the focus is on law. Other disciplines will be important, especially political theory and the academic study of religion, but the central concern will remain law and legal interpretation. Before the book is described in greater detail, however, a word should be said about where experts do *not* disagree.

Common Ground

There is some common ground, even in this contested field. Of course, no foolproof method exists for identifying points of agreement. But the examples in this section should spark little controversy. If that prediction is right, then there are at least a *few* points of commonality amid our intense polarization on questions of religion and state.

Most fundamentally, religious freedom itself is a foundational value. This book stresses its importance. In fact, it holds that current constitutional law actually *underprotects* free exercise by providing too few exemptions from general laws. For that reason, it supports the federal Religious Freedom Restoration Act (RFRA), the law that was at issue in the *Hobby Lobby* case. So the book starts from a premise of foundational agreement with advocates of strong religious freedom.[23]

For example, the Supreme Court held in 2015 that a Muslim inmate had a right to wear a short beard for religious reasons, despite a prison rule that prohibited facial hair. That decision, *Holt v. Hobbs,* was correct. The inmate could be accommodated without any reduction in security and with virtually no cost to the government. And the result was reached under a federal religious freedom law that is similar to RFRA. Such laws provide an important bulwark against government overreaching.[24]

Core equality guarantees also enjoy shared support. Government may not discriminate invidiously on the basis of race, religion, or sex, for example, unless it has an extraordinarily strong objective and no alternative means for pursuing it. Nor may private employers or service providers exclude people on those grounds, so long as the entities are "public" enough to fall within the typical parameters of civil rights laws. Few experts involved in current debates challenge the central guarantees of those laws.

Beyond religious freedom and equality rights themselves, moreover, there is overlooked agreement on certain legal doctrines that *mediate between* the two. Virtually everyone believes, for example, that clergy should have the freedom to solemnize only those unions that comport with their theological tenets. In fact, religious communities may exclude couples from the sacrament of marriage on any ground, including race, religion, national origin, sex, sexual orientation, and gender identity, as later chapters will explain.

And outside the marriage context, there is little dispute that congregations may choose their religious leaders without interference from employment discrimination law, at least when exclusion is required by the group's theology or mission. So Roman Catholic congregations may hire only men as priests, even though employment discrimination on the basis of gender is prohibited by civil rights law. Although there is disagreement over how far this principle should extend, there is unanimity on the core idea.[25]

There is even a great deal of agreement—although falling short of a consensus—around certain exemptions in the context of reproductive freedom. Many Americans believe it is legally permissible to exempt doctors from direct involvement in the termination of a pregnancy. At least where there is no risk to the woman's life or health, there is support for "conscience clauses" or "refusal clauses" that accommodate medical practitioners who have objections grounded in religion or conscience. (Beyond that paradigmatic situation—say, where alternatives are not readily available or where the involvement is less direct—agreement quickly evaporates.)[26]

Finally, Americans tend to agree on the broad outlines of the settlement that has been struck between existing civil rights law and religious freedom. Even in today's polarized political environment, it is rare to hear criticism of federal law on religious freedom and equality in the context of, say, employment discrimination on the basis of race, gender, ethnicity, or religion itself. For example, local congregations can favor members of the faith when they hire an administrative assistant or a janitor, but they cannot discriminate on the basis of race or gender. That exception enjoys stable support, with only a few caveats. Moreover, antidiscrimination law virtually always leaves out small employers, who may have strong associational interests in hiring. Finally, landlords who live in a building with only a few rental units can exclude tenants under the "Mrs. Murphy" exemption from housing discrimination laws. Generally, these settlements between religious traditionalism and civil rights law are accepted by both the profession and the public.[27]

These are not the only areas of overlap between advocates for religious freedom and equality; the discussion in this book builds on others as well. Thus, the question today is not *whether* there will be religion exemptions from civil rights laws; the question is *when* and *how* those exemptions will be afforded. The aim here is twofold: to provide a method for analyzing that question and to suggest actual answers tailored to particular situations.

Plan of the Book

This book has three parts. Part I describes and defends the method of social coherence. That section is best viewed as *relatively* independent from the rest of the discussion. Readers who are less interested in questions of methodology can skip Part I without losing much ability to understand later chapters. Specialists, on the other hand, may want to learn about the method, which unifies and structures the entire work. Part I consists of

Chapter 1, which proposes the approach, and Chapter 2, which defends it against objections from skeptics.

After Part I, work begins on the second goal: offering a substantive vision of how law should mediate between religious freedom and equal citizenship. Nothing about this vision is mechanically determined by social coherence, which provides only a method. If the recommendations can be supported by justified arguments, in addition to raw political contests, that will help to reinforce the attractiveness of the book's method. In turn, the method shows how outcomes *can* be warranted. But otherwise the substantive arguments must stand on their own.

Part II identifies legal principles that can manage tensions between religion and equality. Organizing the discussion around principles makes sense because these general rules tend to cut across discrete legal doctrines and provisions of the Constitution. Each principle also involves multiple areas of antidiscrimination law. Part II proposes four such principles, without claiming that the list is exclusive.

Critically, the four principles *mediate between* religious freedom and equal citizenship. Therefore, those two basic commitments themselves are not included. Again, the book starts from a foundation that incorporates both. But the fighting questions today are not whether religious freedom and equality are important, or how we should understand each of them in isolation, but rather when one should give way to the other in situations where they conflict. Part II draws out the principles that seem to be doing the most work in answering that last question on the ground.

Intriguingly, each principle serves both free exercise and antidiscrimination norms, and none favors one over the other. That makes sense once you understand that they serve a mediating function. So the ambition of these four chapters is to present a framework that is not biased toward either religious freedom or equality aspirations, and therefore is capable of generating surprise outcomes for both sides.

Chapter 3 begins with a commitment that has turned out to be central to thinking about religion and equality—namely, *avoiding harm to others.* That imperative has deep roots, but it returned to the foreground in *Hobby Lobby.* As noted briefly above, *Hobby Lobby* involved a regulation, issued under the Affordable Care Act, that required all employer health plans to include coverage for female contraception without cost sharing. Hobby Lobby, a business corporation with some 13,000 employees, asked for an exemption on the ground that complying with the mandate would violate the religious beliefs of its corporate leaders. Agreeing with the company, the Supreme Court granted the exemption.[28]

The chief obstacle to that ruling was the imperative of avoiding harm to others. Here is the idea (which was developed in collaboration with Richard Schragger and Micah Schwartzman). Normally, when a religious believer asks the government to accommodate his or her observance, any costs of that exemption are borne by the government or by the public. For example, providing halal meals for observant prison inmates may impact the state bureaucracy or treasury. That is unobjectionable. When, however, religion accommodations impose costs on other private citizens, they can raise constitutional concerns. A long-standing principle holds that government may not accommodate religious believers if that means shifting meaningful costs onto other citizens. That rule protects everyone from being forced to bear the costs of someone else's beliefs, and therefore it is rooted in religious freedom itself. Both the Free Exercise Clause and the Establishment Clause incorporate the idea, as the chapter explains.

In *Hobby Lobby,* the principle against harming others meant that the court could not accommodate the company if that meant depriving its thousands of female employees (and female dependents). That risk was real, because simply exempting the company without more would have meant that women covered by its plan would have been deprived of free contraception coverage. Ultimately, the court decided that the administration could fashion a win-win solution that would both exempt the company and provide the coverage. Justice Anthony Kennedy, who provided the crucial fifth vote, wrote separately to underscore the importance of avoiding costs to Hobby Lobby's employees.[29]

Unfortunately, however, the court did not do enough to protect them. Nothing in its opinion *conditioned* relief for Hobby Lobby on protecting the women covered under its plan, and in fact they were harmed. That made the decision unjustified, although not necessarily unjustifiable—other treatments of the harm to third parties were possible, and they might well have been warranted even if mistaken. Key here is simply that the court gave no reason whatsoever for leaving the employees unprotected.

Of course, the court itself emphasized other doctrines. But the third-party harm rule nevertheless should be seen as central to the case and to similar claims for religion accommodations from antidiscrimination laws. That precept alone can do much to manage disputes over religion and equality. And, notably, it enforces *both* the religious and equality interests of third parties, balanced against the converse interests of believers.

A familiar response is that there is harm on both sides—if Hobby Lobby were required to provide contraception coverage, or to drop health insurance for its employees, it would be harmed by virtue of its religion. And that is true—it would face a cost. Many religious actors are deeply committed to their views, and they feel disrespected when they are not exempted from such laws. But a key argument of this book is that the harms are not perfectly symmetrical. Government often burdens citizens, such as when it taxes them or requires them to serve on juries. However, requiring a private citizen to bear the costs of accommodating another private citizen's religious commitments involves a different sort of harm—to equal citizenship regardless of belief or nonbelief. By contrast, when private citizens are asked to obey general laws that apply in the same way to everyone, such as the contraception mandate, they are not being disfavored by government *on the basis of religion.* So equal citizenship is not inevitably at issue on both sides of such disputes—or so the chapters here attempt to establish.

Chapter 4 defends a complementary commitment, *fairness to others.* Although sometimes overlooked in the current debate, this tenet holds that government may not accommodate religious believers if that would be meaningfully unfair to other citizens. Fairness here is independent of harm. Even if the accommodation does not shift costs, it can create unfairness if it extends a freedom to religious actors but not to similarly situated citizens of other faiths or no faith. For example, accommodations for conscientious objectors from the draft cannot be limited to people who have religious objections to war—they must also include pacifists who are nonbelievers. This rule, too, is grounded in both the Free Exercise Clause and the Establishment Clause. And although it does not require every religion accommodation to be precisely neutral, it does require overall evenhandedness. For example, a prison could not offer kosher meals without also accommodating Muslim inmates and vegetarians driven by morality. Governments may level up, providing special meals to all comparable inmates, or they may level down, denying them to everyone, but they cannot favor religious interests over comparable secular interests without offending this principle. Although fairness to others does not feature as prominently as other values in today's debates, it should be remembered and reinforced.[30]

Chapter 5 concerns freedom of association—the right of groups, religious and otherwise, to shape their membership and leadership, even in discriminatory ways that run up against civil rights laws. Virtually everyone agrees that *some* groups should have *some* autonomy from the majority's understanding of equality. Recall that Roman Catholic congregations can hire only men as priests, even though federal law prohibits employment discrimination on the basis of gender. Yet there are limits on the ability of groups to form in discriminatory ways—and setting those limits on the freedom of association has proven difficult.

Differentiating among three sorts of groups, and the constitutional values that protect them, can help rationalize both the political morality of group rights and the constitutional doctrine governing them. First, *intimate relationships* are important to personhood and are protected from civil rights laws. People can choose their spouses and their families on any ground, including rationales that are prohibited in other contexts, because those relationships are so integral to personal flourishing. Second, *community groups* that are tightly knit can support the formation of citizens' impulses and ideas. These close associations need some insulation from government regulation to function as incubators for freethinking members of the polity. But for that reason, they should be narrowly defined. Finally, groups that are larger or looser nevertheless may provide diverse perspectives on questions of social and political import. So *values organizations* may require some autonomy in order to construct and communicate those messages—such as freedom to choose leaders in ways that comport with their mission.

This framework accounts for much of current constitutional law on freedom of association. What is more, it does so without differentiating between religious and secular groups in unjustified ways. Nevertheless, it does require modifying some Supreme Court doctrine in order to harmonize the principle of freedom of association with the concrete cases that best embody that principle, as Chapter 5 explains. It also cuts against some received wisdom among progressives. For example, local congregations should be able to select clergy without interference from civil rights laws, even when the exclusion is not required by their explicit mission. By contrast, values organizations should only be able to discriminate against their leaders when required by their belief systems. This way of understanding freedom of association would advance debates that are stalled today because of intransigence on both sides.

Chapter 6 shifts from government regulation to government speech. The state not only prohibits or allows certain forms of discrimination but also speaks out about religion and equality. What should the government be able to say? A principle that limits state speech on the subjects of religion and equality is *government nonendorsement.* Officials face restrictions when their speech interferes with the full and equal citizenship of individuals. This idea is embodied in various constitutional doctrines under the First and Fourteenth Amendments.

To take a simple example, a city cannot erect a sign that announces, "This Is a Christian Town." That changes the government's legal relationship with people of other faiths or no faith—it renders them subordinated members of the political community. Neither is it permissible for a state or city to declare, "This Is a Town for Whites." That, too, demotes citizens impermissibly, even if no tangible consequences accompany the statement.

Although these two paradigms draw on different constitutional provisions—the Establishment Clause and Equal Protection, respectfully—they embody a meaningful constitutional principle of government nonendorsement. That rule also extends to government speech on electioneering, same-sex marriage, the right to terminate a pregnancy, and more. It does so by drawing on several constitutional provisions. Although not unique to religion, this commitment plays a critical role in mediating tensions concerning religion and equality. It protects citizen standing for religious and nonreligious people alike.

Part III applies these four principles to conflicts on the ground. Chapter 7 begins with the contest between LGBT rights and public accommodations laws like the one at issue in *Elane Photography.* Wedding vendor cases can be resolved by analogizing them to at least two sets of laws. On the one hand, civil rights laws provide relatively narrow exceptions for religious objectors, and therefore they normally would not accommodate a business like Elane Photography. On the other hand, analogizing to "conscience clauses" or "refusal clauses" in the health care context might well suggest that it is appropriate to exempt wedding vendors from participating in an event that has particularly strong religious import for them. Both of these analogies are reasonable.

After assessing the competing paradigms, Chapter 7 concludes that religious claims for exemptions from public accommodations laws are analogous to civil rights laws, not to conscience or refusal clauses. It therefore provides a reasoned justification for the New Mexico Supreme Court's ruling in favor of the couple.

Chapter 7 also continues the argument that the concerns for equal citizenship are not perfectly symmetrical. LGBT people are sidelined by discrimination that targets them directly, while religious traditionalists are burdened but not demoted by civil rights laws that apply to everyone in the same way. While exclusion of same-sex couples by public businesses risks subordination, applying civil rights laws to religious actors alongside other businesses does not carry a social meaning of disfavored status on the basis of religion. Traditional believers may have strong feelings about these issues, and that is something we all should care about, but equal citizenship is not a matter of subjective feelings, as the chapter explains. Stepping back from the particular arguments, moreover, the chapter illustrates how it is possible to find conclusions that are warranted rather than irrational, even in an area as fraught as the conflict between religious freedom and civil rights law.[31]

Chapter 8 moves to the workplace, asking whether religious employers should be accommodated when they wish to differentiate among employees based on sexual orientation, gender identity, or marital status despite civil rights laws that ordinarily prohibit such exclusion. For example, an employer may seek to deny spousal benefits to employees who are married to someone of the same sex or gender. Or, again, a church may wish to exclude members of protected classes from being employed as members of the clergy. Or, to recall the situation in San Francisco, a diocese may want to dismiss teachers in parochial schools who make statements on social media that contradict church teachings, even if local civil rights laws otherwise would bar retaliation for speech outside work.[32]

These cases all concern employment, but otherwise they are variegated and intricate. The chapter analyzes them by reference to Part II's principles—especially, avoiding harm to others and freedom of association. It concludes that in some respects the ability of employers to adhere to their convictions ought to be widened beyond what current law allows. For example, community associations that are closely bound should be able to hire leaders without interference, even if the groups are secular and even if they exclude candidates in ways unconnected to their mission. Yet in many other respects, employers should be limited in their ability to discriminate in contravention of civil rights laws. The chapter ends by proposing a tentative solution to the San Francisco case that harmonizes the church's associational interests with the antidiscrimination rules protecting workers, drawing on existing models in employment law. In brief, teachers of secular subjects have a right to engage in speech outside the workplace, even when they are speaking in public, unless that speech undermines essential educational goals of parochial schools. Whether this tentative solution is accepted or not, the main point is that employment discrimination cases can be approached in a reasoned way despite their complexity.

Chapter 9 considers exemptions for public officials. Both Utah and North Carolina have passed laws that allow government officials to decline to process or celebrate marriages to which they have religious objections. And recall that Kim Davis, the religious county clerk in Kentucky, was temporarily jailed for refusing to process marriage licenses after *Obergefell.* Normally, public officials are obligated to serve all citizens without distinction. And the court was right to penalize Davis when she prohibited her office from issuing marriage licenses.

Yet there may be greater room for accommodation of officials than many believe. After all, judges can recuse themselves from some death penalty cases and abortion proceedings for reasons of conscience, and civil servants must be accommodated in their observances under federal employment law, within reason. Even though there are important differences between judges and county clerks, and even though federal employment law does not extend religion accommodations to elected officials, these analogues nevertheless suggest limited accommodations for people like Davis (although they only entail that accommodations should be permitted, not that they should be legally required). While Davis lacks any power to govern her office according to her religious beliefs, she may be able to withhold personal involvement as long as mediating principles are rigorously observed, including avoiding harm to others and government nonendorsement. Here, too, social coherence suggests a result that progressives might not reflexively adopt.

Finally, Chapter 10 considers the important matter of state funding. Even where a government does not prohibit certain forms of discrimination by religious actors, it can decide to defund them. Excluding religious practices from government support can be an important civil rights tool when the government wishes to discourage but not prohibit illiberal policies. When is this permissible? A paradigm case is *Bob Jones University v. United States,* where the Supreme Court upheld an Internal Revenue Service decision to withdraw tax-exempt status from a religious school because it prohibited interracial dating among students. Although widespread agreement has long been thought to support *Bob Jones,* that consensus has recently been questioned and perhaps unsettled. Serious thinkers have been arguing that *Bob Jones* runs contrary to American pluralism, and that its homogenizing potential is especially dangerous in an era of expanded federal funding.[33]

Another example is *Christian Legal Society v. Martinez.* Recall that a state law school adopted an "all comers" policy, according to which student groups had to open their membership and leadership positions to everyone. CLS could not comply because of its sexual morality policy, which would have excluded most LGBT students. Consequently, CLS was denied recognition by the school. Because recognition came with funding from student activity fees and other benefits, the court treated it as a case about government support and upheld the policy. The justices reasoned that CLS remained free to pursue its activities among students without university support. That decision has been controversial.[34]

Chapter 10 argues that it was correct, however. Doctrine in multiple areas holds that there is a key difference between denying and defunding constitutional rights. Oftentimes, rights can be stripped of support even where they cannot be regulated. For example, policy makers can prohibit government funds from being used for abortion, even though terminating a pregnancy is constitutionally protected. Although there are constitutional limits on the government's discretion to defund protected activities, the realization that government has some leeway is important for mediating the current conflict between religion and equality law.

Conclusion

One lesson of this brief introduction is that the relationship between religious freedom and equality law is complex. It implicates principles as diverse as avoiding harm to others, fairness to others, freedom of association for groups, and government nonendorsement. It involves multiple constitutional provisions, such as free exercise, nonestablishment, free speech, and equal protection. It pits those provisions against several areas of civil rights law, including antidiscrimination rules in employment, public accommodations, government licensing, and funding. And it draws in various institutional actors, including federal and state courts, legislatures, and administrative agencies, not to mention organs of civil society, media outlets, political parties, academics, business associations, unions, and many other social and political organizations. Keeping all of this in mind, it is possible to appreciate the shape and scope of the national conversation.

What does all this mean for Vanessa Willock and Misti Collinsworth? Their case is genuinely difficult. We should hear and understand Elaine Huguenin's objection to photographing same-sex ceremonies for religious reasons. We ought to realize that applying civil rights laws to Huguenin will mean that she has to choose between her deeply held religious views and running a photography business that is open to the public and that includes weddings. American pluralism suggests that we leave room for people like her even after their traditional views on questions like civil marriage have been marginalized by a countervailing tide of public conviction.

Yet applying the method of social coherence can support a different outcome as well, as this book explains. In analogous civil rights contexts, lawmakers have already struck a balance between religious freedom and equality concerns. Sometimes private discrimination is allowed and even protected. Examples include the ability of religious employers to hire only people of the same religion or the ability of congregations to discriminate on additional grounds when hiring clergy. But civil rights law generally does not allow public businesses to discriminate against customers on protected grounds. That is because of harms to equality of opportunity and equal citizenship that civil rights law is designed to eliminate. Even if Willock and Collinsworth find another photographer, they experience social subordination when they suffer the sorts of exclusion that LGBT people still regularly encounter in parts of the country.

So although Huguenin's situation is sympathetic, we should ask whether there is a good reason to rebalance the settlement that has been struck between religious freedom and civil rights. Are religious claims for accommodation in this context different in principle from religious claims for exemptions from laws protecting nonwhites, women, ethnic minorities, divorced people, or believers themselves? Would we allow a wedding photographer to decline to serve an interfaith couple, or someone who wanted to remarry against religious orthodoxy? If the answer is no, then perhaps we should hesitate before refashioning our law, however understandable the claims of people like Elaine Huguenin are in the thick of this cultural moment.

Whether or not this particular conclusion is correct, moreover, the book develops the tools we need to think through such difficult questions of religion and equality. It offers a method for understanding them and it establishes a set of constitutional principles to guide our deliberations. It gives us a framework for talking to each other, whatever our different conclusions might be about particular instances of the existential conflict between free exercise and civil rights law.

I

METHOD

ONE

SOCIAL COHERENCE

WHEN PEOPLE REASON through a new moral problem, they often start with an impulse or intuition about the right result. Sometimes they stop there, but often they subject that initial reaction to examination. They think about it harder.

When they reflect in this way, people frequently compare their current inclination to judgments about other problems that seem similar. Especially if they have thought about those other judgments and hold them with confidence, then they will take comfort if a new solution fits together with them. In other words, they can begin to believe that their solution to the problem at hand is supported by reasons—that it is justified and not just impulsive. On the other hand, if their initial take does not comport with their belief about a familiar situation that seems comparable, they will then want to examine both conclusions to see which is right.

Take, for instance, the case of Vanessa Willock and Misti Collinsworth, discussed in the Introduction. Recall that the couple contacted Elane Photography to inquire whether the company was available to photograph their commitment ceremony. After Elaine Huguenin, co-owner of the business, told them that the company had a policy against photographing same-sex unions for religious reasons, the two women brought a successful civil rights challenge. The court found that the business was a public accommodation that could not discriminate on any protected ground, including sexual orientation, and that no exemption was available on either religion or speech grounds. Was that decision correct?[1]

To answer that question, it seems natural to consider whether courts would grant an exemption based on religion or speech in analogous situations, such as where the objection was to a remarriage or an interfaith ceremony. After all, civil rights laws also often prohibit discrimination on the basis of religion and marital status. It also makes sense to ask whether there are other situations where the law would grant an exemption to a religious provider, such as where a medical professional is asked to participate in a procedure to terminate a pregnancy against his or her conscience, and to ask whether *Elane Photography* is similar in relevant ways. Later chapters suggest answers to these questions—for now, the point is simply that these are the natural questions to ask.

This chapter describes the coherence method, first laying out the basic approach and then detailing the specific version proposed here. Among other things, it explains what the social element adds to familiar coherence theories. For the most part, the chapter presents the affirmative case for the social coherence method, leaving until Chapter 2 a detailed defense against objections.

The Basic Method

John Rawls, the political philosopher, made the coherence approach famous when he described moral reasoning as the search for a "reflective equilibrium." When people think through existing arrangements and search for answers to new problems, they evaluate their convictions by asking whether they fit together with each other. Beginning with judgments about concrete situations—not just impulses or intuitions, but conclusions to which they have given some thought—they then ask whether those judgments cohere, using comparisons and analogies. If their judgments do not hang together, that gives people cause to ask whether they are mistaken. But if they do comport with each other, then moral actors can have some confidence that their conclusions are warranted, that they are backed by reasons.[2]

Simultaneously, people abstract from their concrete judgments to form more general principles. They do that for several reasons. The search for principles promotes examination, meaning it requires people to evaluate their judgments and identify which aspects or dimensions are most important or compelling. General tenets can also provide an "overall account" of an area of law that bolsters a conviction that some problems in that area have correct answers. And principles encourage efficiency of thought and action, because they can guide our response to a new situation, making it unnecessary to perform laborious analogies to other concrete cases.[3]

So when people think about moral problems, they incorporate not just discrete judgments, analogizing them to each other, but also abstract values that account for their particular conclusions. They then work back and forth among these convictions, seeking harmony among their judgments and general principles. When they encounter contradiction or lack of fit, they then alter principles and judgments, seeking a state where all elements hang together—at least within a single subject matter, if not more broadly. Their objective is not only to describe what they *actually* believe, as T. M. Scanlon has put it, but also to discover what they *should* believe. Coherence, even local coherence, gives them reason to think that their judgments are justified or warranted. It can even support a stronger conviction that their conclusions are demanded or determined by reasons.[4]

Seven Clarifications

That is the basic method. People who succeed in harmonizing their convictions can claim that they are warranted or justified. And they can say, against the skeptics, that their choices are not conclusory, ad hoc, irrational, arbitrary, or rudderless. But certain clarifications are needed to specify the particular version of coherence that is given here; this section offers seven.

First, "fitting together" means something more than simple consistency in this context—it means mutual reinforcement. Conclusions gain credence through this process not just because they avoid contradicting each other but because they support one another. Joseph Raz illustrates this idea of mutual reinforcement by giving an example of someone who has two beliefs: (1) John was seen going into Emily's house, and (2) John has long wanted to visit Emily. If either of these beliefs is questioned, it can be bolstered by the other. That John entered Emily's house is some evidence that he wanted to visit her, and that he wanted to visit Emily helps to support the belief that he entered her house. Even if empirical beliefs work differently from moral beliefs, the point is simply that coherent convictions are mutually supportive.[5]

The second clarification is for those attuned to moral philosophy. The argument here is only that coherence or equilibrium supports a claim that conclusions are justified or warranted. And the terms *justified* and *warranted* indicate simply that the conclusions are backed by reasons. When questioned, an actor can offer analogies to other conclusions, and adherence to general principles, to account for the judgments at hand.

Beyond justification, the argument here has no necessary implications for moral *ontology*, meaning the status of a moral claim or belief as real or true. That matter is quite different from the question of justification. Of course, someone may claim that a conclusion that fits together with her other convictions is not only justified but also deeply true. And it might even be possible to develop a coherence theory that has implications for such profound questions. But the argument here is narrower: it is just that we can reach moral conclusions that are supported by reasons.[6]

Showing that a conclusion about religious freedom is rationally justified or warranted is enough to ward off skepticism. Chapter 2 defends that argument in full. For now, it is enough to say that the skeptics' charge of irrationality is most powerful when it means that conclusions cannot be backed by reasons—and that is exactly what coherence theory addresses and denies.

Third, the system of beliefs is dynamic. No element is foundational and every element is subject to revision in light of new information or new understanding. People may find that their existing conclusions need to be revised in light of a considered position on a new problem. They will work back and forth among beliefs, testing each one against the others and seeking a resolution where their positions make sense taken together. Of course, there will be judgments that have withstood sustained reflection and practical testing and are unlikely to change. But in theory everything is revisable.[7]

Fourth, the elements of a moral system may occupy any level of abstraction. They could be judgments about how ground-level disputes should be resolved, or they could be abstract principles that account for those concrete recommendations.[8]

Fifth, coherence or equilibrium is best understood as an ideal that is not likely to be achieved. What gives its components force is not that they are part of a worldview that is fully worked out in every detail. Instead, claims of justification gain power from the process of reflection and testing—a process that is best understood as ongoing. Moreover, it is not just the *fact* of that process that gives its conclusions authority, as Scanlon points out, but rather the *quality* of the judgments that are made along the way. To see whether a position is justified, we have to work through the analogies to other cases and the deductions from principles that generate its persuasiveness.[9]

Sixth, nothing about the method is inherently backward-looking, conservative, or atavistic. While it is true that the process "begins" with existing convictions about which people have some level of confidence after reflection, it does not stop there. People can and do critique inherited conclusions in light of new practices and newly discovered principles. In fact, promoting reflection and testing of inherited arrangements is close to the whole point of the method.[10]

Seventh, the equilibrium approach is well suited to law and it has a recognized application there. In fact, many people see a resemblance between the coherence technique and common-law reasoning, with its analogies to existing cases and its application of legal principles to new situations.[11]

A broader question is how coherence is related to legal interpretation more generally. Perhaps the best answer is that legal interpretation, or making sense of legal ambiguity, involves moral reasoning. And one way of understanding that moral reasoning is as a search for coherence, including harmony with nonlegal convictions. Making the case for this relationship between moral argument and interpretation of laws is well outside the scope of this book, as the Introduction mentioned, though the work has been done elsewhere. In particular, Ronald Dworkin's interpretive theory resembles the approach here. Those who take a different view of legal argument may not find the method as attractive.[12]

But for those who do accept that morality plays a role in legal interpretation, the method of reflective equilibrium or coherence makes it possible to manage areas of law that involve multiple values. Laws on religious freedom incorporate a range of commitments that are complex and sometimes counterpoised. Judges and lawyers emphasize the importance of individual freedom to believe and practice, of course, but they also guarantee the separation of church and state, a prohibition on government endorsement of religious truth, freedom of association for congregations, antidiscrimination on the basis of faith, and so forth. That complexity has contributed to Supreme Court decisions that are routinely condemned as confused.[13]

The question is what to do about it. Some have argued that the only way to bring consistency to the doctrine is to find a single tenet or rubric that can guide legal decision making. But it has proven difficult to formulate any one idea that can resolve cases across the full range of free exercise and nonestablishment topics. Those who have tried have either failed or have ended up practicing something closer to value pluralism when they address ground-level disputes. And, of course, the skeptics have argued that there is no way to bring consistency to religion-clause jurisprudence.[14]

Coherence theory responds to this situation by proposing a form of deliberation that is capable of handling variegated values. Oscillating among judgments and principles gives legal actors a way to reason through problems that are highly intricate. Oftentimes, they will achieve equilibriums that are only local, not comprehensive. Patricia Marino has pointed out that moral reasoning is pluralistic in two interrelated senses: it involves plural values, and those values are understood and prioritized differently by different people. But neither form of pluralism makes the approach unworkable or worthless.[15]

Notably, this response consists of a method or way of thinking, not a substantive theory of religious freedom. Those who propose a single religious freedom value might rely on the method, but so too could people who argue that only a multivalent approach can generate an attractive account of the religion clauses. While perhaps some substantive theory or another is capable of winning a consensus, nothing about that choice is mandated by a coherence method. What coherence avoids is only the skeptical view that warranted outcomes are impossible.

Social Dynamics

Of course, religious freedom law leaves plenty of room for disagreement. Actors will recommend different solutions to a particular problem, and they will offer ways of making sense of those recommendations given other cases and commitments that are widely taken to be authoritative.

Disagreement can take the form that the other side's arguments are incoherent—meaning they conflict with each other or with legal authorities. Or it can take the form of a charge that the opposition's arguments are reasonable but mistaken—because they put the relevant authorities together in the wrong way by, say, prioritizing values incorrectly or drawing analogies improperly. The first type of disagreement charges an individual actor with inconsistency or irrationality, while the second presents a situation of reasonable disagreement.[16]

When they are faced with criticism, constitutional interpreters must then examine their own reasoning. They must decide whether they have left out some important precedent or principle, or relied on ones that are unreliable, and they must evaluate their judgments about how everything fits together. If they have made errors, they will be forced to adjust.

But if they examine their own reasoning and find it sound, then interpreters can push back against their critics and try to convince them to change their minds. They can put their own reasoning up against the arguments of others. Over time, if not immediately, their way of understanding can persuade their opponents. This is true even if constitutional actors start from the position that their proposals are not just supported by reasons but demanded by them. Rational conversion is possible.

But if that does not happen, the mere fact of disagreement does not give constitutional interpreters a reason to change their mind once they have examined their own judgments. Scanlon rightly makes this point. What matters is the process of trying to reach a coherent position, either local or global. If someone examines the judgments that brought them to a particular conclusion and finds them to be solid, then they should conclude that their understanding of the problem is warranted, even in the face of persistent disagreement.[17]

Social coherence brings out an aspect of the method that has been noticed but not emphasized in the philosophy literature—namely, its context. When people reason through moral and legal problems, they do so from a particular location in history, culture, demography, geography, and politics. Their perspective and purposes influence the way they put together their commitments on questions of constitutional significance. Such forces shape not only their interests but also their information—the facts and arguments that they consider when they work through some new problem. And they gain information through the full range of social mechanisms, including interactions with social movements, political mobilizations, media coverage, political party platforms, legislative acts and, of course, judicial decisions that are sufficiently visible. Dworkin has noted that "judges think about law . . . within society, not apart from it," and the same is true of all constitutional actors. Even people who critique law as unjust, or mistaken beyond hope of interpretive repair, do so from within the zeitgeist.[18]

Social setting impacts coherence reasoning in several ways. For one thing, it provides precedents—not just judicial precedents, but political and social ones as well—and it makes them salient. When citizens ask whether their intuitions are correct about the right resolution to *Elane Photography v. Willock*, for example, the judgments and principles they remember and review are provided by culture and politics, in addition to law. Moreover, their evaluations of whether and how cases are analogous or principles are applied reflect their experiences. Arguments shape their thinking, but not in a neutral way; people take more seriously points made by those they have come to consider trustworthy or sympathetic.

That people are influenced by their location does not mean they are not thinking, and it does not mean that reasons do no work. As Marino explains, "this social element to moral belief is compatible with the use of moral reason: social and cultural interactions inform the way people direct and prioritize among the things they care about." Doubtless there are other ways that the search for equilibrium or coherence responds to social and political pressures, but these are among the most important.[19]

Why emphasize the social dynamics of moral reasoning? Two reasons stand out—one defensive and one more constructive. The defensive aim is to anticipate and mollify the worry that because coherence reasoning is inevitably influenced by social and political forces, it cannot generate warranted outcomes. That is mistaken. Just because people experience moral problems from a particular viewpoint does not mean that they cannot reflect on the judgments they have made.

And disagreement with others forces constitutional actors to examine the conclusions they have drawn. When people argue about whether a conclusion is justified, they sometimes do so across different social perspectives. In fact, one strength of this method is that it shows exactly how reflection is possible, even when people's judgments about coherence are partly the products of contingency and circumstance. It describes how interpreters can gain some perspective on their inherited perspectives.

The more constructive rationale for emphasizing coherence's social dimension is that it bolsters the method's appropriateness for constitutional law, which draws part of its legitimacy from responsiveness to popular will. Showing how moral reasoning on questions of religion and equality happens within society and politics helps to connect abstract arguments over moral justification or rationality with constitutional concerns about democratic authority. Because people reason through such problems from a particular perspective that is shaped by social and political action, their arguments and conclusions will reflect such influences—and properly so. Democratic engagement and moral engagement properly go hand in hand, at least when it comes to questions of constitutional import. Of course, there are good reasons to be skeptical about the practical conditions for democratic legitimacy, but the relationship between popular will and the coherence method is nevertheless worth remembering.[20]

Nothing about this social dimension requires actors to actively consider public opinion before coming to conclusions about constitutional problems. In some sense, then, the arguments in this section are really about what constitutional actors actually do rather than about what they ought to do.

Nevertheless, the social element of the method can be understood to have an evaluative aspect. It can help defend coherence against some of its critics, as Chapter 2 explains in detail. One possible criticism is that coherence allows people to label as justified certain worldviews that are unacceptable, so long as they can argue that they hang together. For example, white supremacy can claim to be justified, according to this critique, as long as it achieves internal consistency. But the social element helps to show why that is wrong. White supremacy cannot cohere with basic constitutional commitments that are taken to be binding by the vast majority of Americans. Social coherence is grounded in constitutional understandings that are virtually uncontroverted, irrespective of whether those understandings are true in any ontological sense and even if they can change in theory and have changed throughout history. Chapter 2 explains how widespread social commitments can ground legal interpretation in the beliefs of the people.

Conclusion

To see how social coherence works in practice, think back to *Elane Photography*. Someone trying to figure out the right answer to that issue would look for guidance to analogous situations and governing principles. And different interpreters might view those analogies and principles from different perspectives. A person inclined to be sympathetic to the company, for example, might think first of *Burwell v. Hobby Lobby Stores, Inc.* In that case, as Chapter 3 describes more fully, a business corporation won a religious freedom exemption from a government requirement that all employee health plans include coverage for contraception. Because providing that coverage would have contravened the religious beliefs of the company's leaders, and because the employees could be protected by the government, the Supreme Court ruled that an exemption was required by the Religious Freedom Restoration Act.

Elane Photography could argue that it deserves a similar exemption, using the method described here. It could contend that no one should be required to support a religious sacrament, like a wedding, if doing so contravenes a sincere religious conviction. Otherwise, the photographers would have to choose between their beliefs and their livelihood. That principle should apply even to commercial actors providing services, at least in situations where those services are readily available from other providers.

Free speech precedents and principles are available to wedding vendors as well. After all, the First Amendment protects not only against censorship, or being prohibited from saying something, but also against compelled speech, or being required to say something. On that understanding, Elaine Huguenin cannot be forced to beautify a ceremony that offends her beliefs, whether they are religiously grounded or not.

Using these comparisons and others, Elane Photography could argue that ruling in its favor is rationally justified. Victory for the company could cohere with precedents and principles in both religious freedom law and also in doctrine concerning the freedom of speech.

Stepping back a bit, the company could add that marriage equality proponents have effectively won the culture wars and that they should be magnanimous in their victory. David Brooks made that plea in his column for the *New York Times*. It is time to make peace, and that means accommodating the few wedding vendors who object to serving same-sex ceremonies.[21]

On the other side, the couple could argue that their perspective hangs together as well. They could begin by comparing the company's claim to other requests for religion exemptions from civil rights laws. Businesses that object to weddings on other protected grounds—say, because they are interracial or interfaith—do not receive exemptions. And in an early case, *Newman v. Piggie Park*, the Supreme Court rejected as "patently frivolous" a business owner's claim for a religion exemption from a public accommodations law.[22]

Civil rights cases are different from conscientious refusals to participate in terminations of a pregnancies, they could also say. "Conscience clauses" or "refusal clauses" in the health care setting are limited to situations where alternatives are readily available to the pregnant woman, ideally if not in practice. By contrast, civil rights laws invariably apply even where the customer could receive the service from another provider. Why the difference?

The reason, they would argue, is that civil rights laws like the one in *Elane Photography* do not only protect against incursions on the ability of lesbian, gay, bisexual, and transgender (LGBT) citizens to obtain a photographer. They are partially about economic opportunity. But that is not all. They also protect the equal standing of members of protected groups. An insight of the civil rights struggle, ratified in landmark statutes, is that citizens can be relegated to second-class status not just by government action but also by privately owned businesses and nonprofits. When a restaurant or retailer discriminates against protected groups with the government standing by, that sends a message of disfavored membership in society and in the political community. And that is true even if the exclusion represents a minority view among Americans generally and therefore is disfavored by their representative government. Unless and until the government disallows that kind of discrimination, the risk of unequal citizenship remains real.[23]

Thus, Elaine Huguenin could not exclude couples on the basis of their sex or sexual orientation even if alternative providers were available. Yet public accommodations laws are limited in scope; they only apply to businesses that decide to open their doors to the public. They do not apply to private clubs, and they do not apply to intimate associations. So Elaine and her business partner retained a choice: they could decline to offer their services to the public, or cease working weddings altogether, but if they decided to market themselves as wedding photographers they then had to abide by civil rights laws (and many other regulations that apply to entities that are open to the public whether they operate for profit or not).

For a similar reason, the company's speech interests were not, on this view, unduly burdened. Compelled speech is indeed forbidden by an important constitutional principle, and photography certainly is expressive. But the business here retained a choice, though a difficult one: either violate the owners' sincere religious beliefs or give up running a public wedding business. That meant that their speech was not compelled.

How should we evaluate these opposing claims for coherence? We should examine the judgments that support each of them and see which set is stronger (or whether some other combination of judgments is more compelling than either). Chapter 7 examines these arguments in detail and concludes that, while the case is close, the principles backing up the civil rights approach apply to this situation.[24]

But supporting that conclusion is not the main point of this chapter. Here, the lesson is that, however the debate is resolved, charges of *necessary* irrationality are out of place. The mere fact of disagreement is insufficient to conclude that people's choices invariably will be arbitrary. Of course, social influences matter, and politics matter too. Those influences are inevitable and even salutary in a constitutional democracy. And, again, reasonable disagreement is a permanent feature of American politics. But that does not mean that constitutional actors cannot evaluate and make arguments in a way that is rationally justified. This is where social coherence does real work.

Some will resist. They will argue that although reasons can be given that support ruling for Elane Photography or the couple, the ultimate choice between these two sides will be impossible to justify. They will insist that arbitrariness is an ineluctable part of our decision making. They will say that special features of religious freedom law, like its dual debts to Christian theology and to enlightenment rationality, make it particularly vulnerable to contradiction. And they will conclude that such worries provide a reason to leave such questions to legislatures and to political decision making, free of considerations of constitutional principle. That is a reasonable disagreement about whether reasonable disagreement is possible. Chapter 2 takes it up.

TWO

THE SKEPTICS' OBJECTIONS

TODAY, AN IMPORTANT challenge to religious freedom law is coming from skeptics who generally favor legal solicitude toward religious traditionalism. These scholars argue that religious freedom cases can only be resolved in ways that are conclusory, irrational, or arbitrary.

As noted in Chapter 1, the case law on free exercise and nonestablishment is regularly condemned as confused and contradictory. Skeptics contend that justified outcomes are necessarily unavailable. Although scholars may give careful reasons for each side of a religious freedom dispute, they ultimately just decide which side is more convincing without offering reasons for that final decision. They announce it in the style of an ipse dixit. And, the skeptics continue, conclusory reasoning should not be enough when the issue is the government's use of coercive force.[1]

Some skeptics also argue that a convincing *theory* of religious freedom is impossible. After all, a central aim of such theories is to account for particular outcomes in a way that makes sense across a range of cases. But deep discontinuities frustrate that effort, and necessarily so. According to these thinkers, then, no theory of religious freedom is attainable.[2]

Accepting the skeptics' main argument would be a mistake. Social coherence is designed, in part, to show exactly how thinking on religious freedom can be defended with reasons. Chapter 1 contended that even exceedingly complex moral and legal judgments about free exercise and nonestablishment can be made and implemented in a manner that is rationally justified or warranted. Confusion and conflict will persist in any robust democracy, but that is not a reason to conclude that constitutional interpretations are *necessarily* conclusory or arbitrary. Those judgments can be made by courts as well as by legislators, executive officials, administrators, and a variety of private actors.

This chapter anticipates some of the more potent objections that will be raised against social coherence. First, it defends against the complaint that the method does not really address the most serious charge of the skeptics—namely, their argument that it is impossible to give a reason for the ultimate choice between outcomes in hard cases. The chapter responds by distinguishing between two versions of the charge of irrationality and by arguing that one of them is addressed by coherence and the other cannot and need not be answered.

Second, the chapter defends against the objection that the coherence approach is individualistic—because abhorrent worldviews can be made coherent—and it answers that a version of the method that is socially sensitive and specific to law can be grounded in shared understandings without appealing to foundations. It also rejects the related argument that coherence does no real work because it merely describes an ordinary method of moral or legal reasoning.

Finally, the chapter argues that the method of reflective equilibrium is appropriate not just for coming up with an overall account of religious freedom but also for justifying particular proposals made by particular individuals.

Two Forms of Irrationality

Does social coherence really answer the main critique of the skeptics? Does it show that conclusions on the subject of religious freedom are not necessarily irrational or arbitrary? Even if reasons can be given for each of two opposing outcomes in a hard case, can reasons really be given for choosing one over the other?

These questions implicate deep issues in moral philosophy concerning the nature of rationality. And their answers depend on what we mean by the terms *rationality* and *irrationality*. Yet fortunately, we can put aside the most profound philosophical questions and just distinguish between two ways the skeptics might be using the terms.

One thing skeptics might mean is that constitutional judgments must be grounded in truths that have objective or ontological status. That is, they could be demanding that in order for claims about the proper interpretation or implementation of the religion clauses to be rationally justified, they must be sufficiently connected to propositions that are universal and timeless. You can think of this as a demand that such claims have something akin to theological status.

But this version demands too much. There simply is no authority that is available or accessible to ground judgments about the meaning of the First Amendment in this way. In other words, even if there is such a thing as moral truth, something on which this book takes no position, it is hard to know how it could be accessed and applied without controversy. Not even theological tenets could provide this kind of grounding, because they, too, require interpretation and implementation, generating disagreement and debate. For reasons similar to these, Ronald Dworkin rejected what he described as the external form of skepticism.[3]

A more serious challenge comes from the other understanding of what the skeptics mean when they charge interpreters with irrationality—namely, that interpreters have not been able to give reasons for the ultimate choice of one outcome over another in hard cases. Nor will they ever be able to provide such explanations, on the skeptical account. Talented scholars can parse the reasons that support outcome A and they can understand the reasons that support outcome B. They can decide that overall A is more attractive than B. But they cannot, on this skeptical view, give *reasons* for choosing A over B; that is a matter of subjective preference or mere intuition. Choosing one of these results over the other can only be a matter of irrationality. Dworkin called this "the internal form of skepticism," and he took it seriously.[4]

Social coherence provides a satisfying response to this second form of skepticism. When people conclude that a solution to a religious freedom dispute is the right one, they are not merely saying that the reasons behind that solution seem to them to be stronger than the reasons behind the alternatives. Rather, they are saying that the solution coheres with their other constitutional commitments and that the alternative does not.[5]

Even more strongly, they may conclude that one outcome is *demanded* or *determined* by reasons, not just that it is supported by them. Coherence makes that strong kind of argument available too.

Of course, coming to any such conclusion requires making decisions about how it comports with other judgments about ground-level cases and how it is accounted for by higher-level principles. And those decisions can be challenged in conversation with people who disagree. But the end result is that the chosen solution fits together with interpreters' other convictions, on whatever level of generality.

Having worked through the process, the actor then can conclude that his or her solution to a problem of religious freedom is rationally justified or warranted. What does that mean, exactly? It means that the claim is backed by reasons. The interpreter has arrived at a prescription that makes sense against the background of existing paradigms and principles. Moreover, the alternatives have been rejected as inconsistent in one way or another with those examined beliefs. It is true that the force of the recommendation will depend on the quality of the judgments made along the way. Those judgments are open to examination and testing. But if (and only if) they survive, the conclusion they support can claim to be rationally justified. Choosing it over alternatives can be explained.

Can positions A and B both be warranted? The answer has to be yes. People can have conflicting views about how a case would best be resolved, or even about how the relevant legal authorities demand it be resolved. And both of those views can be internally coherent. That said, people who hold them can still critique one another, either for ignoring relevant arguments or authorities, for improperly prioritizing the ones they do consider, for drawing inappropriate analogies to other cases, or for misapplying general principles. Put differently, advocates of outcome A can criticize supporters of B for a variety of errors.[6]

A related way of understanding the distinction between these two forms of irrationality is to say that inconsistency or arbitrariness *within* an actor's worldview is avoidable—individuals can come to conclusions that are supported and consistent, even in this complex area of law—while disagreement *among* individuals must be an expected feature of public life, because people will exercise their judgment in different ways. But again, all that is necessary here is to establish the first point: that individuals can arrive at conclusions in these areas that are well defended.[7]

Of course, it is always possible that a particular individual will run into difficulty solving a particular problem in law; the relevant precedents or precepts might be vague, or two commitments might be competing and equally important, or values might point in different directions yet be incomparable—so different that they cannot meaningfully be traded off against each other. Such problems very often can be overcome by shifting the technique from analogy to precedents, on the one hand, to deduction from principles, on the other. But sometimes there will be roadblocks or dead ends. That is to be expected. All that is necessary to answer the skeptics, again, is to show that it is *possible* to come to reasoned conclusions in this area.[8]

As an example, consider a discussion from Kent Greenawalt, one of the leading proponents of the view that religious freedom jurisprudence incorporates plural values. His critique of the decision in *Good News Club v. Milford Central School* has drawn criticism from skeptics. In that case, the Supreme Court ruled that a public school that opened its facilities after hours for use by community groups could not exclude religious groups that otherwise qualified to use the space. The court based its ruling on the Free Speech Clause, reasoning that barring only religious organizations would constitute viewpoint discrimination, which is prohibited by the First Amendment. The government is not required to open its school buildings for use by any part of the community, but once it does so it cannot exclude groups based on the particular viewpoint they espouse. And nothing in the Establishment Clause sanctions that kind of discrimination under the circumstances.[9]

Greenawalt criticizes that result; he thinks that certain features of *Good News Club* make it different from other cases where the court has prohibited exclusion of religious speech in the school setting. First, the primary school contained young children who were likely to be more impressionable than the older children involved in earlier cases concerning high schools. Second, the Good News Club was an outside group, not an internal student club, and it was seeking to evangelize. Third, the meetings happened directly after school, a circumstance that school administrators might reasonably have thought would pressure young students or their parents to stay for the meetings, particularly if their peers were doing so. Greenawalt calls these "disturbing features" and he concludes that this was a situation where the nonestablishment values, if not the black-letter law of the Establishment Clause itself, were strong enough to allow the school latitude to decide that allowing the group to meet in school buildings directly after the school day would have made some students feel compelled to attend. It would also have created the risk of a perception that the government was endorsing religion.[10]

Steven D. Smith, who is among the most influential and accomplished of the skeptics, calls Greenawalt's conclusion unreasoned, noting, "Sometimes these declarations are—or at least look like—bald pronouncements." But from the perspective of social coherence, that criticism loses some bite. In fact, Greenawalt compares the facts of the case to precedents—distinguishing it from them—and he then tests his conclusion against Establishment Clause values or principles, such as individual freedom from coercion on matters of faith and government nonendorsement of religious messages. Moreover, his conclusion about *Good News Club* mutually reinforces those specific judgments and general principles.[11]

So, in sum, the example of *Good News Club* helps to show that complex judgments on First Amendment questions can be rationally justified. Of course, some may defend the court's decision, perhaps arguing that it better harmonizes with existing doctrine and constitutional values. Yet, again, the mere fact of disagreement is not enough to establish that conclusions on either side are unwarranted. Still less is it enough to establish that warranted conclusions are not even possible when it comes to the First Amendment.[12]

Before concluding this discussion of irrationality, it is worth considering what the stakes might be. Regardless of whether you are convinced that irrationality does not necessarily plague the endeavor, why does it matter? At root, two concerns seem to be driving the skeptics when they accuse others of irrationality. One is arbitrariness—that people are generating outcomes in a manner that is haphazard or patternless, and that their erratic decision making damages the rule of law or otherwise is inappropriate when state power is being exercised to coerce citizens. Another is bias—that unreasoned decision making allows the personal or political preferences of the interpreter to drive the analysis sub rosa.

Yet social coherence is designed to combat precisely these dangers, among others. Eclectic decision making need not be erratic. Urging people to test their initial impulses against uncontroverted cases and rules works to ensure consistency across cases and to temper individualized influences on constitutional decision making. Moreover, the fact that these precedents and principles are socially located, and not idiosyncratic, bolsters the bulwark against arbitrariness and bias. In fact, it might not be an exaggeration to say that the main point of social coherence is to force constitutional actors to justify their decisions, and to justify them on grounds that incorporate collective commitments, thereby helping to combat contradiction while at the same time leaving room for social evolution and moral change.

Individualism

Some have criticized coherence approaches in moral philosophy by arguing that they are too individualistic. Can it really be the case, they ask, that any worldview that hangs together is for that reason justified? Imagine a white supremacist who is internally consistent, or a male chauvinist who believes he has a coherent worldview that includes the Constitution. Surely such people cannot claim to have views that are rationally justified. Yet coherence or reflective equilibrium seems to lack the resources to resist their claims.

Joseph Raz, for instance, has questioned whether coherence lacks a "base" from which to criticize positions that are internally consistent but morally idiosyncratic. Without such a common set of references, the concern goes, coherence can at most offer grounding for local solutions. Similarly, Patricia Marino imagines someone with a coherent defense of slavery, and she admits that coherence methods lack the resources to condemn that position. "This means," she continues, that the coherence approach "must rest on, and cannot ground, a theory of what counts as a moral value." Raz adds that an inability to offer general solutions could be a particular problem when it comes to law, which must be a collective enterprise.[13]

Yet the social understanding of the coherence method resists this critique. Any conception of constitutional law must take into account precedents and principles that are authoritative among contemporary American jurists. For that reason, people with radically inegalitarian views on race and gender will not be able to successfully resist the charge that their claims are incoherent as interpretations of the Constitution because they contravene basic legal principles. Some have argued that general morality is individualistic in this way, but regardless of whether they are right, constitutional law cannot be radically individualistic.[14]

To be warranted, a constitutional interpretation must be able to claim that it is an understanding of the *United States* Constitution, not a blueprint for some other charter. And in order to make that claim in a convincing way, the interpreter must assimilate uncontroverted features of the jurisprudence. Those features include not only the text and history of the Equal Protection Clause but precedents like *Brown v. Board of Education* in the race context and parallel decisions that render discrimination legally suspect in the gender context. Obviously, then, white supremacy, subjugation of women, and even heteronormativity cannot be harmonized with those features, and those ideologies are unjustified as understandings of American law.[15]

Social coherence therefore occupies a middle position on the problem of individualism in legal interpretation. On the one hand, it rejects the idea that individuals can claim justified any legal conception that they believe hangs together internally. The approach has the resources to critique, say, racist interpretations as unjustified. On the other hand, however, social coherence does not demand that this commonality has any ultimate or ontological status nor even that it has a foundation outside the network of constitutional understandings themselves.

Instead of either of these extremes, social coherence references constitutional understandings. Meanings that are deeply rooted and sufficiently widespread carry interpersonal authority in legal practice—they are not merely subjective. Yet in principle they can be changed, and historically they have in fact undergone repeated transformation. To take only the most recent example, consider the country's turnabout on whether the Constitution protects civil marriage between two women or two men. People can promote those kinds of changes by engaging in critique; for example, they might argue that a legal rule is out of step with other fixed features of the constitutional system. Those shared convictions do ground the enterprise in a commonality that transcends the individual, if only for this society at this particular historical moment.

Methods and Theories, Theories and Judgments

It is possible to argue that while coherence is an appropriate method for developing a *theory* of religious freedom, it is not well suited to generating *judgments* by individual actors regarding specific cases.

But there is no reason cases cannot be resolved in this way. Social coherence can readily be understood as a methodology for generating judgments and principles that are rationally justified or warranted. It describes a reasoning process that, depending on the quality of the judgments that are made, generates conclusions that are backed by reasons. Accordingly, T. M. Scanlon conceptualizes reflective equilibrium as a method for determining "what we ought to think" about particular cases and not just general principles or abstract theories.[16]

Still, no theory of religious freedom is proposed in this book. Plenty of other scholars have recommended frameworks that they believe can rationalize the doctrine across all areas of free exercise and nonestablishment law. Although several of these are attractive, none of them has succeeded in convincing enough decision makers to unify the law. Rather than adding to these efforts to develop a *theory*, the idea here is to describe a *method* that puts individual judgments on a firmer footing. It both provides a defense against skepticism and gives actors guidance on how to think about resolving even complex questions about new situations.

Social coherence also accounts for what many constitutional actors are already doing. In practice, leading experts regularly seek equilibrium when they go about deciding concrete cases. This is true regardless of their particular theory of religious freedom. When they tackle cases on the ground, the most sophisticated and persuasive writers oscillate among precedents and accepted principles, trying to find solutions to concrete problems that make sense in light of their other commitments.[17]

So while it may be possible to construct a theory of religious freedom that brings unity to the doctrine across the full range of First Amendment areas, the effort here is different and more modest: it is just to account for the method that the most persuasive thinkers are already using to drive conclusions to difficult new problems of religious freedom, as well as to reexamine inherited paradigms. Of course, it is still possible and necessary to criticize people for failing to consider all the relevant paradigms and principles in the right way. Yet social coherence gains power and persuasiveness from similarity to the actual practices of constitutional actors.

Conclusion

As Chapter 1 briefly explained, social coherence is about justification, and rationality in that sense, and not about ontology. In other words, it provides a method for supporting moral conclusions with reasons, or for ensuring that such conclusions are reflective rather than impulsive. Although again nothing prevents someone from developing coherence into a theory of moral reality, that is not the objective here.[18]

What it really is necessary to show is that the method provides a defensible way of thinking about how people can and should give reasons for their decisions on questions of religious freedom, and that those reasons can and often do bolster the choices themselves, rather than just providing ex post rationalizations for personal preferences. And that is what these two chapters have attempted to establish. The rest of the book deploys the method to propose a substantive vision of how today's conflicts can be resolved.

PRINCIPLES

THREE

AVOIDING HARM TO OTHERS

WHAT PRINCIPLES should guide our thinking about conflicts between religious freedom and equality law? Part II addresses that question. It describes four primary commitments that run through defensible constitutional decisions in this area, without denying that there may be others.

Although the chapters that follow use the method of social coherence described above, they can be understood without any knowledge of it, so even readers who skipped Part I can easily appreciate the rest of the book. Actually, that accessibility is part of the appeal of social coherence: it resembles the way people already think about the Constitution by analogizing to precedents and by applying principles. Recall too that social coherence provides the rest of the book with a useful technique for thinking through these cases, but it does not determine outcomes. Only by examining the chapters' actual reasons is it possible to evaluate their recommendations for how to resolve the tensions between religious freedom and equality law.

Also important to realize is that the commitments described in Part II do not map neatly onto provisions of the Constitution. They cut across the Free Exercise Clause, the Establishment Clause, and the Free Speech Clause—and some of them even draw on the Equal Protection Clause and the Due Process Clause. Nor does each one abstract from a particular factual situation. Rather, these four chapters draw together lessons from disparate doctrines and decisions, connecting them on the level of general values. Yet they are not vague ideals or aspirations. They have the status of constitutional law.

This particular chapter begins with the imperative of *avoiding harm to others,* while Chapter 4 concerns a related but independent idea, *fairness to others.* Chapter 5 offers a principle of *freedom of association* that protects the ability of groups to form themselves, relying on both free exercise and freedom of speech, and Chapter 6 concludes Part II by defending a principle of *government nonendorsement,* which limits the ways officials can support ideas, both with government speech and with government funding.

The Principle

Normally, when the government accommodates religion by granting an exemption from some general law, any resulting costs are borne by the state itself or by the public. That presents no special constitutional difficulty. What becomes problematic is when the government shifts the costs of accommodating the religion of one private citizen onto another private citizen. Forcing one person to bear the burdens of accommodating the religious practices of another person can work a basic injustice. This chapter describes that principle, grounds it in the doctrine of both free exercise and nonestablishment, shows how it works in practice, and defends it against objections.

Because some commentators have questioned whether this principle even exists in our law, the chapter does important work, especially in the context of the current conflict between religious freedom and equality law. Yet the chapter goes further, showing how the principle would work in practice and how it should be limited. Many of the ideas presented in this chapter were developed with Richard Schragger and Micah Schwartzman.[1]

The chapter offers an example—the Supreme Court's landmark decision in *Burwell v. Hobby Lobby Stores, Inc.* There the court famously ruled that a business corporation could refuse to provide contraception coverage for its employees, as required under Affordable Care Act regulations, because of the religious objections of its owners and managers. It is important to note that the case did involve a conflict between religious freedom and equality—the ability of the company to operate consistent with the beliefs of its owners, on the one hand, and the rights of women in the workplace, on the other. And *Hobby Lobby* implicated harm to others, also known as third-party harm, because it involved an accommodation for the company (the "first party"), granted by the government (the "second party"), with the potential to harm employees (the "third parties"). At least in part, then, the case concerned harm to others.

Ultimately, the court decided that it could exempt the company from the contraception mandate without affecting the employees. It reasoned that the Obama administration had a remedy available that could cover them, as the chapter will explain. Justice Samuel Alito, writing for the court, implied that the impact of its ruling on employees would be "precisely zero."[2]

This apparent win-win solution actually suffered from two interrelated problems. First, the employees were in fact harmed. It took about a year for the Obama administration to implement a solution that would cover employees, and presumably those employees did not receive coverage during that time. Therefore, the impact on them was greater than zero. Those affected included not just female employees but female dependents of all employees. And they included not only workers at Hobby Lobby itself, which had some 13,000 employees, but also those employed by other companies that withheld contraception benefits in reliance on the decision. Although the loss of insurance was temporary, lower courts recognized that the harm to women who are denied free contraception coverage could be significant and irreparable.[3]

Second, the court's decision had troubling implications on the level of principle. Arguably, the court reaffirmed the rule against third-party harms in its decision—a majority of justices, and maybe *every* justice, signed on to that core idea. Yet the court failed to make its decision *contingent* on the absence of harm to employees. And that means that in other conflicts there is a continuing risk of rulings that trench on third parties, so long as the government can in theory avoid those costs. Looming conflicts include not just other challenges to Obamacare's contraception mandate, but also challenges to other laws protecting women's equality. And of course the principle has implications for marriage equality laws and additional civil rights protections for lesbian, gay, bisexual, and transgender (LGBT) citizens.

This chapter therefore argues that the court's decision in *Hobby Lobby* was unjustified. It also defends the principle of avoiding harm to others against challenges, including the arguments that the rule is insufficiently grounded in doctrine, that measuring harm depends on a baseline assumption that is hard to defend, and that the rule cannot account for protection for certain religious businesses, such as kosher delis. These are serious challenges, and they mean that the rule must be nuanced, but they are not incapacitating. Avoiding harm to others is too central to be written out of the American constitutional law of religious freedom.

Why Avoid Harm to Others?

It may seem like an obvious rule of political morality that officials should lift government burdens on religious citizens only when that does not harm others. But when government officials are seeking to protect a basic constitutional liberty, such as religious freedom, they must think hard about *why* exactly they should face limits, and how stringent those limits should be.

Let's begin with some history. A core motivation for the Establishment Clause was to prohibit the federal government from setting up an official church like the one in England during the colonial era. One of the reasons that the framers and ratifiers of the Constitution rejected the idea of an official church was simply to protect against government favoritism on the basis of religion. A related rationale was their opposition to the practice of taxing all citizens for the benefit of one particular religion. In other words, the founding generation of Americans committed themselves to the idea that the costs of accommodating the faith of some citizens should not be imposed on citizens of other faiths or no faith.[4]

On the free exercise side, historians disagree about whether the framers contemplated religion exemptions from general laws, meaning those that applied in the same way to everyone. Regardless, they were concerned about the impact of such exemptions on other citizens. Thus, James Madison famously said that religion should be immune "from civil jurisdiction," but only "in every case where it does not trespass on private rights or the public peace." And Thomas Jefferson, who admittedly was not directly involved in the constitutional drafting process, remarked that accommodating religious beliefs in many situations "neither picks my pocket nor breaks my leg." At least implicitly, leaders of the founding generation contemplated limits on religious freedom that negatively impacted other members of the political community.[5]

Avoiding harm to others, particularly when the government is protecting religious freedom, has been a recurring theme among constitutional interpreters in America, even after the founding. Justice Robert H. Jackson wrote, "My own view may be shortly put: I think the limits [on religious freedom] begin to operate whenever activities begin to affect or collide with liberties of others or of the public." Presumably, imposing the costs of someone's religious practice on someone else does "affect or collide with" the freedoms of those others—especially their right to evenhanded government treatment on the basis of religion.[6]

Justice Anthony Kennedy expressed a related idea when he wrote in the *Hobby Lobby* decision, "Among the reasons the United States is so open, so tolerant, and so free is that no person may be restricted or demeaned by government in exercising his or her religion. Yet neither may that same exercise unduly restrict other persons, such as employees, in protecting their own interests, interests the law deems compelling."[7] And, of course, the dissenters in *Hobby Lobby* strongly emphasized the importance of leaving others unharmed when accommodating religion. Although the majority in *Hobby Lobby* questioned the existence of the principle of avoiding harm to others in a footnote, it limited that observation to dicta. The next section will have more to say about the doctrinal support for the principle; the point here is simply that it has roots in American constitutional thought.[8]

Building on this brief intellectual history, three basic propositions seem stable. First, government in the United States may not establish or endorse a particular faith. Concerns about both favoritism and coercion drive this basic proposition, among other foundational commitments. Second, government may (and sometimes must) accommodate religious practitioners—exempting them from general laws so they may observe their faith does not itself amount to an impermissible establishment of religion. Accommodating religion is not necessarily the same as endorsing it, and any related burdens are generally shouldered by the government itself or by the public. Third, however, government accommodation of the religious beliefs or practices of certain private citizens raises constitutional difficulties when it shifts costs to other private citizens. Imposing such costs on citizens with different beliefs starts to look uncomfortably similar to the first situation: government establishment or endorsement of religion. Both favoritism and material disadvantage may result. So the principle of avoiding harm to others has a firm moral foundation even if real work remains to be done to establish its scope and contours.

It should be emphasized that imposing such harm on others is a violation of religious freedom itself; it represents a form of government compulsion and unfairness on the basis of religion. It should also be noted that not *every* accommodation that results in harm to others presents a problem of constitutional magnitude. Later sections in this chapter will draw limits around the principle; here it is important only to recognize the existence of the tenet itself.

Reviewing this basic account, we can see that the principle has two aspects. Think of the ban on taxation that supports another's faith. The first problem is a special kind of coercion. Although the government can and often does tax citizens to support programs with which they do not agree, the Constitution recognizes a different kind of harm when tax revenues fund an established religion. Why? Partly the notion may be that supporting a particular religion imposes a harm on other citizens that is different from when the government taxes them to support other kinds of programs with which they might disagree.[9]

Another part of the rationale must be that when the government imposes the costs of one religion on others, it takes sides on a basic matter of identity that divides citizens. Religion has salience among Americans, and government favoritism with regard to belief risks deep division in the *political* community. It creates classes of Americans along religious lines, and it advantages some of these classes over others. Government bias regarding any important identity characteristic or comprehensive commitment can run that risk, but religious stratification presents a paradigmatic example of American concerns about unequal citizenship.[10]

When the government merely lifts a burden it has imposed on religious citizens, that concern is not necessarily present. It can recognize the distinct concerns of certain citizens without differentiating or subordinating others. For example, a prison may allow inmates to grow beards for religious reasons despite a grooming policy that otherwise prohibits facial hair. But when policy makers shift a burden to other private citizens—when they *do* pick Jefferson's pocket—worries arise about unequal status on the basis of religious identity. This is not a matter of how disfavored citizens feel, subjectively; it is a matter of their legal standing before the government and relative to one another.[11]

So there are two main reasons why the government should avoid harm to third parties when it accommodates religious freedom. First, imposing the costs of another's religion compels citizens not only to support an idea with which they disagree—something that happens all the time—but it also requires them to support an article or manifestation of faith. Second, and just as fundamental, is the conviction that government should not advantage or disadvantage particular believers over other believers or nonbelievers. That risks dividing and stratifying the political community along religious lines. When government simply lifts burdens on certain believers, concerns about evenhandedness do not necessarily arise, but when it shifts those burdens to others they do become pressing. These concerns have become embedded in constitutional doctrine and have the status of law, as the next section will contend.

The Principle as Law

The long-standing principle that government may not accommodate religion when that means shifting meaningful harms to identifiable others is best understood to be current law, rooted in both the Free Exercise Clause and the Establishment Clause.

For the Establishment Clause, the leading decision is *Estate of Thornton v. Caldor.* There, a Connecticut statute required employers to allow all employees who observed a sabbath to take that day off from work. That proved to be seriously disruptive to many employers and employees, who had to scramble to comply with a law that allowed virtually no exceptions. Sabbath observers had to be accommodated, whatever the impact on others. The Supreme Court struck down the statute, ruling that it violated the Establishment Clause. The court explained that because the Connecticut law gave "unyielding [weight]" to the interests of sabbath observers, it "contravene[d] a fundamental principle of the Religion Clauses."[12]

Here is how the court set out that principle: "The First Amendment . . . gives no one the right to insist that, in pursuit of their own interests, others must conform their conduct to his own religious necessities." This established the principle as law. Although some scholars now read *Caldor* to apply only in situations where the government places "unyielding" weight on the religious interests of some citizens at the expense of others, the more natural reading reinforces a more straightforward principle of avoiding harm to others.[13]

Other decisions reinforce that reading. For example, the court in *Cutter v. Wilkinson* upheld a federal law, the Religious Land Use and Institutionalized Persons Act (RLUIPA), that gave religious freedom protection to inmates and landowners. Although in *Cutter* the court held that the law did not violate the Establishment Clause as a general matter, it conditioned that holding on a requirement that the statute not burden third parties, such as other inmates. Justice Ruth Bader Ginsburg, writing for a unanimous court, was careful to say that judges applying RLUIPA "must take adequate account of the burdens a requested accommodation may impose on nonbeneficiaries," such as inmates who do not share the same religious beliefs. She cited *Caldor* as support.[14]

That, too, represented binding constitutional law. Justice Ginsburg explained that the particular application of RLUIPA was constitutional partly *because* it did not impose burdens on other inmates. That the accommodation did not impose harm on others was essential to the reasoning that supported the outcome of the case, and that made it part of the holding. Some scholars have questioned that conclusion, saying that Ginsburg's language might have been inessential speculation about future cases and therefore nonbinding dicta. But that resistance seems to have faded in light of the stronger reading—that avoidance of harm to others was essential to the unanimous opinion.[15]

One Supreme Court decision approved a religion accommodation in the face of an Establishment Clause complaint that it harmed others, but that decision turned out to be particular to the context of congregations. In *Corporation of the Presiding Bishop of the Church of Jesus Christ of Latter-Day Saints v. Amos,* the court upheld a provision of federal employment law that allows religious organizations to hire only people of their own faith. In other words, Congress created an exemption from the normal rule that employers cannot discriminate on the basis of religion, but only for religious organizations and only so that they could favor members of their own religion. That exemption is an example of the balance that civil rights law strikes between religious freedom and equality concerns for workers.[16]

Frank Mayson, who brought the suit in *Amos,* worked for sixteen years as a building engineer at the Deseret Gymnasium, a nonprofit facility open to the public and run by the Mormon Church. He was fired when he lost his certification of church membership. The court in *Amos* ruled for the church, arguing that Congress could accommodate religious organizations by allowing them to hire only church members. The justices explained that the accommodation protected the church's associational rights—its ability to form a community of believers. They stressed that Deseret Gymnasium was a nonprofit organization that was owned and run by the church so that, in the words of the gym's dedicatory prayer, "all who assemble here, and who come for the benefit of their health, and for physical blessings, [may] feel that they are in a house dedicated to the Lord." Moreover, the justices noted the church's argument that the gym's activities were in fact "expressive of the Church's religious values," and they stressed the dangers of second-guessing that determination. In that situation, employees are normally on notice that the religious organization is limited to members of the church.[17]

Whether the Establishment Clause would permit the accommodation for an organization that was *disconnected* from religious values or engaged in vigorous commercial activity is doubtful. As justices William Brennan and

Sandra Day O'Connor said in their concurring opinions in *Amos*, associational interests are strongest for churches and closely affiliated nonprofits. They are also strong where the organization is involved in noncommercial activities that are related to the mission of the church, but they can be overbalanced by other concerns when the entity is serving the public in a straightforwardly commercial manner.[18]

So the exception in *Amos* should be limited to churches and closely affiliated nonprofits that are not engaged in significant commercial activities. And again, the *Amos* rule is an exception from the doctrinal rule against religion accommodations that shift harms to others.[19]

A similar rationale distinguishes *Hosanna-Tabor Evangelical Lutheran Church and School v. Equal Employment Opportunity Commission*, a more recent decision where the Supreme Court endorsed the "ministerial exception"—the rule that congregations can hire and fire clergy without interference from employment discrimination laws. More will be said about the case in Chapters 5 and 8, but for now the key point is just that it appears to accommodate religious employers despite the fact that pastoral employees bear a cost. And that seems to violate the principle of avoiding harm to others.[20]

Yet *Hosanna-Tabor*, too, should be considered a case about the associational interests of religious congregations. It is different from *Amos* because the congregation's ability to choose its leaders is broader. Chapter 5 will explain why and how far freedom of association protects the ability of community groups to form themselves, including their choice of leadership. Here it is important to understand mainly that freedom of association prevails over the principle of avoiding harm to others, at least in this instance.

Scholars have cited the conscientious objector cases from the 1960s and 1970s as additional counterexamples, but those cases are at least compatible with the rule against harming others, and perhaps even support it. In two decisions, *United States v. Seeger* and *Welsh v. United States*, the court considered an exemption from the draft for people opposed to war in all forms on religious grounds. The justices interpreted the exemption to cover people with *nonreligious* objections to war, despite the language of the statute. One reading is that the justices did that precisely to avoid an Establishment Clause violation that would have resulted if other draftees had to pay the price for conscientious objectors' religious beliefs. So on that reading, the decisions strongly support the principle that *religion* exemptions cannot shift meaningful harms to others. Another reading, however—and probably the better one—is that accommodating conscientious objectors does not shift demonstrable harm to other draftees. Whether any individual is put in harm's way depends on too many factors to draw a causal connection between a particular conscientious objector and a particular draftee. On either of these readings, *Seeger* and *Welsh* do not stand against the commitment of avoiding harm to others.[21]

All of this leads to the conclusion that the Establishment Clause mandates avoiding harm to others. But it does not stand alone in supporting the principle.[22]

Free exercise law also includes concern for religion accommodations that shift harm to others. Here, the leading decision is *United States v. Lee*, where an Amish employer, Edwin D. Lee, was theologically opposed to paying Social Security taxes on behalf of his employees. A unanimous court declined to grant him an exemption. The justices reasoned that relief for Lee would have imposed unacceptable costs on his employees: "When followers of a particular sect enter into commercial activity as a matter of choice, the limits they accept on their own conduct as a matter of conscience and faith are not to be superimposed on the statutory schemes which are binding on others in that activity. Granting an exemption from social security taxes to an employer operates to impose the employer's religious faith on the employees." So in the free exercise context as well, the court observes the principle that religion accommodations cannot be granted where they work to "impose [one citizen's] religious faith" on others.[23]

Congress also endorsed this idea. After the court handed down *Lee*, the legislature responded by enacting a religion accommodation to the payment of Social Security taxes. But when it did so, it was careful to limit the accommodation to situations where employees would not be harmed. Lawmakers seem to have embraced the court's teaching about the importance of avoiding harm to others.[24]

Likewise, in *Tony and Susan Alamo Foundation v. Secretary of Labor* the court turned away a claim for a religion exemption from the minimum wage and other labor protections in the Fair Labor Standards Act, reasoning that the requested accommodation would harm employees both within the religion's commercial businesses and in competing firms. Even though many of the employees apparently shared their employer's faith and declined the act's protections, that might not have been true of all employees. Moreover, the court warned that unequal bargaining power could pressure employees to waive those rights, and that the resulting competitive advantage to the business could depress labor standards for the entire sector.[25]

Not only the Free Exercise Clause itself but also statutes that protect religious exercise—the Religious Freedom Restoration Act (RFRA) and RLUIPA—incorporate the imperative of avoiding harm to others. Even contemporary critics of the Establishment Clause rule now seem to acknowledge that these statutes themselves require judges to avoid harm to nonbeneficiaries. And the court in *Hobby Lobby* reinforced the impression that RFRA does not provide accommodations that would result in harm to others. Even if the majority was equivocal on the point, Justice Kennedy said something similar in his crucial concurrence.[26]

So case law under both the Establishment Clause and the Free Exercise Clause suggests that when government accommodates religious freedom for some citizens, it must avoid harm to others. But that is not all there is to say. We need to know not only that this principle exists but how it works. What counts as harm to third parties? And *how much* harm should trigger the prohibition?

What Counts as Harm to Others?

Some supporters of Hobby Lobby have argued that depriving employees of contraception coverage should not count as a harm at all. They reason that the company had a preexisting right to religious freedom under RFRA, and therefore Congress and the Obama administration could impose the contraception mandate only subject to that right. Therefore, they believe, Hobby Lobby's employees had no right to contraception coverage in the first place, and they could be harmed when the company was accommodated, even if they lacked coverage afterward. That objection is powerful and important. But is it correct?[27]

It is not. To understand why, it is helpful to realize that the objection presents a classic baseline argument. Its force depends on a particular answer to the question, compared to what? If the normal state of affairs is that employees do not have contraception coverage, then the argument is right and they cannot be harmed by an exception to the contraception mandate. They never had a right to that coverage in the first place, so lacking it cannot count as a harm. But if the baseline for comparison is that almost all American employees receive comprehensive contraception coverage without cost sharing, then Hobby Lobby's employees were harmed—gravely and perhaps even irreparably—when they lost coverage. Which baseline is correct?

We should determine whether others have been harmed by taking into account all the values at play—commitments to protecting religious freedom, on the one hand, and to protecting equality, on the other hand, along with any other countervailing convictions. Only by thinking carefully about these values in each situation can we set the baseline for measuring a burden on others in a way that is appropriate and attractive. This normative inquiry may be complicated, but the alternatives are unworkable.[28]

One alternative is to set a libertarian baseline, which imagines a world with no government regulation or funding whatsoever. On this model, a loss of government support or protection can never be considered a burden.

But naturalizing this state of affairs would be a mistake. First of all, American lawyers during the New Deal learned that there is no neutral point of comparison for thinking about what should count as a burden in constitutional law. Imagining a libertarian state of government nonintervention carries normative implications just like any other baseline.[29]

Second, adopting a libertarian baseline would conflict with precedent. After all, the employees in *United States v. Lee* would have suffered a harm if the employer had been exempted from paying Social Security taxes on their behalf, according to the court, even though Social Security is a government creation. Under a libertarian approach, that would be incorrect; the employees could not have been harmed by the loss of a government benefit. Yet few today are arguing that *Lee* was wrongly decided. So the libertarian baseline cannot be squared with settled law.

Yet it would also be a mistake to adopt the opposite alternative—namely, that government programs *always* set the relevant baseline for measuring burdens on religious freedom. Instead of either of these extreme approaches, the most powerful and sensible way to set baselines for measuring burdens on the right is to consider the substantive values at play. Only an approach that considers the underlying purposes of protecting a right can establish baselines in a consistently defensible way.

When Are Harms to Others Permissible?

Once we know that a third party has been burdened, the next question is when that burden ought to defeat the religion accommodation. Are all burdens on others unacceptable? Or are there situations where they should be tolerated, because they are relatively light compared to the interference with religious freedom that the accommodation is designed to remedy?

Think, for instance, of Mary Stinemetz, who needed a liver transplant because of a serious condition called primary biliary cirrhosis. Because she was a practicing Jehovah's Witness, she was opposed to the standard transplant procedure, which required a blood transfusion. There was an alternative technique, called a "bloodless" transplant, that was acceptable to her. Apparently the procedure also was medically accepted, but it was considered slightly less safe, and no hospital in Kansas offered it. A hospital in neighboring Nebraska did provide the procedure, but that would mean transferring Stinemetz, which would be costly. Kansas's Medicaid plan refused to cover the cost, as it was legally entitled to do. So Stinemetz filed a religious freedom claim, arguing that she deserved an accommodation under the Kansas free exercise provision and due process. She won in state court, but too late—by the time the litigation concluded, she had declined further and she was no longer medically eligible for a transplant. She died within a year of her legal victory.[30]

Accommodating Stinemetz would have imposed a burden on the insurer. In the actual case, that would not have implicated the principle of this chapter, because she was insured by the government through the Medicaid program. So accommodating her would only have burdened the public, not another private citizen. Yet imagine that Stinemetz had been covered instead by a private insurer. Would the burden on the insurer have been impermissible? It seems comparatively light, when set against her own concerns related to health and religious observance. Most people would probably agree that she should have been accommodated, despite the burden on her insurer. And that suggests that a standard is needed for determining when—and not merely whether—burdens on others will be permissible.

In other words, once we recognize that *some* burdens on others should be tolerated so the government may protect religious freedom, we need a method for determining *how much* burden shifting is acceptable. One possible standard has been proposed by the two scholars who advocated for the principle against harm to others earliest and most thoughtfully, Frederick Gedicks and Rebecca Van Tassell. They argue that harm to others should be constitutionally prohibited when it is "material." They draw the materiality standard from other areas of law, particularly the common law of torts, and they define a material harm as a cost significant enough that private actors would take it into account in determining their response. This standard has real advantages: it is familiar from other areas of law, where judges have experience administering it, and it would allow the least objectionable religion accommodations to go forward.[31]

But the materiality standard has drawbacks as well. In our hypothetical variation on Mary Stinemetz's case, for example, it might well defeat the religion accommodation. A private health insurer could alter its decision making in response to having to pay to transfer her to a neighboring state. That cost seems to be material. Yet Stinemetz should be accommodated, given the seriousness of her claim compared to the cost of transferring her. And that suggests a difficulty with the materiality standard.

An alternative—the one proposed here—is the undue hardship standard taken from another area of law, employment discrimination. It has several advantages over the alternatives. First, the undue hardship standard has been interpreted by the Supreme Court to address the problem of shifting harm to others.

A second advantage is that the undue hardship standard, although it sounds even tougher than materiality, has actually been interpreted by lower courts in a sensible way—allowing religion accommodations when they impose comparatively negligible harms but not when they work to impose the belief of one private citizen on another. Under that standard, Mary Stinemetz would have been accommodated, in our hypothetical variation on her case. Let us unpack those two advantages, taking each in turn.

Title VII of the Civil Rights Act of 1964 is the main federal law protecting against employment discrimination on the basis of race, sex, religion, and national origin. With regard to religion, its main function is to prohibit employers from targeting workers for adverse treatment simply because of their beliefs—for example, by refusing to hire members of a particular faith. Early in the history of the law, however, the question arose whether employers also were required to take *affirmative* steps to accommodate religious practices. For instance, employers asked whether they were required to ensure that employees could observe the sabbath on the day of their choosing. In response to such questions, Congress revised the law to clarify that employers did have some obligation to accommodate religious practices. Under the amended law, employers must "reasonably accommodate" religious practitioners unless doing so would result in "undue hardship on the conduct of the employer's business."[32]

But Congress's requirement that employers take some measures to accommodate employee beliefs and practices raised an immediate question.

How much impact on an employer and other employees would constitute undue hardship? The Supreme Court addressed that question in a case concerning Larry Hardison, an employee who observed the sabbath on Saturdays as required by his denomination, the Worldwide Church of God. Hardison worked for the airline TWA, which had a collective bargaining agreement with its union. Under the agreement, days off from work were apportioned according to a seniority system. Hardison did not have sufficient seniority to avoid working on all Saturdays. Moreover, attempts to find him another position within the company, or to find workers who would volunteer to swap days off, were unsuccessful. Hardison brought an action and asked for a religion accommodation.[33]

In *Trans World Airlines v. Hardison,* the Supreme Court ruled against Hardison because allowing him to take off every Saturday would impose an undue hardship on TWA, the union, and other employees. Justice Byron White, writing for a 7–2 majority, explained that accommodating Hardison would mean denying other employees their chosen days off from work. And because some of those other employees were senior to Hardison, they had a right to their scheduling preferences under the agreement. Denying them that right would impose real harm.

And that harm to other employees would be based on religion, in violation of the principle against harm to others. "[T]o give Hardison Saturdays off," the court explained, "TWA would have had to deprive another employee of his shift preference at least in part because he did not adhere to a religion that observed the Saturday Sabbath." And that, the court concluded, was not required by Title VII. In a key passage, the court explained, "It would be anomalous to conclude that by 'reasonable accommodation' Congress meant that an employer must deny the shift and job preference of some employees, as well as deprive them of their contractual rights, in order to accommodate or prefer the religious needs of others." To implement its conviction, the court articulated a new standard—or a new interpretation of the undue hardship standard. It said that no religion accommodation under Title VII could impose more than a de minimis burden on others.[34]

In announcing its interpretation of the undue hardship standard, the court emphasized the principle of avoiding harm to others. Addressing Hardison's suggestion that TWA could replace him by moving supervisory personnel from other departments, or by paying premium wages to replacements, the court explained that both of these would involve impermissible costs to TWA. "To require TWA to bear more than a de minimis cost in order to give Hardison Saturdays off is an undue hardship," the court explained, because it "would involve unequal treatment of employees on the basis of their religion." Under Hardison's proposal, in other words, "the privilege of having Saturdays off would be allocated according to religious beliefs." And that is impermissible. The de minimis standard, therefore, was developed by the court precisely to address the problem of shifting harm to others.[35]

It is true that the court in *Hardison* interpreted Title VII without relying on the Constitution. That itself is not necessarily a problem—the principle defended in this chapter is grounded not only in the Constitution but in political morality and in civil rights law. Yet the court's interpretation of the undue hardship standard is probably best understood to reflect constitutional commitments too. After all, the argument had been made that ruling for Hardison would violate the Establishment Clause, and that argument had been accepted in the trial court. There, the judge quoted Learned Hand and warned, "'The First Amendment . . . gives no one the right to insist that in the pursuit of their own interests others must conform their conduct to his own religious necessities.'"[36] Justice White used substantially the same reasoning when he developed the undue hardship standard for the Supreme Court, though without addressing antiestablishment.

Moreover, the undue hardship standard not only fits together with the principle this chapter has been defending but also promotes an attractive parity between employers and employees. If religious *employees* will be denied accommodations whenever they impose undue hardship on others, why should not religious *employers* like Hobby Lobby face the same standard when they seek relief from general regulations that benefit workers? Employees should not only be disadvantaged by the standard when they are seeking accommodations, but they should also be advantaged by it when their employers are seeking exemptions from regulations designed to benefit workers. That seems only fair.

Although the undue hardship standard seems harsh because it appears to require courts to deny all but the most innocuous claims by religious actors, it actually has been applied in sensible ways by lower courts—often, if not always. They have stressed that the inquiry is context-specific and that they will look at both the fact and the magnitude of alleged hardship. And they consider both monetary and nonmonetary costs on employers and other employees.[37]

Consider the case of Herman Tooley, a Seventh-Day Adventist who objected to paying union dues on religious grounds. That was a problem because his workplace was governed by an agreement under which workers were required to pay dues to the union. He suggested an accommodation, under which he would contribute an equivalent amount to a charity. That would have removed any financial benefit to Tooley, but it would have introduced another problem: the union would have lost dues from Tooley and the three other workers who had voiced religious objections. So the religion accommodation would have imposed a cost on the union. Was that cost enough to defeat the objection?

A lower court held that Herman Tooley should be accommodated. Even though the union would be deprived of dues, that cost was considered de minimis. The court explained that the union had enjoyed surplus reserves for the previous three years, and that the reserves exceeded the dues that would be lost by accommodating the four employees who had voiced religious objections to paying them. Although an accommodation that deprived the union of funds necessary for its maintenance or operation might constitute an undue hardship, that circumstance was not present in the actual case. Other courts have extended that holding to situations where the union was not running a surplus but would lose dues from just a few workers.[38]

Moreover, the court in *Tooley v. Martin-Marietta Corporation* considered not just the cost to the union and the employer but also unfairness to other employees. In particular, employees could complain that the accommodation allowed Seventh-Day Adventists to support a charity of their choice, whereas other employees were required to give that money to the union even if they, too, would have preferred to donate it to charity. While this effect was real, the court reasoned, it was not strong enough to defeat the accommodation. It held that the accommodation did not advantage observant employees "in a manner so substantial and direct" that it should be denied. For the court, that "disparate treatment of employees . . . is not necessarily unreasonable" so long as it does not amount to preferential treatment on the basis of religion. Similarly, another court found that accommodating a Saturday sabbatarian was not impermissible simply because other employees could not take Saturdays off to spend time with their families. (Unfairness of this sort is the subject of Chapter 4.)[39]

Finally, and notably, the court in *Tooley* considered the precise concern we have been tracking—namely, that the accommodation benefited religious employees "at the expense of their co-workers" in violation of the

Establishment Clause. It responded that "[a] religious accommodation does not violate the Establishment Clause merely because it can be construed in some abstract way as placing an inappreciable but inevitable burden on those not accommodated." The question is how great such a burden can be before it amounts to impermissible burden shifting. Although the court did not answer directly, it did hold that imposing a de minimis burden was *consistent* with the Constitution under the circumstances.[40]

Other courts have come to similar conclusions—granting religion accommodations even though they would result in some cost to others. One court emphasized that "grumbling" by other employees is acceptable, and that "undue hardship is something greater than hardship." So where other employees complained about having to take up the slack for a Seventh-Day Adventist who could not work on Saturdays, their objections did not necessarily amount to an undue hardship without a seniority system in place. Still other courts have endorsed the view that mere differential treatment of other employees cannot be enough to defeat a religion accommodation.[41]

Under this approach, Mary Stinemetz would have won her hypothetical case. Even though the cost to the insurance company would have been real, and certainly material, it would not have defeated the exemption. That is because the undue hardship test—at least as a normative matter, and perhaps as a description of what lower courts are actually doing—offers the most appealing interpretation of the test for whether a third-party harm prevents the government from accommodating religion.

So, in conclusion, the principle of avoiding harm to others does not necessarily prohibit religion accommodations whenever they result in costs to third parties, however small. Only accommodations that impose an undue hardship on others will be prohibited by this principle. Although the Supreme Court's interpretation of that standard—as prohibiting costs on others that are more than de minimis—sounds exceedingly rigorous, lower courts have developed a body of case law that allows sensible religion exemptions. That doctrine is tailored to situations where providing relief to religious claimants works to impose their religion on others.[42]

Many religion accommodations will still trigger the principle, however. Think, for instance, of a hypothetical that is commonly posed by opponents of the principle. They believe it demonstrates that core protections for religious actors will be defeated by a rule against shifting harm to others.

Could a kosher deli and caterer refuse to serve nonobservant customers, or could such a business decline to cater nonobservant weddings? Public accommodations laws prohibit discrimination on the basis of religion, among other grounds, so the worry is that a principle against shifting harm to others would drive kosher providers out of business.

But that is highly unlikely. First of all, a caterer that only serves a particular community—such as a Hasidic group in Brooklyn—might not be deemed a public accommodation in the first place, and so it would not be subject to civil rights laws. Even if it were, refusing to serve events held by nonobservant people might not be held to be discrimination on the basis of religion, because the exclusion would affect many Jews as well. So it is possible that the business would escape the laws for this reason too.

Finally, however, a kosher deli or caterer that truly did serve only Jews would have to follow any civil rights laws that applied to it—and rightly so. Exempting it would shift a cost to others that counts as undue hardship. Probably, people other than observant Jews would not want to hire a kosher caterer for their events, and they might not choose to patronize a kosher deli. But if they did, their right to do so on a nondiscriminatory basis should be protected by any civil rights laws that apply. Serving kosher food need not entail serving kosher food only to Jews. Once a business decides to enter public commerce, it must abide by the rules and regulations that govern it—including civil rights laws. An accommodation for kosher delis and caterers would harm others in an appreciable way.

Similarly, most religion accommodations that shift harm to others would not find relief under the undue hardship standard. That is because most of them would impose the religious beliefs of some private citizens on other private citizens, and that violates a basic principle of religious freedom in American law.

Harm to Others and the *Hobby Lobby* Decision

So there exists a principle that religion accommodations may not shift meaningful costs to others, and that principle has the force of law. At first glance, *Hobby Lobby* might be seen as yet another example of that principle being faithfully applied by the Supreme Court. But on closer inspection, the court did not do enough to avoid harm to the company's employees.

The court in *Hobby Lobby* seemed to reaffirm the rule against harm to third parties. Justice Alito, writing for the majority, said that judges applying laws like RFRA must take "adequate account" of harm to others, quoting the earlier case, *Cutter*. Moreover, he emphasized that in this situation the

Obama administration had an available mechanism for protecting the employees, and he implied that the burden on employees would be "precisely zero." As noted above, Justice Alito did question in a footnote whether it could be the rule that any burden on others could automatically defeat a religion accommodation, but that discussion was implausible and unconvincing. As explained at length elsewhere, the hypotheticals the court offers there are better handled by an approach that measures harm using a baseline that is set by normative considerations. And in any event the footnote was nonbinding dicta, because it concluded that there would be no burden on employees in this case. So, technically, the court left the rule intact.[43]

And if there were any doubt about that, Justice Kennedy's concurring opinion removed it. Kennedy provided a fifth vote for the majority opinion, but he also wrote separately. And in his opinion he emphasized that avoiding harm to the employees was a premise of the decision. He said that religion exemptions may not "unduly restrict other persons, such as employees, in protecting their own interests, interests the law deems compelling." When you put this together with the opinion of the four dissenters, who explicitly adopted the principle against harm to others, it becomes hard to doubt that the imperative of avoiding harm to others remains good law.[44]

Nevertheless, the court did not do everything it should have done to vindicate that principle. In particular, it did not make relief to Hobby Lobby *contingent* on the company's employees retaining contraception coverage. Justice Alito merely said that the Obama administration could make the employees whole, not that it must do so. That falls meaningfully short of vindicating the principle of avoiding harm to others.

And in fact, Hobby Lobby's employees were harmed. As mentioned above, it took the Obama administration roughly a year to implement a fix that covered them. During that time, Hobby Lobby's workers almost certainly were not receiving contraception coverage. Harm must have resulted, and it may well have been irreparable.[45]

For one thing, the Obama administration's rule was not retroactive, and could not have been under the court's own precedents. For another, any harm suffered by employees may have been impossible to remedy with money. As judge Richard A. Posner explained in an opinion for a lower court, scientific and medical evidence shows that "the provision of . . . contraceptives without cost to the user can be expected to increase contraceptive use and so reduce the number both of unintended pregnancies and of abortions." So damage was predictable.[46]

Moreover, courts have reinforced the connection between reproductive freedom and equality for women. Judge Posner pointed out that the harm that the Obama administration sought to avoid by providing contraception coverage has an impact on women's equality because "'women who can successfully delay a first birth and plan the subsequent timing and spacing of their children are more likely than others to enter or stay in school and to have more opportunities for employment and for full social or political participation in their community.'"[47]

So it is possible to say with some confidence that serious, irreparable harm was shifted to Hobby Lobby's employees because of the religion accommodation imposed by the court. Because the company has some 13,000 employees, many of whom are female or have female dependents, the number of people affected was large. Furthermore, other companies may have been withholding benefits to their employees in reliance on the *Hobby Lobby* decision. So even though it was temporary, the burden on employees was, in all likelihood, real.[48]

This analysis means that the court's decision in *Hobby Lobby* was unjustified, but it does not mean that it was necessarily unjustifiable. It is possible to formulate a narrow reading of the third-party harm doctrine that is consistent with what the court did. For example, it has been argued that the doctrine only applies where the government forcefully imposes harm on third parties, not where it merely allows harm to be imposed through private actions. That is not the best reading of the cases—there is no relevant difference between a government action that accommodates religion, knowing that the private religious actors intend to use that freedom to shift costs to others, and an action that enforces their wishes more forcefully—but it is an available one. And it might make the outcome reasonable or warranted, even if incorrect.[49]

Justice Ginsburg, joined by justice Sonia Sotomayor, later reiterated her view that the *Hobby Lobby* court had made a mistake. In a concurring opinion in *Holt v. Hobbs,* the case about the Muslim prison inmate who wished to grow a beard, she wrote, "Unlike the exemption this Court approved in [*Hobby Lobby*], accommodating [the inmate's] religious belief in this case would not detrimentally affect others who do not share petitioner's belief. On that understanding, I join the Court's opinion."[50] This statement is important for two reasons. First, it reminds us that not every religion accommodation will shift harm to others—the inmate exemption in *Holt* did not. Arkansas was unable to show any increased safety risks from short beards worn by inmates for religious reasons. Second, Justice Ginsburg reminds us of other truths: that some accommodations do shift serious harms to others, that *Hobby Lobby* involved one of those, and that the court should have done more to protect the principle that every single justice ostensibly endorsed.

Conclusion

Avoiding harm to others will remain a central commitment for mediating the conflict between religious freedom and equality law. Since *Hobby Lobby,* it has featured in debates concerning Utah's decision to protect LGBT citizens against discrimination in housing and employment, but with significant religion protections; Indiana's controversial state-level religious freedom law; Arkansas's halting attempt to enact something similar; and Louisiana's effort to exempt religious businesses. All of these efforts have triggered concerns over harms to others.[51]

Yet it is important to realize that so far the debate still partly concerns whether the principle exists in U.S. law at all. This chapter contributes to the effort to show not only that it exists but that it has roots in the American founding and in long-standing case law. Key to that effort is to establish that the principle is workable and has limits. But until the rule is recognized more widely, the project will continue to be foundational.

FOUR

FAIRNESS TO OTHERS

AMID ALL the controversy surrounding the principle of avoiding harm to others, commentators sometimes forget another, equally important principle—namely, *fairness to others.* Even if a religion accommodation imposes no appreciable harm on anyone else, it can work unfairness if it lifts burdens that other citizens in a similar situation would also like to avoid. This is an independent constitutional commitment.

Burwell v. Hobby Lobby Stores, Inc. could be understood as implicating this principle, though the case has not been debated that way. There, as previous chapters have explained, a business corporation was granted a religion accommodation from a rule that required all employers to include coverage of female contraception in any health insurance for workers. So far, the public debate about *Hobby Lobby* has focused on issues like the substantiality of the burden on the company, the importance of the government's interest, and the impact on employees.

But there is another, overlooked constitutional aspect to the court's ruling—namely, that it may implicate the principle of fairness to others. There may well be employers who object to providing contraception coverage for secular reasons that reflect profound convictions. If that seems far-fetched, remember that Hobby Lobby only refused to cover forms of contraception that it thought resulted in abortions—including, for example, emergency contraception drugs such as Ella and Plan B. And it is widely appreciated that opposition to abortion can be motivated by secular commitments as well as religious ones. Can the government accommodate Hobby Lobby but not secular employers with similar objections?[1]

In fact, the Supreme Court has enforced a principle of fairness to others. This chapter will set out rationales for the rule and describe its principal precedents. The discussion will be brief, because this commitment has not played a primary role in contemporary debates over the conflict between religious freedom and equality law. Nevertheless, fairness to others must be included in any full picture of the political morality and constitutional law surrounding those disputes.

Religion and Equal Citizenship

Why would it be problematic for the government to lift regulatory burdens on religious citizens but not similarly situated secular citizens? After all, laws accommodate people differently all the time. Draftees who oppose war in all forms are exempt, but those who oppose only particular wars are not, even if their opposition is equally sincere and profound. Parents who resist vaccinating their children on philosophical grounds are exempt in many states, but parents who believe that vaccinations are medically unsafe are not. Homeowners can deduct some mortgage interest payments when they file their tax returns, but renters cannot deduct their monthly housing costs. Citizens who object to these inequities have a political remedy—they can seek to exert pressure on their elected representatives to enact a better policy—but they do not generally have a constitutional argument. Why should it be any different for religion accommodations that omit secular claims of conscience?

One answer is that religion has an importance for membership in the social and political community that other grounds for accommodation may not. Official favoritism on the basis of religion can therefore affect the standing of citizens relative to each other and before their government, while unevenness on other grounds may have no such impact. So parents who are skeptical about vaccination safety may be disappointed when they are not accommodated. But if nonbelievers who are conscientiously opposed to war in all forms are not exempted from compulsory military service, even though religious objectors are accommodated, they may suffer subordination in their legal relationship with the government and with other members of the political community.

In other words, government favoritism on the basis of religion risks a particular kind of unfairness. Speaking in terms of familiar political theory, that kind of partiality may harm the right of others to *equal citizenship.*

Chapter 6 will describe this concept in greater detail; for now, the key idea is that government favoritism on the basis of religion has a powerful salience because of the role that religious identity plays in membership or belonging. This is a matter of social meaning, which will be particular to American history and culture, not necessarily a timeless and universal truth. Moreover, it is not special to religion, as Chapter 6 will also show. Unequal citizenship can result from government differentiation on other grounds, such as race, gender, ethnicity, sexual orientation, and gender identity.[2]

Equal citizenship, as discussed here, is not the only principle that a liberal democracy must observe. Also important is *full citizenship*—the idea that citizens must be able to exercise basic social and political freedoms, such as free speech, political participation, sexual and reproductive freedom, and so forth. Freedom of religion is one of these basic liberties that is essential to full citizenship, at least in American constitutional democracy. And oftentimes, the government exempts religious actors from a burden that it has imposed on everyone else in order to further its commitment to the value of religious autonomy. That is laudable in many circumstances, such as in *Holt v. Hobbs,* the case in which a Muslim prison inmate was allowed to grow a half-inch beard for religious reasons despite prison grooming rules. Not every religion accommodation presents a problem of political inequality.

But where other citizens would like to engage in the same practice for reasons that are comparably profound and worthwhile, granting only a religion accommodation can become unfair and can impermissibly trench on citizenship guarantees. This is not a matter of balancing; it is a binary rule that prevents government from granting special privileges on the basis of religion, even where those accommodations are enacted to preserve religious freedom, itself a core commitment. In response, government can either "level up" by exempting comparable secular actors as well, or it can "level down" by removing the religion exemption. By itself, fairness to others has nothing to say about this choice. All it insists is that officials cannot accommodate religious actors in ways that harm the equal standing of all citizens before their government and in relation to each other.[3]

Fairness to Others as Law

That government must not grant a religion accommodation that results in unfairness to others has been recognized under both the Free Exercise Clause and the Establishment Clause.

Probably the leading cases are two decisions about conscientious objection to the draft during the Vietnam War era, *United States v. Seeger* and *Welsh v. United States.* Although neither of them drew explicitly on the Constitution, they have come to be widely understood to be rooted in the First Amendment. And although they addressed a circumstance that has not arisen recently—military conscription—they continue to be cited and discussed by courts and scholars with a frequency that is notable. Apparently, these cases expressed an important commitment in constitutional law.[4]

Congress enacted a law that accommodated draftees who objected to war in all forms, but it limited the exemption to those whose opposition was grounded in religion. Daniel Andrew Seeger invoked the exemption, even though his pacifism did not stem from a recognizable religious tradition. He made some attempt to argue that his belief system was religious, understanding that term quite broadly. Elliot A. Welsh II, however, more boldly—though again not completely clearly—grounded his opposition to the war in convictions that were unconnected to religion. Both times the Supreme Court ruled in favor of the objectors, even though their beliefs could be counted as religious only with difficulty. The court purported to base its decision on a broad interpretation of the term "religion" in Congress's statute.[5]

Because the court's interpretation of the statute was tortured—Welsh in particular really did seem to be an atheist or agnostic—most courts and commentators have taken the decisions to be grounded in a constitutional objection to Congress's decision to limit the law to religious objectors. This is now the orthodox reading of the cases, in fact. But what constitutional principle was at play, exactly? There are at least two choices.[6]

One is that the court was avoiding a shift of harm to others on the basis of religion. (Chapter 3 described and defended this principle.) If Congress had exempted only religious objectors from the draft, that would have meant that other draftees would have had an elevated risk of facing danger in a combat situation. By broadening the exemption to include nonreligious objectors as well, the court avoided a violation of that constitutional principle. Harm was still shifted, but it was not shifted *on the basis of religion.* Draftees who had to serve in the place of objectors could no longer complain that they were being forced to bear the costs of another citizen's religion, specifically.[7]

A second principle that could explain the cases, however, is the one this chapter is defending—fairness to others. Granting a conscientious objection exemption only to religious citizens would be intolerably partial; it would involve the government in favoritism on the basis of an identity characteristic that is recognized to be socially significant. Consequently, it would constitute nonreligious objectors as disfavored citizens based on their deepest commitments. Put plainly, the idea is that it would be unfair to exempt religious objectors to the draft without also exempting nonbelievers. Atheists and agnostics deserve parity even if we do not think that atheism and agnosticism fall within the definition of the term religion. This second reading, that the cases reflect the constitutional principle of fairness to others on the basis of religion, is common today.[8]

Yet *Seeger* and *Welsh* are not the only decisions vindicating fairness to others. In another opinion, *Texas Monthly, Inc. v. Bullock,* the Supreme Court considered a Texas law that exempted religious publications from sales taxes. *Texas Monthly,* a secular publication that did not receive the exemption, argued that it violated the Establishment Clause, and the court agreed. Justice William J. Brennan Jr. wrote for a plurality, "The core notion animating the requirement that a statute possess 'a secular legislative purpose' and that 'its principal or primary effect . . . be one that neither advances nor inhibits religion,' is not only that government may not be overtly hostile to religion but also that it may not place its prestige, coercive authority, or resources behind a single religious faith or behind religious belief in general, compelling nonadherents to support the practices or proselytizing of favored religious organizations and conveying the message that those who do not contribute gladly are less than full members of the community." In other words, accommodating only religious publications harms equal citizenship: it constitutes secular citizens as "less than full members of the community." As Justice Brennan concluded, "It is difficult to view Texas' narrow exemption as anything but state sponsorship of religious belief." Vindicating the principle of fairness to others provides an alternative rationale to the one offered in Chapter 3: that *Texas Monthly* cannot be forced to bear the costs of accommodating only religious publications.[9]

Justice Harry Blackmun, joined by justice Sandra Day O'Connor, agreed that the Texas exemption should be invalidated. He reasoned that the exemption would have been unproblematic if it had also benefited publications that addressed profound questions from a secular perspective. But as it was, the law violated the Constitution. "A statutory preference for the dissemination of religious ideas offends our most basic understanding of what the Establishment Clause is all about," he wrote.[10]

Not every religion accommodation has been found to be impermissible, however. Consider *Cutter v. Wilkinson,* the case that upheld the Religious Land Use and Institutionalized Persons Act (RLUIPA). Prison inmates who were members of religious minorities sued to obtain various accommodations from Ohio authorities. In response, prison officials argued that RLUIPA violated the Establishment Clause because it advanced religion. The court rejected that argument, saying that "religious accommodations . . . need not 'come packaged with benefits to secular entities.'" It pointed out that government often relieves religious actors from burdens it imposes on others without triggering nonestablishment concerns. The court pointed out that Ohio allows inmates to assemble for worship, but not for political rallies.[11]

What is the difference between religious accommodations for conscientious objectors or publications, on the one hand, and inmates, on the other? Why were the former held to be unconstitutional, but the latter was not? Can these cases be reconciled? Perhaps they can, once it is recognized that only the first cases implicated equal citizenship.

When a prison relieves a burden on religious practice, it allows practitioners to observe their faith even though the government has almost complete control over their environment. That respects the importance of a fundamental freedom. That political rallies are not also permitted may reflect security concerns; the difference does not constitute secular inmates as disfavored citizens. In situations where the parallel is stronger, however, such as where atheist inmates have sought to hold meetings, courts have protected them under the Establishment Clause. Likewise, only government favoritism can explain accommodation of religious publications but not secular ones, or religious pacifism but not pacifism grounded in nonreligious morality. The difference between these cases is contextual—it is a matter of social meanings—but it is consequential because it separates out government unevenness that merely disadvantages some citizens from government unevenness that is unfair because it renders them disfavored.[12]

Stepping back, then, constitutional law recognizes the principle of fairness to others in addition to the rule of avoiding harm to others. Although religion accommodations need not always be accompanied by accommodations for secular actors, exemptions that constitute them as unequal citizens are invalid.

Conversely, exemptions that lift burdens on deep and worthy secular commitments of conscience can violate the fairness principle if they neglect comparable religious objections. A statute that protected nonreligious objectors to the draft but not religious ones would risk this kind of bias. Yet not every accommodation for secular commitments would implicate the principle; only those that selected out comparably profound commitments so that religious actors would suffer a degradation of citizenship status. Thus, accommodating medical disabilities that prevented people from serving in the armed forces but not any kind of conscientious objection would not work unfairness, though it may well violate other guarantees of constitutional law and political morality, such as freedom of conscience itself. Here the important point is just that fairness to others can work both ways, protecting both religious and nonreligious actors, although the focus here is on the latter.[13]

An Application

Think back to Elane Photography, the wedding vendor that objected to serving same-sex couples. Imagine that the state had crafted a religion exemption from its public accommodations law, so that religious wedding vendors—and *only* religious ones—could refuse to serve at weddings that violated their theology.

Some states have proposed such accommodations. Indiana, for instance, considered a religious freedom restoration act that was designed to apply to cases like *Elane Photography v. Willock.* That version did not survive as law. Yet some states have accommodated those with religious objections to lesbian, gay, bisexual, and transgender (LGBT) unions, so the hypothetical poses a real issue, as Chapter 7 will explain.[14]

Imagine further that another wedding vendor also objects to same-sex marriages, but for reasons of secular morality rather than traditional religion. This is really quite counterfactual, because so much opposition to marriage equality is grounded in religion. Nevertheless, that business would not be able to invoke the accommodation, and it would be subject to public accommodations law. As a consequence, it would have to choose between violating its moral convictions, closing its operations or at least the wedding photography portion of its business, and ceasing to serve the public.

Does the secular Elane Photography have a constitutional argument? On one understanding, it has not suffered harm. So while the couples have been disadvantaged—they face restricted choices of wedding photographers, or even no choices in some circumstances, and an accompanying risk of higher prices—vendors with secular objections to serving protected classes of customers arguably do not face a material cost.

Yet arguably they suffer unfairness. Government has relegated them to a disfavored status to the extent that it has validated the objections of religious vendors but not secular ones. This favoritism makes the claim somewhat analogous to the argument of *Texas Monthly,* the secular publication that was denied a sales tax exemption offered to religious publications. But the analogy is not that the secular Elane Photography has suffered a competitive disadvantage, but rather that it has received a government message that its opposition to civil rights laws is less worthwhile or understandable than Elane Photography's. That damages its relationship to the government, and its standing in the political community.

Faced with a determination that it has violated the principle of fairness to others, the government has a choice. It can either level down and deny any exemption from civil rights laws, or it can level up and offer protection to both religious and nonreligious objectors alike. Leveling up, however, imposes a greater impact on equality for LGBT citizens, in possible derogation of the principle of avoiding harm to others defended in Chapter 3, and doing so may well increase the political cost of providing any exemption at all from core civil rights protections like public accommodations laws.

Conclusion

Alongside the principle of avoiding harm to others, which has featured in debates over the conflict between religious freedom and equality law, there exists a second principle of fairness to others. Supported by the political morality of equal citizenship and grounded in the constitutional law of free exercise and nonestablishment, this principle is basic: it holds simply that government may not accommodate religious actors when that relegates similarly situated secular actors to disfavored status. Probably the clearest paradigm here is conscientious objection to military conscription, which cannot be limited to religious objectors without offending the Constitution. As Justices Blackmun and O'Connor noted in another context, selective accommodation of religious ideas and practices "offends our most basic understanding of what the Establishment Clause is all about."[15]

Not that statutory accommodation of religion always does that. There are many situations in which religious practices are relatively unusual, and lifting burdens on them does not require evenhandedness toward secular analogues. Consider the use of peyote in sacred rituals, which Congress protected by statute after the Supreme Court declined to do so in *Employment Division v. Smith*. There is almost no recreational market for peyote, because using it has unpleasant side effects. Accommodating its use only in sacred rituals by Native Americans is not unfair. Or consider *Holt v. Hobbs*, the prison grooming case. Allowing Muslim inmates to grow a half-inch beard for religious reasons is permissible, even though secular inmates might like to grow a beard for aesthetic reasons. No unconstitutional unfairness results from that disparity. But where a secular need really is comparatively pressing and principled, government may not exclude it from an accommodation without an unfairness that amounts to a constitutional violation.

Again, this principle of fairness to others is not as central to current concerns over LGBT rights, women's equality, or reproductive freedom. But it should be kept in mind, because in situations like the hypothetical variation on Elane Photography described above, government may face a choice between protecting all moral objections in an evenhanded way or applying the law to everyone without accommodations for objectors.

FIVE

FREEDOM OF ASSOCIATION

MANY OF THE CLAIMS for exceptions from civil rights laws feature not just religious individuals but religious groups. Churches, hospitals, social service agencies, prayer groups, elementary schools, universities, and now even business corporations—all of these have sued as organizations. Should political morality or constitutional law give protection to groups as such? And if so, should religious groups get distinctive protection, as compared to secular entities?

Surprisingly, neither political theory nor constitutional law has offered clear answers to these questions. Yet they matter a great deal at this moment in American intellectual and political history. Increasingly, religious groups are arguing that they have a right to exclude certain classes of people. An essential part of freedom of association, they say, is the ability *not* to associate with certain people. And some of those arguments surely are correct.

For example, the Roman Catholic Church has a constitutional right to hire only men as priests, even though employment law prohibits discrimination on the basis of gender. The Supreme Court has endorsed this constitutional judgment, which enjoys widespread support. Furthermore, citizens have a right to form (and sever) intimate romantic and family bonds for any reason—even bias. Constitutional law protects their ability to do that. And again, that principle is virtually uncontroverted among Americans.

Cases like these suggest an important principle of *freedom of association*. People can form certain relationships with each other, and their right to do so is strong enough to overcome even core equality protections. Yet although there is widespread and long-standing agreement about the *existence* of that commitment, its *strength* and *scope* remain remarkably unclear. That confusion troubles the relationship between religious freedom and equality law. This chapter sets out to clarify the boundaries of associational freedom.

Below, the discussion begins with normative political theory. Its argument is that only a disaggregated approach to freedom of association can satisfactorily capture its contours. At least three types of groups should be differentiated according to their distinctive values, both for individuals and for democratic society. First, *intimate associations* ought to be able to resist state regulation of their formation, although organizations that are larger and looser receive more limited protection. Second, *community groups* should be shielded because of their importance for the incubation of interests and ideas among citizens. Finally, national bureaucracies that are organized around ideas ought to have some freedom to select their leaders because of those groups' importance to public debate. This chapter refers to them as *values organizations.* Sorting groups into these types should not involve a rigid sort of formalism—on the contrary, we should be guided by the *purposes* of associational freedom when we work to determine the scope and strength of constitutional protection.

The argument then shifts to law, making the case that the disaggregated approach to associational freedom is reflected in existing constitutional doctrine—though some significant modifications are necessary. Notably, those changes provide somewhat *stronger* protection against civil rights law for community groups, as compared to existing law, but *weaker* protection for more diffuse religious organizations. While some liberals will resist the former conclusion, it is suggested by a coherent account of the freedom of association.

It is important to note that the principle defended in this chapter applies to religious and nonreligious groups alike, with only a few exceptions, and it cuts across several provisions of the Constitution, including the religion clauses, freedom of speech, and due process. The conclusion points toward places in Part III of the book where the principle will be applied and tested.

Why Protect Associations That Discriminate?

Why should a constitutional democracy protect the right of people to form groups at all? That might seem like a silly question in the abstract. Of course, people should be able to join together in families, civic organizations, political parties, nonprofits, business corporations, and all manner of clubs and societies. Yet when those groups are formed through exclusion of people who regularly face societal discrimination, the question quickly moves from silly to serious. We need a rationale for freedom of association so we can appropriately set its limits.

This topic is huge, and hugely complex. This chapter begins to address it by focusing on the interaction between religious freedom and equal citizenship at this historical moment in the United States. (It therefore leaves to one side entire areas, like multiculturalism and multilingualism, treatment of indigenous people, and legal pluralism.)

Distinguishing between types of associations is necessary to describe and defend the reasons for protecting associations against civil rights laws. In other words, a central argument of this chapter is that disaggregation among varieties of groups is essential to understanding the scope and strength of American commitments to freedom of association. Actually, it is possible that further differentiation will be needed as our understanding of this complex area grows—the contention here is that *at least* three categories should be considered.[1]

First, intimate relationships should be protected simply because they are basic to personhood, to being fully human. Constitutional law has long recognized this, though sometimes only implicitly. People can choose their spouses for any reason, however reprehensible, without interference from the state. Similarly, people can choose—and exclude—members of their families without a good justification.[2]

This feature of political morality is often overlooked or downplayed, but it is fundamental. If government were able to regulate these relationships, they would lose their essential character. Sometimes the term *privacy* is used to describe their immunity from official scrutiny, but that term is purely negative and fails to fully capture the concept. People need to be able to freely form these bonds not because the government has no interests there but also because doing so is essential to their humanity or personhood.[3]

Of course, even the closest and most primary groups can be regulated in certain ways. Government can and must prevent spouses from subjecting each other to grievous harm, for example. It can remove children who suffer abuse or neglect. It can protect minors by prohibiting them from marrying until they reach adulthood. It can outlaw prostitution because of concerns about that occupation's systematic exploitation of sex workers. Yet when it comes to antidiscrimination law, our focus here, the freedom to select our spouses and other close relations is virtually absolute. A government could not prohibit someone from forming these relationships for invidious reasons, including racial discrimination.

Second, groups that are not intimate, but still contained and close, enjoy significant immunity from state intervention as well. Voluntary associations like these serve as sites of identification, they build up social capital, and they influence citizens' ideas and impulses. Examples of community groups characterized by bonds of trust and identification might include religious congregations and private clubs. While perhaps not essential to personhood as such—a debatable point—these groups nevertheless provide context for the formation of individuals' conceptions and basic commitments. Not just through education but through conversation, socializing, and shared pursuit of projects, they help to cultivate citizens and they enrich the wider political community. Individuals' perspectives and passions on the most fundamental questions of personal and political morality owe much to their participation in these groups.[4]

Crucially, independence from the influence of government, powerful organizations, and other citizens can be strengthened in such settings. Robert Cover was right to emphasize the importance of associations for the genesis and cultivation of norms that can be independent of the state and the market. Political and social life might be possible without community groups, but it doubtless would take a form that is different, diluted, and even desultory. These groups are not only important because of the role they play in democracy—in addition, they bolster personal identity and the exercise of a range of human capacities—but they do perform a crucial function for constitutional law and politics.[5]

These community associations ought to be able to constitute themselves without interference from the state, presumptively even where they practice selection or exclusion that is not connected in any obvious way to their values or mission. The rationale for this immunity, however, *is* connected to the role of these associations in the formation of wills and worldviews. Community groups deserve a guarantee against government intervention because and insofar as they foster persons and citizens. However, it would be a mistake to require them to articulate a mature vision as a condition of protection, because they require room to explore and elaborate on their ideas and impulses. Were we to demand a connection to mission before exempting these groups from civil rights laws, that could imperil the *processes* of principle formation that such groups enable. And that, in turn, could flatten the diversity of discourses that a vibrant democracy needs—both to formulate good policy and, critically, to check the government through dissent.[6]

Several limits surround this imperative of immunity for community groups, however. An implicit requirement is that they must qualify as relatively close, a requirement that should be rigorous, so that few groups will satisfy it. Bonds of trust and identification are necessary for the effective exploration and experimentation with impulses and ideas. Therefore, groups that do not feature such interpersonal identification ought not to qualify. We can use the formation of ideas and impulses as a powerful criterion for when groups ought to qualify for constitutional protection. That said, it is helpful to have at hand criteria that are more specific and administrable, if only as proxies for the kinds of associations that can claim this extraordinary guarantee against civil right laws.[7]

One way to depersonalize relations is to commercialize them. But that is not the only way. Not just groups that are primarily commercial in their nature or activities but also true nonprofits may be disqualified, even though they may be committed to the pursuit and promulgation of ideas, because (and insofar as) they are too diffuse or dispersed to provide the conditions for the mutual constituting of citizens. Although there is no formula for distinguishing these groups, factors for identifying them may include size, bureaucracy, selectivity, exclusivity, commercialism, and orientation to the expression or implementation of ideas or values. These factors are drawn from doctrine on whether a group is subject to public accommodations law, but they also can work to describe the kinds of groups that require constitutional protection in order to form and foster normative worlds independent of government. None of these factors is dispositive. Again, identifying groups that qualify for this sort of First Amendment protection ought not to be a formalistic exercise; rather, it should always relate back to the purposes for protecting community groups in a democratic society.[8]

Relatedly, the immunity of community groups from government regulation ought to be presumptive only. Sufficiently compelling public reasons can outweigh the importance of group autonomy for the wider social and political community. Certainly these reasons must be strong in order to prevail; if even civil rights laws can be suspended, then many other government regulations likewise will be insufficiently strong. But space must be left for the possibility that such interests can overbalance the value of associational freedom. In addition, immunity from regulation is not the same as entitlement to support—policy makers may decline to subsidize groups that they could not force to stop discriminating under conditions that will be described in Chapter 10. Likewise, government leaders can denounce such groups through official communications, within the limits that are explored in Chapter 6.[9]

A third and final type of association describes those that, although larger and looser, are still deserving of some protection from antidiscrimination rules. *Values organizations* can be crucial to the diversity of viewpoints that is necessary for probing debate on pressing questions of self-governance. And certain forms of selectivity may be necessary for them to communicate those perspectives with clarity and coherence. Think here of Catholic Charities, the social service organization, or the Boy Scouts of America. Discrimination in the employment of leaders—hiring only clergy, and thus only men, to lead a large religious university or hospital, for instance—may be essential to the mission of such groups. And again, their visions can enrich a democracy, even when (or because) those policies are illiberal.

Yet here political morality demands stricter limitations. These constraints follow from the rationale for protection in the first place. Most important, such groups *do* have to show that any discrimination is required by their organizational values or purpose. After all, the point of suspending antidiscrimination laws here is to allow these entities to compose and communicate their missions effectively. So where exclusion would not further the mission of the organization, it does not deserve immunity.

Moreover, autonomy for these groups normally extends only to policy leadership, not to the employment of people in administrative roles. Only employees who are involved in mission development and communication need to be shielded from civil rights laws for the entity to play its role in democratic life; employees with other duties should be free from bias. Finally, the immunity is only presumptive here, too, and therefore it can be overbalanced by sufficiently strong government interests.

Overall, this disaggregated approach—or one that is further developed along these lines—can be both nuanced and powerful enough to articulate the main commitments of political morality to freedom of association, at least when set against civil rights guarantees. A few general points should be kept in mind. First, remember that this framework applies equally to religious and secular organizations. Not only congregations but civic organizations generally can play critical roles in the formation of wills and worldviews among citizens. Not only nationwide denominations but also large secular organizations can influence national debate on key contemporary issues. In other words, virtually every substantive argument for freedom of association applies evenhandedly to religious and secular groups. At least in this area of political life, religion is not special.[10]

A second general comment is that there can be *interaction* between community groups and values organizations, particularly where a local group is part of a larger national association. Many churches are organized this way, and so are some nonreligious groups that are active in local life. And of course the larger group can have an important impact on the principles and perspectives that are developed by local affiliates. For example, in *Jaycees* a chapter began admitting women as regular members; it sued when the national organization threatened to revoke its charter. So umbrella organizations can have an important impact on the ideologies of local groups. However, it usually is not necessary for national organizations to have complete discretion to exclude leaders on discriminatory grounds for them to be able to play that role. Most of the time it is sufficient to allow these umbrella organizations to choose policy leaders for reasons *connected* to their mission for them to provide the structure—institutional and ideological—within which local groups can engage in processes of will formation that are so critical to citizenship.[11]

A third observation is more tentative—namely, that these normative arguments justify certain associational rights not only in the noncommercial realm but also in commerce. There is no obvious reason why business associations ought to be automatically excluded, whatever their other attributes. This contention is bound to be controversial, but it appears to follow from the moral commitments described and defended above. Commercial enterprises are not likely to be characterized by bonds of trust and identification, but where they *do* approximate community nonprofits in their scale and substance, they too may deserve protections from government interference. And when commercial concerns have an even broader reach—where they are regional or national—they nevertheless can claim protections where they are organized around ideas whose communication can enrich democratic debate.

Keep in mind the difference between commercial and noncommercial organizations and activities; that can help illustrate why it is hard to make a normative case for treating commerce as categorically different. Nonprofit organizations can be involved in commercial activities, for instance. Large hospitals can have thousands of employees, an even greater number of customers/patients, and budgets in the hundreds of millions of dollars. Without a doubt, they are engaged in commercial activity, even if they are structured as nonprofits. Universities, too, offer a service for a fee. Of course, both types of entities also have important noncommercial purposes, but they cannot easily be classified as solely noncommercial in nature. In fact, the activities of nonprofit and for-profit organizations are sometimes indistinguishable.

Now, it may make sense for legal doctrine to use the distinction between nonprofit and business organizations as a proxy for associational closeness. But conceptually and normatively, there may be no good reason why a commercial entity need *necessarily* be unable to promote the goods identified in this section. That an entity is engaged in commercial activity may be *some* evidence that its purpose is primarily profit oriented or instrumental rather than values based or expressive, but it is not dispositive. And much the same may be said for the fact that an entity is organized as a nonprofit rather than as a business; it can be suggestive of associational dynamics, but not more.[12]

If the arguments above are correct, then political theory should distinguish among (1) intimate associations, which are essential for personhood; (2) community groups, which promote the formation of citizens' wills and worldviews; and (3) larger or looser organizations designed around values, which play an important role in public debate. Each of these can justifiably claim a different sort of protection. Intimate relationships need the ability to exclude in order to preserve basic humanity and personhood. Community or civic groups may draw the boundaries of their association without reference to the ideas that they establish the conditions for cultivating, but they will be narrowly defined. And values organizations need protection only insofar as necessary to construct and communicate their convictions in public debate. Again, the difference between government treatment of the last two groups is justified because tight associations can and should be incubators for the formation of concepts and commitments, without any need to show results, while more bureaucratic organizations ought to be able to engage in illiberal targeting only where necessary to promulgate established convictions. Distinguishing among these groups will be specific, fact intensive, and worthwhile insofar as freedom of association law comes to serve the values that animate the doctrine in the first place.

Something like this framework is reflected in contemporary constitutional law. That is not sufficient to conclude that the framework is correct, but its coherence with case outcomes that are thought to be defensible, after reflection, can bolster a conclusion that its conception of freedom of association is warranted. That said, the interests that drive the framework also generate significant *critiques* of existing law.

Freedom of Association in Law

Contemporary association law can be understood as differentiating among different types of associations—intimate relationships, community groups, and values organizations—although courts do not consistently conceptualize the doctrine that way.

First, there is a doctrine of intimate association, usually located in the Due Process Clause, which does provide virtually absolute protection to form such relationships. People have a constitutional right to marry whom they like, even on discriminatory grounds, free of government interference. And that right is fairly strictly limited to truly intimate groups.[13]

Second, associations that could be called community groups enjoy significant protection. Various doctrines embody this principle. For one, the ministerial exception allows religious congregations to select clergy free of employment discrimination law. The Supreme Court embraced that rule, which had long been observed by lower federal courts, in *Hosanna-Tabor Evangelical Lutheran Church and School v. Equal Employment Opportunity Commission.* There, the court held that both the Establishment Clause and the Free Exercise Clause forbid civil rights law from interfering in churches' leadership decisions. In particular, the justices ruled that a Lutheran school could fire a teacher for taking her complaint about discrimination to the EEOC rather than resolving it internally, as required by church rules. (She believed that the school had taken employment actions against her because of a medical disability, which if proven would have been illegal under civil rights law.) That ruling shielded the church from antidiscrimination law, which otherwise may well have protected the teacher's decision to seek help from civil rights authorities.[14]

Similarly, in *Boy Scouts of America v. Dale,* the court ruled in favor of a local troop that excluded a scoutmaster because he was gay, even though New Jersey civil rights law otherwise would have protected him against that form of discrimination. The court accepted that sexual morality was essential to the group's articulated mission, and that the group had to be able to select leaders that would embody and promote those beliefs. Whether the Boy Scouts really did hold beliefs about sexual morality as part of its essential purpose was a question in the case—the court deferred to the group on this issue, to a significant extent—but the principle of the case seems plain.[15]

So both religious and secular community groups can discriminate when they select leaders, albeit in different ways. Other doctrine, embodied in civil rights laws rather than the Constitution, allows congregations to favor people of the same religion when they choose not just leaders but other employees. For instance, Title VII of the Civil Rights Act of 1964, the main federal civil rights law on employment, contains a provision, Section 702, that allows religious organizations to discriminate in favor of coreligionists. This exemption is quite limited, however. Section 702 only allows groups to discriminate on the basis of religion—not race, sex, gender, and the like—and it allows them to do so *only in favor of members of their own faith.* So while a Catholic church could use this doctrine to limit employment to fellow Catholics, it could not exclude, say, Lutherans alone. The idea is that the free formation of ideas may require hiring members of the same faith, but not other prohibited discrimination—at least not as directly. And although the doctrine allows groups to discriminate even against employees with no responsibility for policy or preaching, the exemption only applies to religious organizations themselves, not to business corporations, even if they are owned and operated by believers.[16]

The leading case on Section 702, *Corporation of the Presiding Bishop of the Church of Jesus Christ of Latter-Day Saints v. Amos,* illustrates the last two features of Section 702. First, the employee there functioned as a janitor, not as any kind of policy leader. Second, while the organization in *Amos* was a gymnasium, it was owned and operated by a religious organization.[17]

So while there are borderline cases—consider what happens if an employee is terminated for becoming pregnant in violation of religious teachings, where the congregation claims it is firing her for straying from orthodoxy rather than for being a woman—on the whole, Section 702 is relatively narrowly limited to discrimination in favor of coreligionists by nonprofit religious organizations themselves.

In recent times debate about the Section 702 exception has continued. Currently, federal civil rights law does not protect against discrimination on the basis of lesbian, gay, bisexual, or transgender (LGBT) status in employment. Congress has long considered adding sexual orientation and gender identity to the list of protected classes, alongside characteristics like race, gender, religion, and national origin. That proposed legislation, the Employment Non-Discrimination Act (ENDA), included a widened religion exemption that would allow congregations not just to favor employees of the same faith but also to disfavor LGBT employees. In 2015 the Obama administration considered that sort of broad exemption when it prohibited employment discrimination on the basis of LGBT status by federal contractors, but it ended up retaining the existing, narrower religion accommodation modeled on Section 702. At around the same time, several large LGBT advocacy groups withdrew their support for ENDA in Congress, citing concern about the broad religion exemption in the bill. So the scope of this exemption for religious employers is a matter of active debate among Americans. In 2015, progressive groups suggested that an exemption in the style of Section 702 should not necessarily be required for all religious organizations receiving federal funding through the faith-based initiatives program.[18]

Here the crucial point is that civil rights law already recognizes the ability of congregations to shape their associations in illiberal ways. Some of these exemptions apply to secular groups as well. Federal employment discrimination law gives free rein to groups with very few employees, allowing them to select, hire, and fire people in any way they like. Many state and local employment laws are more restrictive, applying even to small employers, but they, too, recognize some ability of very small employers to associate on their own terms.[19]

Moving beyond employment, houses of worship can deny *membership* on virtually any ground without legal interference. And public accommodations law does not apply to private clubs, as Chapter 7 will explain in detail. These legal rules seem to reflect a commitment to associational freedom for civic groups. In one decision from the civil rights era, the Supreme Court held that a local chapter of the National Association for the Advancement of Colored People could not be forced to divulge its membership lists to Southern authorities; the First Amendment protected its ability to define membership without official penalty. In these ways, membership decisions by community groups are constitutionally guaranteed.[20]

Again, however, there are limits. New York City's public accommodations law, for instance, prohibits discrimination even by private clubs that have more than four hundred members and engage in certain commercial activities, such as serving food and renting out their space to nonmembers. So the Racquet and Tennis Club on Park Avenue excludes women, even today, but it must remain relatively small and noncommercial in order to avoid civil rights restrictions. And again its employment practices are even more constrained.[21]

In several respects, then, existing antidiscrimination law recognizes the ability of community and civic groups to associate in ways that are inegalitarian—not only in membership but even in employment to some degree. This reflects, presumably, the importance of such groups for the formation of citizens whose thinking can remain independent of each other and of the state.

Looser organizations—the third and final category of associations—receive certain accommodations when they are organized around values that are significant and substantive, and when an exemption is needed for the group to further those values. For example, the ministerial exception applies even to large bureaucracies—some that are national in scope and relatively attenuated in their affiliations. If a religious university requires its president to be ordained, and if the clergy is all male, that can effectively exclude women from consideration for the position. Similarly, religious hospitals or social service organizations may have leadership that is limited to male clergy members. And these are all employment relationships that would normally be regulated by federal and state civil rights laws that prohibit discrimination on the basis of sex or gender.

Secular values organizations receive similar protection in their selection of leadership under the doctrine of expressive association associated with the First Amendment's Free Speech Clause. Recall that in the *Dale* case, the Boy Scouts were protected when they decided to exclude a scout leader because he was gay, even though New Jersey's civil rights law otherwise would have protected him. Here the group was required to show that the exclusion was connected to its mission, though the court gave substantial deference to the Boy Scouts' determination about whether condemnation of LGBT people was required by its organizational purpose. Although the case involved a local troop, the same rule would apply to the national organization.[22]

Moreover, religious organizations receive the accommodation in Section 702 of the federal employment discrimination law—the one that allows them to favor coreligionists in employment—even if they are large and highly bureaucratized. This exemption is, however, narrow. Recall that it allows only discrimination in favor of members of the same faith, not against particular other faiths. And it does not permit discrimination on other protected grounds, such as race or sex, even when that is required by the group's theology. Finally, it should not allow discrimination against employees engaged in theologically prohibited conduct—such as pregnancy outside marriage or divorce and remarriage—if that would amount to discrimination on protected grounds other than religion, such as sex or gender. The next section suggests further modifications.[23]

Where law prohibits discrimination on the basis of sexual orientation and gender identity, the scope of Section 702 is a salient question today. Think of President Obama's executive order banning employment discrimination on the basis of sexual orientation by federal contractors, which contains a narrow religion exemption patterned on Section 702. Would that exemption allow religious contractors to fire employees who marry someone of the same sex in violation of their theology? The best reading of current law is that they would not have that right. Section 702 and its analogues allow only discrimination in favor of members of the same faith, not employment action against people who engage in conduct that is closely associated with, or tantamount to, membership in a protected group.

In sum, then, American law does reflect strong protection for intimate relationships, significant protection for community and civic groups, and even some leeway for large values organizations. This roughly reflects the importance of each type of group for citizens, for the society, and for democratic government. However, the congruence between political morality on the freedom of association and existing law protecting that freedom is imperfect. To better reflect democratic values, modifications in existing law should be considered.

How Freedom of Association Law Should Change

Several reforms of current law would help to align it with the principle of freedom of association. With regard to close community groups, a category that is not sufficiently recognized in American law, the changes pertain mostly to employment.

Religious congregations already have constitutional latitude to choose their leaders without interference from employment discrimination laws. Although the Supreme Court did not speak to the point, lower courts have long held that this autonomy extends even to discrimination that is *not required* by the group's theology—and even to discrimination that may be *prohibited* by the faith. Why would courts do this? Their main rationale seems to be that the relationship between congregation and clergy is so close that government interference would be inappropriate.[24]

But that rationale is deficient in important respects. For one thing, the ministerial exception applies even to denominational bureaucracies that are national in scope and diffuse in their structure. Even with regard to community or civic groups, moreover, it fails to capture the strongest *rationale* for immunity in clergy employment. After all, these groups are not intimate in the way that marriages or families are—relationships in them are not necessary for basic personhood in the same way. Rather, freedom to choose a leader is important because local congregations are crucial incubators for citizens' conceptions and convictions. And whether and how those commitments are fostered depends greatly on local leadership. Therefore, courts are right to protect community groups' leadership decisions without regard to ideology.

They should not, however, make this protection specific to *religious* community groups. And under current black letter law, secular groups may choose leaders only in ways that are required by their mission. Think of the Boy Scouts, who were asked to show that excluding a gay scoutmaster was required by their teachings. At least for exceedingly close-knit community groups, that requirement is inappropriate. Such groups should not have the burden of showing that their ideas are already sufficiently developed to require a certain form of differentiation among leaders. And *in practice,* if not unequivocally in theory, that is close to the law. After all, the Supreme Court deferred to the scout troop's understanding of its own belief system. Courts should conform their doctrine to that practice. And that goes not just for voluntary leadership—James Dale himself was a volunteer—but also for employment of leaders.

That change would bring the law for secular close associations into congruence with the rule for religious congregations. And in areas where there is no good reason to treat religion differently under the Constitution, as here, that congruence is needed.

When it comes to larger values organizations, however, congruence should be achieved in the opposite way—by bringing religious groups in line with secular ones. Citizen convictions are not shaped by bureaucratized organizations in exactly the same way they are by community groups. And even if they sometimes are, such groups do not require latitude to develop the ideas and ideologies that do that work; they are already fully elaborated, presumptively. Routinization tends to promote mature ideological elaboration in these institutions (which nevertheless can further develop their commitments through established processes). Citizens may still be influenced in profound ways by these organizations, but not because the group itself is still engaged in a process of establishing and elaborating its core tenets.

Similarly, the ability of diffuse organizations to enrich public debate on issues of the day does not depend on choosing leaders without regard to their ideology. That is, the arguments in political morality for protecting association by civic organizations without regard to mission do not apply to larger bureaucracies, as we have seen. To the extent that these larger groups should be insulated from employment laws when they choose their leaders, they should bear the burden of showing that such insulation is necessary for them to construct and communicate their values.

Currently the ministerial exception contains no such distinction between close associations and values organizations—but it should. Denominations whose theologies prohibit discrimination against, say, women should not be able to exclude candidates on the basis of sex or gender when they choose national leaders. That limitation may require courts to inquire into the belief systems of faiths, but that should be fairly straightforward and familiar when large, established groups are at issue. After all, judges already must determine whether a "religion" is at issue to apply religious freedom provisions.[25]

Similarly, secular organizations that operate beyond local communities should be required to show that any discrimination in their choice of leadership is required by their expressive purpose. And deference to those claims is properly limited.

Changes to Section 702 would also be worthwhile. Again, that provision allows religious organizations to discriminate in employment in favor of members of the faith, even outside of leadership positions. In *Amos*, remember, the court protected the ability of a church-owned gymnasium to fire a janitor whose church membership had lapsed. This doctrine seems appropriate for local congregations and even for religiously owned and operated nonprofits that are community based; they require such latitude to create and maintain a community that is capable of cultivating the ideas and ideals of engaged citizens.

Yet large, diffuse organizations have less reason to engage in employment discrimination that favors members for positions that are unconnected to the formation or implementation of the group's mission. A full-service hospital, for instance, does not need the ability to limit all employment to members of the faith, even if it qualifies as a religious organization, as did the gymnasium in *Amos*. Large hospitals serve everyone, and their objective is to heal people. They do not require the ability to limit all employment to coreligionists, even if they are affiliated with a religion and even if their purpose is connected to religious values.

Certain employees of these organizations, however, may well need to be members of the faith. Workers who set or implement the core policies of the institution, for example, may be required to share the basic tenets of the religion with which the institution is affiliated. This distinction connects the doctrine around Section 702 to the underlying purposes of freedom of association for values organizations.

Recall that these organizations deserve some protection in their ability to associate because of the role they play in diversifying and driving public debate on consequential issues, as well as to effectively implement their convictions by serving the public on the ground. The hospital example suggests that such organizations may not only need the ability to exclude nonmembers from employment just to craft and communicate their mission but also to pursue their purpose of promoting public health. Yet even so, that rationale does not require giving values organizations the ability to exclude nonmembers from employment positions that are unconnected to institutional policy.

Another important change to Section 702 is to make its provisions equally available to sacred and secular organizations. None of the arguments that have been offered in this chapter differentiate between religious organizations and nonreligious ones, and this discussion of Section 702 is no exception. Ideally, community and civic groups of all sorts would be able to limit employment to people who are members of the group. This would be just as necessary for will formation by secular entities as it would in the religious context. And, again ideally, larger values organizations would enjoy that immunity from civil rights laws only for the employment of people who are engaged in policy formation, implementation, and communication—not for employees without those responsibilities. Equality of opportunity, a central goal of employment discrimination laws, is too important to be sacrificed where an organization cannot give good reasons for needing to limit employment on prohibited grounds.

Normally this will not be difficult, because secular groups can limit employment to members without running afoul of antidiscrimination laws in the first place by virtue of the fact that secular ideology is not a prohibited reason for adverse employment action. (Recall that Section 702 does not license exclusion of protected classes other than membership in the belief group—and there is no reason why its secular analogue should not be limited in the same way.) Yet the arguments for freedom of association are important to remember in case situations arise in which secular groups find themselves restricted in their ability to shape employment according to their membership—for instance, where an employee can make out a claim for retaliation for speech. Then the protection for freedom of association that Section 702 affords might become relevant to secular groups as well.

Outside of employment, as well, some changes to current law may be necessary to preserve the freedom of association. Currently, private clubs generally can already shape their membership because they are specifically excluded from public accommodations laws. But not all community groups qualify as private clubs—the Boy Scouts troop in *Dale* is one example of an organization that did not.

Generally, the arguments given here point toward significant protection from public accommodations laws for such community groups. However, it should be noted carefully that this only applies to close associations, and it applies most strictly to membership decisions, and much less strictly to employment policies that implicate the state's interest in equal economic membership for all citizens. And for groups that provide services to the public, it does not apply to discrimination among beneficiaries, which involves weaker associational interests for the group and strong interests of equal access for the state. Yet within those boundaries, the freedom of association provides somewhat greater protection from public accommodations law than does current law.

All in all, then, existing law roughly tracks the arguments for freedom of association, and for its limits, that this chapter has described and defended. However, certain changes to existing law can eliminate inconsistencies and bring the legal doctrine into closer conformity with the underlying rationales for protecting the ability of groups to form and exclude. Obviously, additional and more detailed work will be necessary to implement this vision, and Part III begins that work. But setting out the parameters of the principle is an important first step.

Freedom of Association for Corporations?

Whether these protections—for community groups or values organizations—should be available only to nonprofits is a difficult question that requires further analysis. Arguments that draw on the importance of citizen formation, or that trade on preserving the richness of public debate and committed action, would seem to apply to any group that pursues ideas and values as a central part of its purpose, regardless of whether it is organized as a nonprofit corporation, a religious corporation, a sole proprietorship, a partnership, or a business corporation. What matters, on this conception, is whether its purposes and activities are values based or commercial. On the other hand, whether a group is organized as a nonprofit may be a useful proxy for whether its ideas and endeavors are commercial in nature. And law often deploys proxies like these, despite their moral inaccuracies, because of their benefits for administrability and general workability.[26]

Moreover, and more profoundly, whether business corporations have access to the freedom of association should depend on the purposes of such legal entities, if we are to avoid a mechanical formalism that treats corporations differently without good reason. And, it turns out, there is profound disagreement among experts in corporate law on that point. Perhaps the wisest view is that corporate entities serve multiple purposes. All of this requires further investigation.[27]

Conclusion

What *is* clear from this discussion is that changes should be made to current doctrine to bring it into harmony with the principle of freedom of association once that principle is clearly and fully understood. Although the law already reflects and reinforces a disaggregated view of the freedom of association, it does so with complex doctrines that are hard to rationalize. Making the modifications suggested here will help to make the law more defensible. And current conflicts require a warranted approach that can address them in all their complexity, as Chapters 7 and 8 will illustrate.

SIX

GOVERNMENT NONENDORSEMENT

SO FAR, the principles identified in Part II have all concerned government regulation of citizens in various ways. Avoiding harm to others limits the ability of the government to lift regulatory burdens on religious actors when doing so would shift meaningful costs to other private citizens. Fairness to others restricts the ability of officials to accommodate religious people alone, when nonreligious people also seek to engage in the activity for reasons that are comparably deep and worthwhile. And freedom of association protects groups against civil rights laws that would impair the ability of the group to pursue important interests—or perform critical functions—for individuals, society, and democratic politics. All of these concern the government's power to restrict or compel citizen behavior.

What about when the government is acting not as regulator but as speaker? After all, the government sends messages to citizens all the time: it promotes healthy living, champions national pride, educates children and adults, chastens wrongdoers, promotes health and safety, and so on. And generally, the Constitution gives it wide latitude to convey those messages. In fact, the government could hardly function if it faced serious and frequent restrictions on its own expression.

Nevertheless, there *are* constitutional limits on what the government can say, and those limits play a crucial role in ensuring free and equal citizenship for everyone. Restrictions come from the religion clauses, the Speech Clause, the Equal Protection Clause, and perhaps even the Due Process

Clause. And when those restrictions involve religion, constitutional boundaries on government speech can work to mediate the conflict between religious freedom and equality.

Consider a consequential example. In *Town of Greece v. Galloway*, the Supreme Court evaluated a local government's legislative prayer practice. Legislators in the Town of Greece, New York, assembled once a month to pass ordinances, hold hearings, consider petitions from citizens, and conduct other town business. Each of these meetings opened with an invocation from a local clergy member. Apparently, the town clerk selected these ministers by consulting a guide to the town's congregations and going down the list, inviting each clergy member in turn. But the result was that only Christian clergy delivered invocations. Over a ten-year period, every prayer was offered by a Christian priest or minister. (The only exceptions occurred during the year that litigation began, when four of twelve prayers were delivered by non-Christians.) Moreover, many of the messages delivered by Christian clergy were identifiably Christian in content rather than nonsectarian. Atheists sued the town, arguing that the prayer practice amounted to an official endorsement of Christianity and monotheism in violation of the Establishment Clause.[1]

A foundational principle holds that when the government lends its imprimatur to a particular religion, that impairs the citizenship standing of others. Outsiders become, through that very act, disfavored members of the political community, or at the very least they are marked according to their faith. The court has implemented something like this conviction in its "endorsement test" for detecting violations of the Establishment Clause. That test, though much criticized, embodies a basic impulse. Most Americans would agree that it would be impermissible for a municipality to adopt the message "This is a Christian town" as official policy.

But the Establishment Clause does not stand alone in restricting state speech. Government would be equally prohibited from conveying the message "This town is for whites." Although that statement would implicate the Equal Protection Clause rather than the Establishment Clause, it would run up against a similar value—namely, the importance of guaranteeing that citizens stand as equals before their government.

Government nonendorsement, the principle described and defended in this chapter, accounts for that commitment to full and equal citizenship as applied to government speech. Enforcing the rule does not mean that government will not continue to have wide discretion to decide what to say; the principle of government nonendorsement is only rarely triggered. But it nevertheless has conceptual importance for the subject of this book.[2]

After all, marriage exclusion laws are unconstitutional even in states like California, where all the legal benefits of civil marriage are available to same-sex couples through civil union or domestic partnership laws. On the understanding provided in this chapter, that is because government may not relegate lesbian, gay, bisexual, and transgender (LGBT) citizens to a different status in society and in the political community. That is virtually what the court held in *Obergefell v. Hodges*, when it required marriage equality throughout the United States.[3]

By contrast, the court sidelined the principle of government nonendorsement in *Town of Greece*. Its ruling for the town was an anomaly and a mistake, as justice Elena Kagan argued in her pathbreaking dissent. By and large, the court has enforced constitutional limits on what the government can say. And it has done so largely, if not exclusively, to protect the legal stature of all citizens before their government and in the political community.

Note that the government can communicate approval or disapproval in another way as well—namely, through funding or defunding. When it provides or withholds this kind of support, similar legal issues can arise, especially when it subsidizes private speakers. For example, a legislature could not only denounce private discrimination but also defund offenders. It could even contract with private speakers to communicate its message of equality. Although the issues that arise when government acts as funder therefore can be similar to those surrounding its role as speaker, this chapter sets them aside. Chapter 10 considers questions of state spending, drawing analogies to official expression where appropriate.

This chapter begins by illustrating the principle of government nonendorsement in the areas of religious freedom and racial equality. It then extends the discussion to LGBT rights, especially the right to marriage equality. Limits on government electioneering and antiabortion advocacy are rooted more deeply in full citizenship, meaning the ability of people to exercise their basic freedoms, so they are discussed more briefly. Putting all the examples together, the chapter concludes that there are constitutional limitations on what the government can say. Those limitations are multiple and meaningful, even though they are relatively modest, and they play a role in mediating between religious freedom and equality law.

Why Should the Government Be Limited in Its Speech?

A basic principle holds that American government must protect the full and equal citizenship of all members of the political community. *Equal citizenship,* as this book has been arguing in various contexts, means that all Americans stand before the government on the same footing, simply as citizens. There ought to be no second-class citizens or subordinated castes within the polity.

Full citizenship means that all Americans should have freedom to exercise the basic capacities of citizens. It captures the liberty aspects of citizenship. For example, Americans have the rights to speak freely, to vote, to run for public office, to form associations, and so forth.

The chapters in this book not only apply these principles of citizenship to specific disputes and less abstract commitments, but they thereby help to establish and strengthen the case for the existence of full and equal citizenship in a reciprocal fashion. Here, similarly, the discussion of government nonendorsement both implements and supports the commitments to full and equal membership in the political community.

At first glance, the notion that government could affect the capacities and standing of Americans might not seem intuitive. Many people subscribe to the childhood saying, "Sticks and stones may break my bones, but names can never hurt me." But on closer inspection, it turns out that government speech can implicate basic democratic commitments, even when it is unaccompanied by tangible consequences like regulation of private activity or loss of government funding.

In other words, government speech alone can interfere with the ability of citizens to stand before the government not simply as Americans but as differentiated or disfavored members of the political community. And it can interfere with their participation in politics and their exercise of fundamental freedoms. Notably, this principle is not a matter of injured feelings; it protects against a change in the *legal* relationship between government and citizen. Government communications that offend equal citizenship constitute citizens as a matter of law.

Government Endorsement of Religion

Perhaps the paradigmatic example of government speech that violates the Constitution is endorsement of religion. Many people recognize that it would be unconstitutional for an American government to declare its partiality toward a particular faith. While historical establishments among the states typically also included other elements, such as public funding of an official church, today there is a near consensus that state endorsement of a particular faith would violate the Establishment Clause, even if it was unaccompanied by more tangible forms of support.[4]

Supreme Court case law comports with this sense. For example, the court struck down a Ten Commandments display in a McCreary County, Kentucky, courthouse because it had been erected with the purpose of advancing or endorsing religion. And a crèche that was displayed on the steps of a courthouse in Pawtucket, Rhode Island, was invalidated because it communicated favor toward Christians and disfavor toward others.[5]

Admittedly, the "endorsement test" is besieged. Originally developed by justice Sandra Day O'Connor and then adopted by the full court, the test asks whether an objective observer, informed of all the relevant facts, would conclude that a government display endorses a particular faith over others, or religion over irreligion. If the answer is yes, then the government's speech impermissibly renders some members of the political community favored and others disfavored. That approach has been criticized on various grounds, including the difficulty of evaluating the meaning of government speech according to an objective observer. And in *Town of Greece,* the endorsement test went unsupported, even if it was not explicitly rejected.[6]

Still, the best understanding of constitutional law is that meaningful boundaries continue to limit government endorsement of religion, both in principle and in practice. First of all, even if the endorsement test is further eroded or even eliminated, a rule will endure that government cannot engage in core forms of religious speech, even apart from material effects. Of course, minor exceptions will be permitted, for better or worse—"In God We Trust" will remain America's national motto for the foreseeable future, and the Pledge of Allegiance will continue to be permitted in classrooms despite the phrase "One Nation under God." But blatant, outright endorsements will continue to abridge a basic principle of American government.[7]

So although the court approved the prayer scheme in *Town of Greece,* it arguably retained the premise that *if* the scheme had promoted a religion—say, because the town clerk had willfully favored Christian clergy—then it would have run up against the Establishment Clause. In other words, a shared assumption of both the majority and the dissent was that government speech about religion *can* violate the Constitution, even absent concrete ramifications. Their dispute was about what kind of speech crosses that boundary.[8]

Ultimately, then, the most defensible conclusion is that the Establishment Clause of the First Amendment should and in fact does limit government expression on matters of religion. Whatever the future of the endorsement test itself, officials in America will continue to face constitutional limitations on their ability to endorse particular faiths over others or belief over nonbelief. That is a fundamental instance of the principle of government nonendorsement. Yet the principle also applies beyond the subject matter of religion.

Racialized Government Expression

For another powerful application of the principle of government nonendorsement, consider the example of government speech on the subject of race. Official expression that denigrates racial minorities violates citizenship guarantees in a paradigmatic way.

Of course, there is a well-known debate about whether private speech that communicates hatred on the basis of race ought to remain constitutionally protected. Some countries do prohibit certain forms of hate speech, and their courts do not interpret their constitutions to protect that speech. American courts, by contrast, have interpreted the Free Speech Clause in the First Amendment to protect private expression, even when it expresses hatred toward racial minorities.[9]

Yet although the protection of *private* hate speech is debatable, the constitutional status of analogous *government* speech should not be in any doubt. Imagine that Congress issued a joint resolution declaring "America is a white nation." Or imagine a rural municipality posting a sign alongside the main road into town, supporting white supremacy. These official statements would violate equal citizenship in a straightforward way, because they would constitute nonwhite citizens as subordinate.[10]

Notice that nothing in this conclusion depends on how such statements make people feel, subjectively. The harm in racialized government speech is not psychological, in other words, but legal. When the state says such things, it changes the *legal* standing of citizens before their government. This is an objective matter. So while there is a "sticks and stones" argument for protection of private hate speech—convincing or not—there is no such argument when it comes to government speech that subordinates on the basis of race. Its harm is independent of its targets' construction of its meaning.[11]

Racialized government speech is not only reprehensible as a matter of political morality but it also violates the Equal Protection Clause. Perhaps the best place to see this principle at work is in *Brown v. Board of Education*, the famous school desegregation decision. There, chief justice Earl Warren emphasized the importance of public education, as well as the damaging psychological effects of segregation on the basis of race. That reasoning was subsequently criticized on the ground that it was not based in neutral principles of law. But Charles Black famously defended *Brown* by arguing that racially segregated public schooling had an unmistakable social meaning—namely, government subordination of nonwhite citizens. Even if the schools were equal in every material way, and even if students suffered no psychological harm, *Brown* was rightly decided because it prohibited the government from rendering African Americans inferior among the citizenry.[12]

Similarly, in *Loving v. Virginia* the court struck down a state law prohibiting interracial marriage largely because of its expressive import. The State of Virginia defended the law by saying that it impacted everyone equally, since it prevented white people from marrying the person of their choice just as much as it prohibited nonwhite people from doing so. But the court rejected this argument, pointing out that in fact the law only prohibited nonwhite people from marrying white people—it did not block nonwhite people from marrying those who were thought to be in another nonwhite racial category. So the law's structure reinforced its social meaning, which was obvious anyway. To use the court's own language, the Virginia law was designed to bolster a system of "White Supremacy."[13]

Another precedent for the principle that racialized government messaging can violate equal protection is *Shaw v. Reno*, the racial gerrymandering decision. There the court considered an effort by a state to draw the boundaries of electoral districts in order to ensure that minority voters would have their views represented in the legislature. The court struck down the scheme in *Shaw*, holding that the state had drawn district lines in such a way that the only possible conclusion was that race was the predominant factor in the districting, overriding other considerations like urban density, income, political affiliation, age, and so forth.[14]

What was striking about that decision was that voters were not harmed by the districting. Or at least it was possible to hold that view. There was no claim that votes had been diluted; in other words, the "one person, one vote" standard had been observed, and everyone's vote counted equally. In that sense, nonminority voters had just as much influence on their representatives after the redistricting as they did beforehand. If that was right, then the chief harm from the redistricting was expressive. Government was sending the message that race had overriding importance in electoral politics, according to the court—and that message alone violated equal protection. To the extent that reading is correct, *Shaw v. Reno* provides still more support for the notion that government expression alone can violate the Constitution.[15]

Thus, according to both political morality and law, government expression that renders racial minorities subordinate is impermissible, even if it is unaccompanied by any tangible harm. Such government speech alters the legal relationship between minority citizens and their government. Yet there are other examples, too.[16]

Endorsement of Traditional Marriage

Although paradigmatic, these two instances of government nonendorsement—concerning religion and race—do not stand alone in constitutional law. For a more recent example, think of marriage equality for same-sex couples.

Marriage exclusion had an expressive impact. Of course, it also had a tangible impact in many states. A variety of benefits follow civil marriage, including dependents' health benefits, spousal visitation in hospitals, special allowances in estate taxation, and more. In jurisdictions where those benefits were only available to couples who were legally married, exclusion from civil marriage had concrete consequences.[17]

But in several states, all the material benefits of civil marriage were available to same-sex couples through civil unions or domestic partnerships. That was the situation in California, for example, before a federal court struck down the exclusion there. And a Vermont court ordered the legislature to provide all the rights and benefits of civil marriage to same-sex couples. So in jurisdictions like those, the harm was chiefly or entirely expressive. Same-sex couples were mainly just prohibited from using the term *marriage* itself. Moreover, that prohibition only applied to civil law, because couples there could still marry in private ceremonies.[18]

Yet in *Obergefell v. Hodges,* the Supreme Court struck down marriage exclusion laws in all the states, including ones where all the material incidents of marriage were available without regard to sexual orientation. What was its theory of why marriage exclusion laws were unconstitutional even in states with comprehensive civil union or domestic partnership laws?

One theory the court offered in *Obergefell* was that access to civil marriage is a fundamental liberty protected by the Due Process Clause. According to that story, being able to marry in a civil ceremony is a basic capacity of citizens. And the states could articulate no sufficient, nonreligious reason to restrict that freedom. Due process was, in fact, the primary rationale in justice Anthony Kennedy's opinion for the court in *Obergefell.*[19]

Yet that theory had some weaknesses. For one thing, civil marriage has long been restricted in numerous other ways: people cannot marry their siblings, pets, or cars. Were those restrictions also suspect? For another, the due process theory seemed to suggest that a state could not get out of the marriage business altogether, as some state lawmakers proposed in the wake of the decision. In other words, the court's understanding did not treat civil marriage as a discretionary government benefit, which it otherwise seemed to be. Justice Clarence Thomas made this point in his dissent. After all, a state's decision to get out of the marriage business would impose the maximum possible burden on a due process right to civil marriage, and yet most people assumed that it would be constitutional. So the due process theory presented some difficulties.[20]

The court in *Obergefell* did offer another explanation, grounded in equal protection. On that view, marriage exclusions violated the Constitution's equality guarantee simply because they communicated moral disapproval of same-sex spouses and perhaps of LGBT citizens generally. The court seemed to suggest that expressive harm like that would be enough to invalidate the law.

In one passage, for example, the court explained that marriage exclusions should be understood "against a long history of disapproval of their relationships." Especially in that context, their "denial to same-sex couples of the right to marry work[ed] a grave and continuing harm" because the "imposition of this disability on gays and lesbians serve[d] to disrespect and subordinate them." Although the court did not apply this language specifically to laws that worked only expressive harm, the rationale applied fully to them.[21]

In another place, the court addressed the intersection with religious objections to same-sex marriage. While it went out of its way to avoid accusing objectors of animus or bigotry against LGBT people, the court nevertheless adhered to the conviction that allowing such objections to be written into law would work legal disregard of gay and lesbian couples:

> Many who deem same-sex marriage to be wrong reach that conclusion based on decent and honorable religious or philosophical premises, and neither they nor their beliefs are disparaged here. But when that sincere, personal opposition becomes enacted law and public policy, the necessary consequence is to put the imprimatur of the State itself on an exclusion that soon demeans or stigmatizes those whose own liberty is then denied. Under the Constitution, same-sex couples seek in marriage the same legal treatment as opposite-sex couples, and it would disparage their choices and diminish their personhood to deny them this right.[22]

Although this passage appeared in the last paragraph of the due process discussion, and although it included concern for couples' "liberty" and "choices," it also traded on considerations of equal citizenship. The idea that denying same-sex couples the "same legal treatment" with regard to civil marriage "demeans," "disparage[s]," and "stigmatizes" them was classic equal protection reasoning, and it provided a segue to the court's discussion of equal protection itself.

Crucially, then, the court was saying that its ruling should not be understood as an accusation of bigotry against religious reasons for marriage exclusion. It also explained that such reasons are not a permissible ground for policy making. The court dismissed as "counterintuitive" the states' own attempt to explain why the laws were needed—namely, because expanding marriage to include same-sex couples would have promoted a view of marriage that was divorced from procreation and child-rearing, and that in turn would have discouraged *different*-sex couples from marrying. Implicitly, the justices were saying that the only conceivable reasons for marriage exclusion laws were religious or moral, and that those reasons were insufficient to limit an important right.[23]

But the court was saying something else, too—namely, that excluding same-sex couples from civil marriage expressed government disapproval of the practice. Furthermore, that disapproval "serve[d] . . . to subordinate" members of these couples. So although religious people who succeeded in enacting their opposition to same-sex marriage into law were not acting out of bigotry, they *were* drawing the government's "imprimatur" for an expression of disapproval. And that government endorsement of disapproval changed the legal relationship between LGBT citizens who wished to marry in civil ceremonies and the governments that offered those ceremonies. And *that* harm, unlike any material consequences for benefits, was imposed by states that simply denied LGBT people the right to use the term marriage with state recognition.

In sum, marriage exclusion laws did not appear at first to be instances of government expression. They barred same-sex couples from doing something in the manner of a regulation, it seemed, rather than just expressing a perspective like a sign saying "This is a Christian town." But on closer examination, marriage exclusions turned out to have expressive import—and that import was key to the court's rationale in *Obergefell.* Even apart from any regulation of same-sex couples, the laws endorsed disapproval of same-sex marriage. That endorsement alone was enough to violate the Constitution, according to the court. And *Obergefell* therefore stands as an example of the principle of government nonendorsement.

Government Electioneering

Reading the chapter up to this point, it would be possible to conclude that government nonendorsement is an embodiment of equal protection alone. All the examples offered so far—nonendorsement in the area of religion, racialized government speech, and marriage equality—can be understood that way. But in fact, government nonendorsement cuts across a broader range of constitutional provisions. Of course, nonendorsement of religion is most naturally located in the Establishment Clause, and it expresses a commitment to religious liberty understood broadly because it protects the ability of all citizens to believe or not believe according to their convictions. Yet examples outside the religion context also extend beyond equal protection.

Imagine that the government issued a proclamation that read "Vote Democrat" or "Vote Republican." In an era of intense partisanship, it is not so difficult to envision a legislature endorsing that kind of message. Congress issues resolutions all the time, although they usually are not as egregious as an explicit request to vote for a particular party.

But stay with the blatant version for now, just to establish the principle. Most people share an intuition that government itself should not persuade its citizens to exercise their basic political freedoms in one way or another. The commitment to *full citizenship* protects the ability of people to exercise those fundamental capacities without interference from the state.

Reasons for this are at least twofold. First, individuals should be free to participate in elections simply as a matter of political actualization or participation. Part of what it means to belong to a democratic polity is that you can exercise your capacity for opinion formation and the persuasion of others, both inside and outside the government. Engaging that political capacity provides one motivation for citizens to participate in elections at all.[24]

Second, allowing the government to influence electoral politics short-circuits the system of representative government. Normally, citizens elect representatives to carry out their will. They then monitor officials to ensure that they are in fact doing so. And if they are not, citizens have the ability to sanction their agents in government, either through public criticism or by voting against them in the next election. But when public officials use government power to influence elections in a direct way, that process is interrupted. The independence that allows citizens to assess their representatives' performance is compromised, or at least there is that risk. And that undermines both the responsiveness of the system and the perception of responsiveness that is central to its legitimacy.[25]

Of course, many questions and qualifications immediately follow. Government officials act in politically self-serving ways all the time—by pushing policies that have partisan impact, for example. So it can be difficult to tell the difference between ordinary policy making and electioneering. What is more, government officials *can* campaign explicitly for themselves and others while they are in office—they just cannot do that in their official capacity. So the president can say "Vote Democrat" or "Vote Republican" when he or she is speaking as a private citizen or party leader. But, again, it can be hard to tell the difference. Despite these complications, however, the essential point remains uncontroverted: government itself cannot engage in electioneering.

What provision of the Constitution embodies this prohibition? It is difficult to say, because the idea pervades the structure of democratic accountability. Probably the best answer is the Free Speech Clause. Freedom of speech contains not only an individual aspect, guaranteeing a certain form of autonomy, but also a structural aspect, preserving the system of accountability that scaffolds a constitutional democracy. And government electioneering undermines the democratic structures that are fostered by freedom of expression. Consequently, most of those who have recognized a rule against government electioneering have grounded it in the First Amendment.[26]

If that analysis is right, government nonendorsement cuts across not only equal protection and nonestablishment of religion but also the Free Speech Clause itself. And that is not the only liberty-oriented expression of the principle.

Government Opposition to Reproductive Freedom

Another place where government nonendorsement applies outside of equal protection and nonestablishment—and this will serve as the final example—is due process. In particular, it is possible to imagine government speech that is coercive enough to interfere with a woman's right to terminate a pregnancy. Official condemnation like that could well abridge full citizenship in violation of the Constitution.

Recognized by the court as fundamental, the right to terminate a pregnancy was announced in *Roe v. Wade* and reconfirmed in *Planned Parenthood v. Casey*. Today the rule is that government cannot place an undue burden on the ability of women to terminate their pregnancies before viability. It is at least conceivable, though the court has not confronted such a case, that extreme government speech discouraging abortion could run afoul of this legal rule. If the government positioned agents at the entrance to abortion clinics, for instance, and if their job was to shout at women entering the clinic, telling them that abortion is immoral and that they are making a mistake, that could well be unconstitutional as an undue burden. And that could be true even if it consisted purely of government speech, with no legal or material consequences.[27]

Of course, under current law government may express moral disapproval of abortion, and it does so all the time. Laws that defund abortion send that message, for example, and so do laws that require women to be "informed" of certain facts. The court has even held that the purpose of such regulations can be to persuade a woman not to seek to terminate a pregnancy or to express moral judgment. In this way, due process is different from equal protection when it comes to government nonendorsement. While the state may not express disapproval of racial minorities, religious denominations, or people who marry someone of the same sex, the same is not true of terminating a pregnancy.[28]

A sympathetic (and crude) explanation of the difference is that due process protects liberty, which is not abridged by government speech that condemns it, while equality can be violated by simple speech. A response that is less sympathetic to current law is that reproductive freedom itself is essential for the equal standing of women in society, the economy, and the political community.

Either way, government communication that happens close to the time and place of a medical procedure to end a pregnancy could conceivably have both the purpose and the effect of coercion. Such speech happens at the point of greatest vulnerability for the woman. And again, that seems to be its purpose and its likely effect.

At least in theory, then, government nonendorsement has *possible* application to reproductive freedom. And that means it extends, conceivably, to the Due Process Clause, in addition to equal protection, nonestablishment of religion, and freedom of speech. And in due process, as well as in the other settings, the principle has important ramifications not only for individuals' exercise of full citizenship capacities but also for their standing as equal citizens. In that respect, government nonendorsement's application in the area of reproductive freedom resonates with its application in the context of same-sex marriage, where the due process liberty rationale is so closely tied to the equality rationale. In both contexts, government nonendorsement limits what the government can say about fundamental freedoms that also have important ramifications for equal regard in the national community.

Conclusion

Government nonendorsement, then, is the fourth and final principle offered here for thinking about the interaction between religion and equality law in contemporary law and policy. Officials, speaking as officials, cannot telegraph messages that violate guarantees of full and equal citizenship rooted in equal protection, nonendorsement of religion, freedom of speech, and due process. That matters for a range of conflicts involving religion. For example, it limits the ability of states to exclude same-sex couples from civil marriage for religious reasons. And it likewise restricts the ability of governments to implement religious and philosophical opposition to abortion through certain forms of extreme and coercive condemnation of the practice—condemnation that also has an impact on women's equality.

For many of the same reasons, the principle of government endorsement plays an impactful role in debates over religion accommodations in the wake of marriage equality. As Part III details, those debates extend not just to accommodations of public officials with religious objections to processing all civil marriages impartially but also to a range of accommodations of private actors.

The next four chapters—which form the third and final part of the book—apply government nonendorsement to these disputes, together with the other principles articulated here in Part II. Chapters 7 through 10 bring together all four of them in a cross-cutting way. Throughout, the effort is to articulate an approach to new and complex disputes that fits together with our considered convictions about concrete cases and the principles that account for them.

APPLICATIONS

SEVEN

PUBLIC ACCOMMODATIONS

A CORE ASPECT of civil rights law protects against invidious discrimination in what the law calls "public accommodations." The main idea is simple: businesses and other providers that open their doors to the public cannot refuse to serve people on protected grounds, such as race or national origin. Even discrimination on the part of private parties, rather than the government, can harm citizens' social, economic, and political standing. Beyond that basic idea, matters quickly become complex, as will be explained in this chapter. Yet underlying that complexity is a central commitment.[1]

Should religious actors receive exemptions from public accommodations laws? Should Elane Photography be permitted to photograph only different-sex ceremonies and couples, to return to the example from the Introduction? Think too of Barronelle Stutzman, the owner of Arlene's Flowers and Gifts in Washington State, who refused service to a same-sex couple planning their wedding. In another example, an Oregon bakery named Sweetcakes by Melissa was fined by civil rights authorities for refusing to cater a wedding between two women. Or think of Mark and Todd Wathen, who were turned away from TimberCreek Bed and Breakfast when they tried to hold their wedding there. Vendors like these have been among the first to run up against civil rights laws.[2]

But conflicts between public accommodations laws and religious freedom have extended beyond wedding vendors. A decision by the local government in Fayetteville, Arkansas, to extend public accommodations protections to lesbian, gay, bisexual, and transgender (LGBT) citizens has drawn a lawsuit alleging, among other things, that the new law violates the religious freedom of affected providers of public goods and services. And a 2016 law in Mississippi allows providers who have religious objections to same-sex spouses to refuse service to them in a variety of contexts, despite some local laws that protect LGBT citizens from discrimination in public accommodations.[3]

Beyond for-profit businesses, consider religiously affiliated adoption agencies. Should they be able to refuse to place children with same-sex married couples? Or think of marriage counseling services and retreat centers for married couples. Should they be able to limit their services to traditional couples for theological reasons?[4]

These are some of the questions raised by the conflict between religious freedom and public accommodations laws. On the one hand, religious entities argue that serving the public is essential to their religious mission. Think of homeless shelters, educational institutions, or health care facilities. Religious actors often argue that they should not be put to the choice between violating their beliefs and shutting their doors to a needy public. Moreover, they point out that public accommodations laws have expanded in scope, covering not just hotels and restaurants but virtually every entity that serves the public. And they argue that forcing them from public service because of their traditional beliefs on sexual morality renders *them* disfavored citizens.

On the other hand, LGBT advocates remind policy makers that public accommodations laws provide core civil rights protections that are driven by foundational commitments to social and economic equality. Conflict over such arguments could intensify in the coming years.

Another, deeper question is *how* we should think through those clashes. Again, the complexity here is notable. Public accommodations law can cover nonprofits and business corporations; it can be federal, state, or local; and it can interact with common law rules and constitutional limitations. At the moment, for example, antidiscrimination law does not protect LGBT people on the federal level or in about half the states. Yet even in states with no comprehensive protection, cities and towns often do include LGBT people in their local civil rights laws. And there is significant variation in coverage and exemptions. On the other side, religious freedom protections vary depending on whether they are federal or state regulations and on whether they are constitutional or statutory. They can also be specific to certain areas of civil rights law. So the obstacles to comprehensive analysis are significant.

This chapter proposes that we think our way through these difficult questions by using the method of social coherence described in Chapters 1 and 2. Simply, the idea is to resolve new conflicts by comparing them to settlements that have already been struck between religious freedom and equality concerns in familiar areas of law, and about which we have come to have some confidence after experience and reflection. If we can find a solution to a problem of accommodating religious freedom that fits together with precedents in other areas, we are justified in recommending that resolution.

Moreover, coherence should be sought not just with analogous conflicts on the ground, but also with governing principles. Part II described and defended some of those principles, which account for our considered convictions about concrete cases, at least provisionally. Several of them are implicated by the problem of religious freedom in public accommodations, including avoiding harm to others, freedom of association, and government nonendorsement. Nothing about social coherence determines specific outcomes, but it nevertheless can be useful for organizing the debate—even on questions involving multiple areas of law and variegated values.

Applying that method, this chapter contends that solving the problem of how to accommodate religious actors depends on analogies that pull in opposite directions. On the one hand, public accommodations laws provide relatively narrow protection for religious objections when it comes to discrimination on other grounds, such as race, gender, ethnicity, or disability. Drawing a comparison to other areas of civil rights law therefore points toward limited religion exemptions. On the other hand, there are "conscience clause" or "religious refusal" laws that protect doctors and other providers who have theological objections to certain medical procedures, typically including abortion, contraception, and sterilization. These legal provisions generally provide more generous protection. Comparing current conflicts to conscience or refusal clauses points toward broader exemptions for religious actors. So figuring out whether and how to accommodate religious actors when it comes to serving LGBT people in public accommodations might depend on determining which of these analogies is apt. (For reasons of practical manageability, this chapter focuses on LGBT equality, though it addresses other forms of public accommodations in places.)

While there are arguments to be made on both sides, the chapter concludes that exempting religious actors from public accommodations laws protecting LGBT people is closest to exempting them from other types of public accommodations law, such as those protecting women and religious minorities. After all, the analogy is tight: both instances concern civil rights, and the same variety of civil rights at that. And there are meaningful differences between the claim of Elane Photography and the arguments for why doctors should be permitted to opt out of direct participation in, say, procedures to terminate a pregnancy, as this chapter explains. Therefore, the exemptions for religious groups from these new civil rights laws ought to be relatively narrow. But again, the question is close and the answer may vary somewhat depending on the specific scenario.

More generally, the chapter addresses the argument that denying religion exemptions will send a government message that religious traditionalists are disfavored, thereby rendering them marked members of the political community. This symmetry is more apparent than actual; in fact, religious traditionalists and members of protected classes are not positioned in exactly the same way with respect to the principle of equal citizenship. When civil rights laws prohibit discrimination, they do not single out religious traditionalists for special disfavor but instead express disapproval of all discriminatory practices, whether religious or secular. In other words, the purpose and social meaning of equality law does not target religious people, or even religious traditionalists, and it does not alter their citizenship standing on that basis. Instead, it combats discriminatory practices on the part of private actors, whether religious or secular, that work to disadvantage protected classes in the economy, in society, and in politics. Many feel the denial of an exemption acutely and sincerely. But that does not change the social meaning of the law, however contingent it may be.

The first section of the chapter describes the basics of public accommodations law, including the sorts of religion exemptions that typically exist. The second section lays out some types of exemptions that states have already included in legislation on marriage equality, allowing religious actors to exclude same-sex couples from facilities and services even when they qualify as public accommodations. The third section describes the two competing paradigms for thinking about whether and when religious objections should be given leeway: public accommodations laws with respect to other groups, on the one hand, and conscience or refusal clauses in the medical context, on the other. It concludes that the former is comparable, but the latter is not. The fourth section applies principles of avoiding harm to others and freedom of association and argues that they not only do not impede, but strongly support, familiar religion exemptions in existing civil rights laws.

Finally, the chapter briefly notes the objection that businesses like Elane Photography should be protected not because they are religious but because they are engaged in speech. It suggests that wedding vendors are not compelled to say anything because they can always choose not to open their doors to the public in the first place. Therefore, it indicates that the First Amendment principle against compelled speech does not apply.

Why Protect against Discrimination in Public Accommodations?

At first glance, it may not be obvious why we should protect against discrimination in public accommodations at all. At issue here are private actors, not government. And generally, the equality rules that bind government are different from those that regulate private actors. For example, government cannot differentiate among citizens in arbitrary ways, according to basic constitutional law. Private businesses, by contrast, can exclude customers for arbitrary or irrational reasons, according to the conventional wisdom: A restaurant could refuse to serve people with long earlobes or anyone wearing a blue shirt. So why would civil rights law restrict the ability of private businesses to exclude customers, if only when those customers fall into certain protected classes? Why not let the market drive those companies out of business?[5]

Andrew Koppelman has identified three common rationales for antidiscrimination laws. First, allowing economic actors to exclude people in systematic ways can lead to inequality of economic opportunity. While that is not generally a risk for idiosyncratic biases like antipathy toward long-earlobed people, it can present a real danger for members of groups that experience widespread cultural and political exclusion. For example, when the Supreme Court upheld the public accommodations portion of the Civil Rights Act of 1964, it recognized that African Americans found it difficult to travel through regions of the United States because so many hotels and restaurants refused to serve them. Restrictions on travel and on general participation in the economy can hamper not only the basic liberties of non-white citizens, but also their economic opportunities.[6]

Second, civil rights laws protect against social and political subordination. Not only government but private actors can contribute to that phenomenon. Most obviously, when businesses post signs that advertise exclusion, or where they adopt policies that communicate an equivalent message, they not only impair the ability of minorities to actually procure goods and services but also generate and perpetuate a social message of inequality.

Civil rights law, including public accommodations law, stands against the formation of caste differences, even outside government. This danger can exist not only with regard to systemic exclusion but also with regard to more isolated or idiosyncratic instances of discrimination against protected classes.[7]

Third, and finally, equality law sends a message of disapproval and discouragement of unfair discrimination. It seeks to alter social norms, partly through persuasion and endorsement. It is important to note here, however, that the government message is not disapproval of religion, or even of religious traditionalists, but instead condemnation of discriminatory practices, whether motivated by religious or nonreligious convictions.[8]

So there are good reasons to prohibit discrimination against protected classes, even from private providers. But we should also question the conventional view that otherwise businesses may exclude whomever they like. It turns out that at earlier moments in American history, the common law actually required inns and common carriers that were open to the public to serve everyone without irrational exclusion. Joseph Singer showed this in a classic history of public accommodations law. Of course, such businesses could adopt restrictions that were business related. But they could not turn away people with, say, long earlobes under the old rule. The conviction seemed to be that once a business elects to open its doors to the public, it must serve everyone impartially, absent a good reason—that it should not be allowed to pick and choose customers irrationally. Even today, several states retain this common-law rule of equal access.[9]

Moreover, Singer argued that several states had odious reasons for abandoning the equal access approach. After the Civil War and Reconstruction, these states realized that their existing common law could be used to protect the ability of African Americans, including freed slaves, to demand access to public businesses. So they passed statutes that overrode the common law and established the ability of providers to exclude people at will. In other words, the background rule is not natural but historically constructed, and at least in some places it was originally adopted for discriminatory reasons.[10]

In any event, the reasons for protecting *at least* members of protected classes from discrimination by businesses open to the public are strong and commonly accepted. And over time the category of public accommodations has expanded beyond inns, common carriers, and theaters to include virtually any provider open to the public. Even small businesses like Elane Photography must abide by the rules, and they must do so even if there are other providers available to the customer. Public accommodations law also applies to nonprofits, such as hospitals and many social service agencies. Again, because much of this law is state and local, there is quite a bit of variation, but this general picture captures its general contours.[11]

Excluded from public accommodations laws are clubs and other private entities, precisely because they are not open to the public. Clubs can reject members—the equivalent of customers—even on protected grounds. Presumably this discrimination is acceptable because of the countervailing importance of the freedom of association, as described and defended in Chapter 5. Ideological variation among groups is important for the formation of ideas and interests among citizens, and to preserve the richness of public debate on critical questions of policy among people who govern themselves.

Yet there are limits on the ability to discriminate in most jurisdictions. Most simply, entities must be truly private in order to escape civil rights law. Typically, though not universally, they must satisfy several criteria to qualify: they must be selective in membership, they must exclude nonmembers from using their goods and services, they must be controlled by the membership, they must operate on a nonprofit basis, and they must not market their services to the public. Additionally, they must not be too large, especially if they engage in commercial activities. Once an organization reaches a certain size, it ceases to operate solely as a setting for will formation and it begins to implicate the commitments to equality of opportunity and equal social standing that drive antidiscrimination law. Of course, size alone does not perfectly capture this balance of risks and rewards for club autonomy, and so it is combined with other criteria. But because it can function as an administrable approximation, size serves as a limit on many public accommodations laws. To take just one example, New York City's civil rights law requires clubs with more than four hundred members to obey nondiscrimination rules, if they serve meals and rent out their space for commercial activities. So the Racquet and Tennis Club on Park Avenue can exclude women, as it does, but only so long as it keeps its membership below that number, assuming it serves meals and makes its space available for commercial use. Overall, then, public accommodations law appropriately looks to multiple factors to determine whether an entity can escape its requirements because the organization is distinctly private.[12]

Note that courts take into account the nature of an entity's activities in deciding whether it counts as private. For example, the Junior Chamber of

Commerce—known as the Jaycees—was found to be a public accommodation, not a private club, because it was large, it sold commercial goods, and did not have selective membership requirements. The upshot was that the Jaycees could not exclude women.[13]

Religious groups generally are subject to public accommodations laws on the same terms as other businesses and organizations, though there is some variation—they escape nondiscrimination requirements insofar as they are private, but not because of their religious nature. Overall, only a few jurisdictions have treated religious organizations in a way that is meaningfully different from other public accommodations—at least until the recent changes made in the context of LGBT equality.[14]

Remember that the federal government and about half the states still do not protect LGBT people in public accommodations at all. While some localities within those jurisdictions do provide protection, businesses otherwise may exclude LGBT people openly. Presumably, in the wake of *Obergefell v. Hodges*, we will see intensified efforts to expand the category of protected classes to include sexual orientation and gender identity. We can also presume that the effort will be accompanied by arguments for religion exemptions.

Some expansion of civil rights law, with accompanying religion protections, has already been underway. Utah, for example, added LGBT antidiscrimination protection to its civil rights laws for employment and housing in 2015. And it included a broad exemption for religious groups and religiously affiliated organizations. But notably, Utah declined to expand its public accommodations law. And that was true even though Utah was one of the very few states with a broad religion exemption already written into its civil rights law. Apparently, protecting LGBT people in public accommodations was seen as too controversial to be politically viable, even with a strong religion accommodation.[15]

In other states, however, expansion of public accommodations law to include a guarantee against discrimination on the basis of LGBT status will become politically feasible, sometimes in conjunction with arguments for meaningful exemptions for religious groups. What kinds of arguments for exemptions are we likely to see? The next section briefly introduces some of the leading contenders, building on state laws enacted in the context of marriage equality before *Obergefell*. Ensuing sections then evaluate these arguments, exploring both which exemptions are desirable and which ones existing law allows.

Three Examples

What kinds of claims are we likely to see for religion exemptions from public accommodations laws that cover LGBT people? Based on experiences with state legislation in the context of marriage equality, three types of entities seem likely to seek exemptions: church facilities, adoption agencies, and for-profit businesses including wedding vendors. Although several additional areas of conflict are possible and will be mentioned—such as married student housing, retreat centers for married couples, and marriage counseling services—these three disputes seem so far to be paradigmatic. This section will briefly introduce them from a distance, before subsequent sections evaluate them at somewhat closer range. Arguments about these three will have relevance for other disputes over the application of public accommodations laws to religious actors.

Perhaps the most straightforward examples concern religious facilities that are open to the public generally but seek to close their doors to same-sex weddings or receptions. Instances of such conflicts are not numerous, but they have affected how people think about religion exemptions from civil rights laws in the context of marriage equality.

Ocean Grove was a community on the New Jersey shore that had been established to allow Methodists an opportunity to live near the beach in a Christian setting. Between the village and the beach sat a stretch of boardwalk, and in one place the boardwalk was built out into a covered pavilion. Ocean Grove opened the pavilion to the public as an event space, which was then used for a variety of gatherings and celebrations, including beachside weddings. Because the community made the pavilion publicly available, it was eligible for favorable tax treatment from the state. That arrangement continued without incident until two women applied to celebrate their union. After the community denied their request, the couple sued. New Jersey's civil rights agency ruled for the couple, finding that the state's public accommodations law applied to the pavilion, which therefore could not exclude same-sex couples. Subsequently, Ocean Grove apparently limited use of the pavilion to church members and forfeited the tax benefits that it previously had enjoyed.[16]

Although examples like *Bernstein v. Ocean Grove Camp Meeting Association* are not common today, similar disputes have arisen. For example, questions have been raised about whether religious universities must allow their chapels and other event spaces to be used for same-sex weddings and receptions if those spaces otherwise are open to the public. And it is possible to imagine similar difficulties surrounding gymnasiums or theaters owned by religiously affiliated organizations.[17]

That said, churches themselves, along with other houses of worship, may decide which weddings to allow in their sanctuaries. Multiple reasons support that conclusion. One is that houses of worship are not generally held open for use by everyone, and therefore they are not public accommodations. Moreover, serious free exercise questions would hamper a government's effort to force a religious group to open its sanctuary to everyone on equal terms. Therefore, any questions are likely to surround not sanctuaries themselves, but affiliated facilities like Ocean Grove's boardwalk pavilion or university event spaces.

Some states have already exempted religious facilities from antidiscrimination laws in the wake of marriage equality. In fact, virtually all states that passed marriage equality statutes before *Obergefell* provided some protection for religious facilities that objected to hosting same-sex celebrations or receptions on theological grounds. Allowing these exemptions was seen by advocates as a necessary political price for passing marriage equality laws. For example, Hawaii's statute provides that "a religious organization" will not "be required to provide goods, services, or its facilities or grounds for the solemnization or celebration of a marriage that is in violation of its religious beliefs or faith." And subsequent to *Obergefell,* Mississippi moved to protect religious organizations from any law that might require them to provide facilities to same-sex couples seeking to marry. Is this proper, or should public accommodations laws be applied to these facilities?[18]

A second example is the pressing question of whether religiously affiliated adoption agencies may refuse to place children with same-sex couples who are legally married. For example, Catholic Charities of Boston was ordered by Massachusetts authorities to cease excluding same-sex couples from its adoption and other child placement services. Rather than comply, the agency famously decided to shut down its child placement program altogether.[19]

Adoption law is complex and hard to distill, because members of couples can choose to adopt singly or jointly, because agencies are allowed to prefer married couples generally (which until recently meant they could tacitly exclude same-sex couples in many jurisdictions), and because much of the decision making happens at the agency level, or in lower state courts that do not always explain or publish their reasons.[20]

Moreover, adoption agencies are regulated by the states, which usually require them to be licensed. Public accommodations law often intersects with that sort of licensing law. In Massachusetts, for example, it was the state license regime that prohibited discrimination on the basis of sexual orientation. It is usually also state licensing law that requires pharmacies to serve everyone despite any religious objections (though this example pertains to reproductive freedom and women's equality rather than LGBT rights, which are the main concern of this chapter). Because laws on public accommodations and licensing overlap, they should be considered together.[21]

And licensing requirements are similar to accreditation practices, which also may coincide with public accommodations laws. For example, in 2014 Gordon College faced questions from the local accreditation body because of the college's policy of banning homosexual conduct among students following theological prohibitions. Accreditation authorities pointed to their standards' general nondiscrimination requirement when questioning the school's policies. Although the college ended up facing no adverse action by the authorities, the example further underscores the connection between public accommodations laws and licensing or accreditation requirements.[22]

Here, too, some states already have passed exemptions that protect religious adoption agencies in the context of marriage equality. Connecticut, for example, exempts religious adoption agencies from any obligation to serve same-sex spouses, although only if they do not receive public funding. In 2015, after *Obergefell,* Michigan passed a general religion exemption for child placement agencies. It provides that no child placement agency will face negative consequences for declining to provide services that conflict with its religious beliefs. During the debate over the Michigan law, it was referred to as a "conscience clause" for adoption placement agencies.[23]

Other laws are somewhat more oblique. Rhode Island's law, for instance, says that religious organizations and religiously affiliated nonprofits need not provide "services, accommodations, advantages, facilities, goods, or privileges" if those services are related to the "promotion of marriage through any social or religious programs or services, which violates . . . religious doctrine or teachings." Against the background of arguments that providing child placement services does "promote" same-sex marriage, this language could be read to protect Catholic Charities.[24]

In sum, laws like those in Connecticut, Michigan, and Rhode Island raise the question of whether adoption agencies should be able to decline to place children with same-sex couples despite civil rights laws that protect against discrimination on the basis of sexual orientation and marital status in public accommodations.

A final question—perhaps the one with the highest profile—is whether businesses may refuse to serve same-sex couples, especially but not only in the context of wedding ceremonies and receptions.

In the for-profit context, the exemption claim is often grounded in the state's Religious Freedom Restoration Act (RFRA). Patterned after the federal statute at issue in *Burwell v. Hobby Lobby,* state RFRAs provide general religious freedom protection against other state laws. They typically require any substantial burden on religious freedom to be justified by a compelling state interest and a showing that the law at issue is narrowly tailored to that interest—a demanding standard that the government has the burden of satisfying. And after *Hobby Lobby,* it seems possible that many RFRAs will be interpreted to cover businesses under the same kind of reasoning that led the Supreme Court to protect a closely held corporation there.[25]

In *Elane Photography v. Willock,* the court ruled against the company by holding that the New Mexico RFRA only applied against the government, and therefore it did not cover suits between private parties like the litigation between the business and the couple. But courts are split on that question. Some have held that RFRAs should apply in civil rights suits between private parties because the lawsuit is made possible by the public accommodations law, which is enforced in court. So whether businesses will be shielded by RFRAs is very much a live issue.[26]

In fact, the controversy over Indiana's 2015 RFRA was fueled in large part by that issue. Indiana, like other states, took steps to pass a state RFRA for the first time against the backdrop of court rulings in favor of marriage equality for same-sex couples. Its first version of the law, which was in fact enacted, contained language that clarified that the law would apply in actions between private parties. That language seemed designed to reject *Elane Photography* and similar decisions—in other words, its object seemed to be to ensure that Indiana's RFRA would apply in civil rights suits. Although Indiana had no protection for LGBT people in its public accommodations law, some cities within the state did provide comprehensive civil rights coverage to them, so the danger seemed to be real if not absolutely certain to be realized. Reacting to the public outcry over that concern, Indiana amended the law, making it inapplicable to civil rights claims against businesses. That seemed to quiet the furor.[27]

More recently there has been a shift from RFRA laws to what are known as First Amendment Defense Acts (FADAs). These laws provide somewhat more specific protection from public accommodations laws to actors that oppose same-sex marriage on religious grounds, sometimes including businesses. For example, Mississippi's FADA-like statute protects wedding vendors who refuse to serve same-sex couples for religious reasons.[28]

All these examples raise the basic question of whether businesses may turn away LGBT people because of religious objections, either to same-sex marriage specifically or to LGBT people more generally. Is this type of claim something that courts and legislatures should heed? How does it differ from claims in the context of religious facilities or adoption placement? The following sections evaluate those issues.

Two Paradigms

Thinking about whether to exempt these sorts of religious practices from public accommodations laws protecting LGBT people requires comparisons to other places where the law does or does not exempt religious conduct. A coherence method requires these kinds of comparisons in an obvious way, because it looks for harmony among legal solutions in analogous areas. But even a commonsensical approach would look for analogies, to the degree that it aspired to be rigorous and not merely intuitive. Reflective people naturally seek guidance for what they ought to do—and what the law ought to be interpreted to require—by reference to familiar scenarios and principles. This section examines ground-level comparisons, and the next section incorporates the relevant principles from Part II.

As it turns out, there are two main contenders for paradigms or analogies, and they suggest divirgent outcomes.

On the one hand, religion exemptions from public accommodations laws that protect LGBT people might be treated like religion exemptions from public accommodations laws protecting other groups, and from civil rights laws even more generally. That is, we might look to the ways in which civil rights law exempts religious actors from the obligation to serve people without regard to race, gender, ethnicity, and other protected statuses.

Accepting that comparison would point toward rather limited religion exemptions. Public accommodations laws do apply to religious organizations, generally if not uniformly. They also may well apply to adoption agencies, including those that are religiously affiliated. And they certainly include businesses—even small businesses, as the *Elane Photography* court found. Moreover, they do not usually contain special exemptions for actors with religious objections to complying. Nor do courts usually grant such exemptions under constitutional provisions. In one precedent, the Supreme Court abruptly dismissed the free exercise claim of a business that wished to exclude customers on the basis of race for religious reasons, despite the federal public accommodations law.[29]

On the other hand, policy makers may compare religion exemptions from public accommodations laws protecting LGBT people to "conscience clauses" or "refusal clauses" in the context of medical care. These provisions, which are common in federal and state law, protect doctors and other medical providers from participating in certain procedures that offend their religion or conscience. Originally designed to accommodate opposition to abortion in the wake of *Roe v. Wade,* these clauses now commonly also apply to contraception and sterilization. They vary quite widely as to the providers who are covered, with some limited to doctors, and others extending to nurses, and still others including hospitals, pharmacists, and even funders. They also vary substantially in their level of protection for patients. Nevertheless, they share some core features—namely, exemption from participation in certain medical procedures that draw objections on the basis of religion or conscience.[30]

Comparison to conscience or refusal clauses points toward greater solicitude for religious actors who seek exemptions from the requirement to serve same-sex couples. For one thing, these clauses are more politically palatable, even though they exempt religious actors from involvement with what many see as the exercise of a core civil right for women—namely, the right of reproductive freedom. For another, many clauses contain only limited protections for third parties—usually women seeking to terminate a pregnancy. While some clauses are inapplicable in situations where there is no medical provider willing to perform the service, others protect patients only in emergencies, and still others contain no such protections at all, extending a virtually absolute right of refusal to medical providers with religious or conscience-based objections.[31]

If religion exemptions from public accommodations laws are similar to conscience or refusal clauses in the medical context, therefore, the inclination will be to grant them more freely. This analysis could apply in legislatures considering specific exemptions, or in courts applying RFRAs.

Not surprisingly, then, advocates for religion exemptions from public accommodations laws have been urging the comparison to conscience clauses. For example, supporters of the Michigan law, which exempted adoption agencies from antidiscrimination rules that conflicted with their religious convictions, referred to the provision as a "conscience clause." Understanding the two most obvious comparisons makes sense of that choice as a matter of political advocacy. Critics of the adoption legislation, also understandably, referred to it as a license to discriminate, or as a carve out from civil rights laws. Which comparison is correct?[32]

Why the Civil Rights Analogy Is Apt

Generally, though not in every circumstance, the comparison between religion exemptions from public accommodations laws that protect LGBT people should be to public accommodations laws protecting other groups, and to civil rights law more generally, rather than to conscience or refusal clauses in the medical context. Beyond the simple observation that public accommodations laws in this context actually are civil rights laws, and arguably therefore not just analogous but equivalent to public accommodations laws protecting other groups, several distinctions make this comparison compelling.

First, medical exemptions centrally protect providers who are directly involved in the procedure itself. Some statutes, especially the more recent ones, go further and protect hospitals or funders. But the core intuition behind the original clauses was that medical providers should not be forced to perform or assist with a procedure they find deeply objectionable. Directness of involvement was seen to matter.[33]

And some claims for relief from public accommodations laws in the context of LGBT rights do not involve close proximity to a wedding, which is a sensitive ceremony that many consider to be a religious sacrament. Ocean Grove, for example, was asked to rent out an event space located on the border of the community to a lesbian couple on the same terms as other renters. Community members would have no direct involvement in the event.[34]

Admittedly, Elane Photography would have been more proximately involved, because it would have been depicting the wedding itself. It could therefore be distinguished from other types of wedding vendors, such as florists and bakers, who would not need to be present at all. Yet in other ways Elane Photography's claim seems different from a conscience situation in medicine.

A second distinction concerns the personal nature of someone's involvement in protected behavior. In other words, not just directness but individuality seems to be important. Conscience clauses usually protect against personal involvement in a medical procedure, whereas civil rights laws are more likely to affect the activities of organizations or institutions such as employers and commercial businesses offering goods and services to the public. Furthermore, certain provisions in both contexts reinforce this intuition. In civil rights laws concerning housing, for example, the "Mrs. Murphy" exemption recognizes the personal nature of allowing someone to occupy a rental unit in one's own home, at least if the building is small enough.[35]

And in the context of medical exemptions, there is a recognition that claims are weak when made by entities rather than individuals. Consider religion accommodations in the pharmacy context, for instance, where professionals have raised conscientious objections to distributing emergency contraception, among other drugs. The majority approach today allows individual pharmacists to decline to fill prescriptions on grounds of conscience, despite licensing laws, but it limits that exemption to situations where another pharmacist is available. Moreover, this approach disallows exemptions for pharmacies as entities, despite any religion objections by the owner.[36]

So the distinction between personal involvement and impersonal or entity involvement is also important. And although that distinction works within both civil rights law and medical conscience provisions, it also tends to separate them, because conscience or refusal clauses most often concern personal involvement, whereas civil rights provisions usually restrict entity behavior.

Third is the factor of time or duration. Whereas conscience or refusal clauses refer to a discrete event that happens at a particular moment, religious exemptions from public accommodations laws are harder to limit to a point in time. Chiefly, that is because of how the religious argument works. The most compelling objection made by people like photographer Elaine Huguenin is that they view a wedding as a religious sacrament and therefore that they have a special objection to involvement with that event. But it is difficult to see how religious traditionalists could object to same-sex *weddings* on this ground but not to same-sex *marriages*. Both the event and the relationship status have sacramental importance, after all. Yet a marriage is designed to last. And it is difficult to understand why providers of public accommodations would not object to providing goods or services that are specific to a marriage—over the entire life of that marriage.

If that is right, the objection of Huguenin would apply just as strongly to photographing a same-sex wedding anniversary. And that makes the temporal aspect of her claim *somewhat* different from the momentariness of a doctor's objection to participating in a procedure to terminate a pregnancy. Even more obviously, religious adoption agencies object to placing children with same-sex couples who are married, and that objection will last the length of the marriage.[37]

A fourth and finer-grained distinction is that while conscience clauses almost always cover not only religious objections but also objections grounded in morality or conscience, exemptions from public accommodations laws typically are specific to religion, where they exist at all. Take, for instance, the Michigan abortion agency exemption, which protects only objections grounded in religion, not conscience more generally. This specificity strengthens the argument against relying on conscience or refusal clauses as a model.[38]

Some people have resisted the analogy to civil rights law, with its limited religion exemptions, by arguing that religious hesitancy around same-sex marriage is dissimilar to religious objection to interracial marriage. Among the most thoughtful of these is Kent Greenawalt, who has argued that religious objections in the LGBT context are more "comprehensible" because they are more deeply grounded historically and because they have *some* biological foundation insofar as reproduction is not possible for same-sex couples without modern technology. It is probably arguable which of these objections is older, but that question is best left to professional historians. And although biological objections to interracial marriage are also familiar, having played a prominent role in litigation over bans on interracial marriage in the 1960s, it might be best to put the race analogy aside.[39]

Even if we ignore any comparison to racial discrimination, however, public accommodations laws generally also protect against discrimination on the basis of marital status and religion itself. And because practices like remarriage or interfaith marriage violate some theologies, laws prohibiting discrimination on such grounds have drawn claims for accommodations. Yet here, too, religion exemptions are narrow or nonexistent. So regardless of whether the analogy to race is apt, the comparison to interfaith marriage or remarriage after divorce remains. Ultimately, then, the principal objection to the analogy to religious exemptions from other public accommodations protections should not alter the outcome.

We should conclude from this analysis that the correct comparison is between claims for religion exemptions from public accommodations laws covering LGBT people and similar claims for religion exemptions from other aspects of those laws—such as those protecting customers from discrimination on the basis of race, religion, national origin, and marital status. By contrast, the comparison to conscience or refusal clauses in the medical context is unconvincing. Someone following a coherence approach therefore should seek resolutions of these cases that fit together with resolution of claims for religion exemptions in other areas of civil rights law.

While this understanding may not resolve every claim under every factual circumstance, it should govern our general analysis of the main cases considered in this chapter: religious facilities, adoption agencies, and commercial wedding vendors. Those scenarios will be played out in greater detail in a moment.

Principles Governing Conflicts between Religion and Equality

Before returning to the three concrete examples, though, we should seek harmony not just with similar ground-level scenarios but also with principles that fairly abstract from those situations. How does consideration of those principles affect the way we think about application of public accommodations laws to religious actors here? It strengthens the argument for limited exemptions, as it turns out.

Let's start with the imperative of avoiding harm to others. Virtually all of the available religion exemptions from public accommodations laws present this danger. First there is the harm to economic opportunity. Recall that combating economic inequality is one of the three aspirations of antidiscrimination laws. It is conceivable that the couples seeking to marry in Ocean Grove, or adopt a child in Boston, or find a photographer in New Mexico, would have difficulty finding alternatives if religious providers were allowed to opt out. Koppelman points to data suggesting that same-sex marriage will have majority support in nearly every state in the foreseeable future, and he suggests that purveyors in those states will not exclude LGBT people in a systematic way. Even if he is right, however, same-sex couples may face increased search costs. Moreover, they may still encounter systemic discrimination in certain regions or localities within those states. And any difficulty they face finding goods and services likely would count as an undue hardship that they should not be forced to bear as the cost of accommodating another citizen's religious belief.[40]

An independent concern, moreover, stems from another rationale for antidiscrimination law—namely, preserving equal standing within the community. Extending legal solicitude to religious objectors can reinforce differential standing for LGBT beneficiaries. And this is true whether or not beneficiaries can readily find alternate providers of goods and services within the community. For similar reasons, antidiscrimination law does not allow exclusions of customers or clients on the basis of race, religion, or marital status, even where alternatives exist. Once providers make the decision to open their services to the public, they normally must abide by equality requirements. Failure to do so imposes an unjustified indignity on citizens who would otherwise have been protected from exclusion.[41]

So the principle of avoiding harm to others reinforces the conclusion that religion exemptions from public accommodations laws protecting LGBT citizens ought to be narrow, as they are with regard to other groups.

Nor does freedom of association change the outcome fundamentally, though here matters are somewhat more complex. Think of our three examples. Neither Ocean Grove, nor Catholic Charities of Boston, nor Elane Photography has an association-based reason for refusing LGBT couples. But other examples are more intriguing.

Consider golf clubs. May they restrict membership on the basis of sexual orientation or gender identity? (Here the question is limited to access for beneficiaries; employment is considered in Chapter 8.) Imagine not just a traditional club that observes conservative values but also a golf club established for LGBT people who have been excluded from established clubs. Surprisingly, and tentatively, the principle articulated in Chapter 5 could be thought to suggest that *some* of these clubs could engage in exclusion because they qualify as community or civic organizations. At least insofar as clubs are distinctly private and not directly engaged in economic activity, and as long as they satisfy the other criteria of close associations, they may have the right to select members on discriminatory grounds. Further, local clubs can do so without having to show that the exclusion is connected to the group's mission or ideology. Still further, this protection would apply to religious and nonreligious clubs alike. But again this freedom would be limited to clubs that qualify as close associations under the multifactor analysis set out in Chapter 5.[42]

Another example is the Boy Scouts of America. As the Supreme Court ruled in a landmark decision, *Boy Scouts v. Dale,* some local chapters of that organization have the ability to exclude scoutmasters on grounds that are connected to their mission. That decision is best explained as an instance of freedom of association for civic or community organizations. Today the national organization has moved away from a national exclusion of gay scoutmasters, though it still allows exclusion by local troops that are affiliated with religious congregations (as many apparently are). Shaping its membership in these ways could conceivably be important for its engagement with worldview formation on the part of local troops.[43]

Yet organizations that start to look like the Jaycees, where business networking is a primary part of the operation or where commercial transactions become central, would lose protection as sites of citizen formation. Distinguishing them is a matter of individualized, fact-specific determination using the factors described in Chapter 5. Nor would the importance of association extend in the same way to employment, as Chapter 8 explores. Nor does the principle have necessary implications for funding, as Chapter 10 explains. Overall, then, the freedom of association does provide some limited, contextualized limitation on the conclusion that public accommodations laws should reach religious actors.

A final principle, government nonendorsement, may have a role to play—reinforcing the conclusion of this chapter. Consideration of this principle links up with the third purpose of antidiscrimination law—namely, pronouncing government opposition to invidious discrimination and persuading private actors to abandon the practice. While many religion exemptions from antidiscrimination laws carry no particular message of approval or disapproval, some do. And in recent years, attempts to exclude religious actors from such laws have had an evident valence—they have been attempts to protect traditional religious actors in the wake of marriage equality and in anticipation of comprehensive civil rights protections for LGBT citizens. Now, not all of these provisions necessarily endorse discrimination. They may instead simply express solicitude for the plight of people forced to choose between violating their religious beliefs and legal liability that will be costly or may even mean closing the doors of their business. But *some* religion accommodations can carry a message of endorsement under *some* limited circumstances. The court in *Obergefell* seemed to acknowledge this possibility in a telling passage:

> Many who deem same-sex marriage to be wrong reach that conclusion based on decent and honorable religious or philosophical premises, and neither they nor their beliefs are disparaged here. But when that sincere, personal opposition becomes enacted law and public policy, the necessary consequence is to put the imprimatur of the State itself on an exclusion that soon demeans or stigmatizes those whose own liberty is then denied. Under the Constitution, same-sex couples seek in marriage the same legal treatment as opposite-sex couples, and it would disparage their choices and diminish their personhood to deny them this right.[44]

The court was discussing state exclusions from civil marriage, of course, but it is conceivable that religion accommodations could also "put the imprimatur of the State itself" on subordination of LGBT citizens. For example, Indiana's initial RFRA, before it was amended, could reasonably have been understood to be designed to give religious actors in the position of Elane Photography an exemption from civil rights laws. If it had been allowed to stand, that law might have sent a message not only that religious actors are in a tough situation but also that they should prevail in conflicts involving antidiscrimination laws. If that is correct, then there are *some* circumstances, however narrow, under which the principle of government nonendorsement could come into play.[45]

In sum, then, claims for religion exemptions from public accommodations laws generally ought to be evaluated by reference to other areas of public accommodations law, and civil rights law more generally. That is so because the scenarios here comport with judgments that have come to be accepted in those other areas, and not with conclusions regarding conscience or refusal clauses. It is also demanded by the application of principles that account for our concrete judgments, including principles of avoiding harm to others, freedom of association, and government nonendorsement.

Those general normative arguments, however, do not settle the matter of how we should evaluate the three concrete examples this chapter has been tracking. Let us return to them now and see how these arguments shape our legal conclusions on the ground.

Three Examples Redux

Returning to our three examples with the benefit of these analogies and principles, the first one becomes easier to resolve. Religious facilities that are open to the public are subject to public accommodations laws on the same terms as other buildings and event spaces. Houses of worship will not be affected by this rule, because they are not regularly leased or rented to nonmembers, so they will not qualify as public accommodations in the first place. But spaces that are regularly made available to everyone can be required to avoid discrimination against protected classes. University chapels, for instance, may be required to host same-sex weddings if they are generally open for marriage celebrations.

This conclusion simply presents organizations with a choice: they can cater only to members, even on discriminatory grounds, but if they elect to benefit from renting out their spaces to the public, they must do so evenhandedly, without excluding protected groups. That conclusion is bolstered by, and bolsters, New Jersey's decision in *Ocean Grove*. Remember that afterward, the community exercised its option to close the space to the public so that it could restrict its use on theological grounds. Under the analysis here, it enjoys that prerogative. What it cannot do is have it both ways—continue to profit from renting the space to community members while excluding members of classes protected by public accommodations laws.

Likewise, adoption agencies cannot refuse to place children with same-sex couples in states whose laws protect LGBT people. Again, since *Obergefell*, efforts to allow them to do so have stepped up. Michigan passed a law that explicitly protects child placement agencies, as noted above, and so did Mississippi as part of its FADA. These measures mirror provisions enacted as part of marriage equality statutes before *Obergefell*, as we have seen.[46]

Such provisions are regrettable. Adoption agencies should be required to serve everyone, without selectivity that implicates protected groups, when they decide to offer child placement services. Admittedly, agencies are in a somewhat more difficult position than religious event spaces. In most jurisdictions, at least, adoption agencies must be licensed by the state to operate at all. Again, the nondiscrimination requirement is sometimes included in the licensing requirements, independent of public accommodations laws—that was the case in Massachusetts when the Catholic Charities dispute was being resolved.

A consequence of the licensing requirement is that adoption agencies do not have the option of closing their services to the public if they wish to adhere to church doctrine. If they resist serving LGBT families, their only alternative is to shutter their child placement business altogether, as did Catholic Charities of Boston. Or, if they wish to continue to place children with same-sex couples, they may be forced to separate from the church, as some organizations have. Catholic Charities of Illinois, for example, ended its relationship with the Catholic Church rather than terminate its child placement services. The question there was whether the organization could retain state funding, but otherwise the contours of the dilemma were similar. Deciding between these two options may be agonizing for the agency.[47]

Nevertheless, it is difficult to understand why adoption agencies should be able to exclude LGBT couples for theological reasons when they have never had the ability to turn away couples in any other protected category—those who are interracial, interfaith, or remarried—in violation of church teachings, even though religious rationales for those other types of exclusions exist (or have existed at other moments in history). And that policy makes sense, because granting religion exemptions would undercut the rationales for antidiscrimination provisions in this context: ensuring equality of access to services, preserving equal membership in society and in the political community, and encouraging egalitarian practices. If religion exemptions would frustrate those purposes with regard to these other forms of discrimination, it would work against them here, too.

A different kind of difficult choice may be presented if state law protects the ability of adoption agencies to exclude same-sex couples only if they do not receive public funding. Recall that Connecticut imposed this sort of provision during its initial move toward marriage equality. Although that provision, too, will put agencies in a difficult position, it is less restrictive than a flat antidiscrimination requirement in licensing law. And because the more restrictive requirement is permissible, the funding condition should be also.[48]

Third, think again of wedding vendors and other commercial actors. There, too, the issues are hard, but the most defensible conclusion, taking everything into account, is that religion exemptions from public accommodations laws generally should be unavailable. *Hobby Lobby* left plenty of room for that result. Although commercial actors can be protected by RFRAs, they nevertheless may be required to follow civil rights laws, which are driven by compelling government interests. Again, access to services can be a serious problem, even at a time when acceptance of same-sex marriage is spreading, because resistance will continue to be felt in many localities and regions of the country. And the possibility of harm to equal membership is real. In other words, civil rights law should decline religion exemptions by public businesses for the same reasons that it does not accommodate even targeted religious objections to certain kinds of weddings by members of other protected classes.

It bears repeating that cases like *Elane Photography* are not easy. Strong arguments exist for exemptions, especially for small wedding vendors. Those arguments should be considered, and the next section continues that work.

Before turning to it, however, an important protection for religious groups emerged out of the last section, and it should be reiterated. Membership in private clubs and close associations may be limited on grounds of belief, under the freedom of association, despite the arguments of some progressives. This ability is bounded in the ways mentioned above: it applies only to truly private membership organizations that do not conduct significant commercial activity, it applies only to membership and not to employment, and it does not protect against government funding decisions. Additional limits may be appropriate as well, but within them, organizations should have the opportunity to shape the interests and ideologies of citizens through civic organizations that are constituted with bonds of trust and intimacy.

An Objection

Thus far this chapter has argued that religion exemptions from public accommodations laws protecting LGBT people should be construed relatively narrowly, in line with religion exemptions from other forms of public accommodations protection and civil rights law more generally. An objection to this conclusion is that it impermissibly compels wedding vendors in violation of the speech clause.

That objection is particular to the wedding photography situation, and perhaps a few other wedding vendor situations. In brief, the idea is that photography is a form of expression. When a photographer depicts a wedding, she not only documents it but also portrays it in a beautiful, sympathetic light. Therefore, the argument goes, a government requirement that wedding photographers include same-sex unions constitutes compelled speech. It is forcing the photographer to beautify an event that she believes to be the sinful misuse of a sacrament. Although that objection goes beyond religious freedom, and therefore is outside the focus of this book, it makes sense to treat it briefly here.

There is a free speech rule, the compelled speech doctrine, that prohibits the government from forcing citizens to speak. Just as people have the right to speak without government censorship, they also have a right to be silent. For example, a driver successfully sued New Hampshire to prevent it from forcing him to display the message Live Free or Die on a license plate. In the decision, *Wooley v. Maynard,* the Supreme Court relied on the compelled speech doctrine. And Jehovah's Witnesses won their lawsuit against a school that required children to recite the Pledge of Allegiance in violation of theological teachings. Writing for the court in the Witnesses' case, *West Virginia State Board of Education v. Barnette,* justice Robert H. Jackson famously said, "If there is any fixed star in our constitutional constellation, it is that no official, high or petty, can prescribe what shall be orthodox in politics, nationalism, religion, or other matters of opinion or force citizens to confess by word or act their faith therein."[49]

Elaine Huguenin thought that was exactly what was happening in her situation—New Mexico had decided what was orthodox in politics and religion, and it forced her to speak in conformity with liberalism. The difficulty with her argument, according to the New Mexico Supreme Court, was that she was not being forced to say anything. Her obligation to serve LGBT citizens equally was triggered by her decision to make her services available to the public. So the choice remained with her at all times—she could become a wedding photographer in the open marketplace and accept its rules, or she could choose not to photograph weddings. Even if depicting a wedding through photographs constituted speech, therefore, it was not being compelled.[50]

But wait, someone might wonder, didn't the students in *Barnette* and the driver in *Wooley* also have choices? At least as a formal matter, the students and their families could have chosen private school—that was the way religious families often circumvented government messages that they found objectionable in public education. And, again as a formal matter, the driver in *Wooley* could have found some other mode of transportation. Although a public bus would have carried the same license plate, its message wouldn't have been associated with the citizen as an individual. Of course, those choices were more theoretical than real, because the cost of public education and giving up driving may have been extremely high. But the cost to Elaine Huguenin of giving up her wedding business was formidable too. So what distinguished the cases?

Probably the best answer is that the citizens in *Wooley* and *Barnette* were being forced to endorse a government message that was unrelated to the regulated activities. Students were not compelled to recite the Pledge of Allegiance as part of an education program, and drivers in New Hampshire were not compelled to display the government's message on their own cars because of its benefits for road safety. Rather, government was leveraging its regulatory power in these two areas to force private persons to articulate or endorse its messages. Elaine Huguenin, by contrast, was simply required to refrain from prohibited discrimination in the same way as all businesses. That doing so would have had an incidental impact on speech was not reflective of the government's untoward effort to use its regulatory power to compel her to convey its message. It was an effort to guarantee economic opportunity and equal citizenship to all citizens.

Even if that argument is right, however, are there businesses that *do* need special protection from public accommodations laws? Think of a professional speechwriter. Must she accept clients with whom she fundamentally disagrees, simply because of civil rights laws? (Let's assume that she qualifies as a public accommodation, and that her state includes LGBT protection in its civil rights laws.) That is a difficult case, but one possible response is that she must serve all clients without distinction on the basis of race, gender, sexual orientation, gender identity, and other protected grounds. But this would not mean that she could not reject clients based on their *political views*. There is an argument that civil rights law does not prohibit that, and that the First Amendment protects it. What civil rights law does prohibit is discrimination on the basis of protected identity.

Where those two criteria collapse into each other, she may be confronted with a difficult choice, just as Elaine Huguenin was. If, for instance, the speechwriter was asked to draft a toast to be delivered by a newlywed at a same-sex wedding, on this view, she could not refuse on the ground that she was religiously opposed to LGBT weddings, because that would be tantamount to refusing to serve LGBT people. To see this, imagine she resisted serving an interracial wedding. One does not have to believe that opposition to same-sex weddings is equally odious as opposition to interracial weddings to see that the form of the argument has the same structure—and it is vulnerable for similar reasons.

This discussion is tentative, and outside the focus of this chapter. Nevertheless, it gives us *some* reason to think that the New Mexico court was right to turn away Elane Photography's speech claim. Further thought is necessary to be completely confident.

Conclusion

Some of these issues are troubling. Whether and why Elane Photography and other wedding vendors should be required to abide by public accommodations laws protecting LGBT people, despite their sincere religious opposition, is not obvious. They say they are looking for a narrow exemption that would only apply to direct participation in weddings, which they consider to be a religious sacrament, and that the exemption would only affect a handful of cases nationally. Especially in places where LGBT couples can find alternative wedding photographers and bakers, why shouldn't that limited accommodation be allowed?

This chapter has provided a way of thinking about such problems following the method of social coherence and examining the analogies and principles suggested by that approach. It has concluded that, generally, religious actors should be exempted from public accommodations laws (and related licensing laws) only narrowly, in line with how they are treated under existing civil rights regimes. That argument does not resolve every particular dispute, however, because questions will remain about how exactly that approach should be applied in particular situations. Accreditation of colleges with traditional religious rules on sexual conduct, for example, is complicated because it concerns not just whether universities *may* adopt antidiscrimination regimes but whether they *must* do so. With respect to the three examples this chapter has been tracking, however, exemptions would not be available in most situations.[51]

Although conclusions for other areas of civil rights law may draw on similar reasoning, they will not necessarily fall out in exactly the same way. Employment law, for example, presents some discrete questions. Chapter 8 addresses them.

EIGHT

EMPLOYMENT DISCRIMINATION

CHAPTER 7 CONSIDERED one major area of tension between lesbian, gay, bisexual, and transgender (LGBT) rights and religious freedom in the current climate—namely, civil rights laws that protect against discrimination in public accommodations. It argued for an approach to religion exemptions that is relatively consistent with other areas of public accommodations law. What about civil rights laws that concern employment? Does the calculus change when our focus shifts from customers, patients, or clients to employees? It turns out it does change quite a bit.

To see the basic issue, consider the case of Flint Dollar. He was a music teacher at Mount de Sales Academy in Macon, Georgia. Although he was effective and popular during the four years he taught at the school, he was fired after he announced on Facebook that he planned to marry his partner, another man. The school is run by the Roman Catholic diocese, whose bishop expressed concern that Dollar's presence would undermine church teachings. Dollar's ensuing legal challenge was not dissimilar to that of Matthew Barrett, who lost a food services position at Fontbonne Academy, another religious school, after it was discovered that he was married to a man. And in Detroit, Aimee Stephens claims she was fired by a funeral home after it learned that she was transgender; the funeral home raised a successful religious freedom defense in the trial court. Moreover, these cases are not the only employment suits that have arisen.[1]

Other issues do not concern LGBT citizens as such, but rather speech in favor of them. Recall the situation in San Francisco's Roman Catholic schools, described in the Introduction: apparently the church became concerned when it learned that teachers were posting messages on Facebook supporting marriage equality and LGBT rights. Although the statements were made outside the workplace, they threatened to undercut the schools' teachings about sexual morality. Therefore, the church announced a new employee rule that prohibited public statements contradicting church teachings, even outside school. Quite possibly, California law protects workers against this kind of retaliation for speech outside the workplace. A question in the conflict is whether the church can claim an exemption on the theory that the teachers are "ministers."[2]

Notably, conflicts between religious freedom and equality in employment extend beyond schools, beyond LGBT issues, and beyond any one faith. Of course, the contraception mandate cases—*Burwell v. Hobby Lobby Stores, Inc.* and *Zubik v. Burwell*—both concern equal employment opportunities for women who use contraception. And in less prominent cases, individual women have challenged religious restrictions in the workplace. For instance, a teacher named Emily Herx lost her position at a religious school after she attempted to become pregnant using in vitro fertilization. Similarly, Coty Richardson, a teacher in exercise science at Northwest Christian University, was fired in July 2015 after she became pregnant without being married. She brought suit, alleging discrimination based on sex, pregnancy, marital status, and religion, among other legal violations. Such cases are not uncommon.[3]

Not only employers but also employees are raising religious freedom claims. For example, two day-care workers in Houston, Texas—Madeline Kirksey and Akesha Wyatt—were fired after they refused to address a transgender child by his preferred name and gender pronouns. They cited their religious beliefs that condemn changes in gender identity. And they pointed out that employment discrimination laws prohibit discrimination on the basis of religion alongside other protected categories.[4]

Still other LGBT disputes involve not outright job loss, but employment benefits. For example, a class action lawsuit was filed against Walmart in July 2015. Jackie Cote claimed that the company refused to extend health insurance coverage to her wife, Dee Smithson, even though the two had been legally married in Massachusetts since 2004 (soon after the state high court mandated marriage equality). Smithson had been diagnosed with breast cancer and ovarian cancer, so her health care costs were high—too burdensome for the couple to cover on their own. Walmart subsequently elected to begin offering benefits to same-sex spouses, so the couple was seeking to recover damages sustained in the intervening years. But it is easy to imagine religious employers continuing to refuse such benefits on religious grounds, especially in jurisdictions that are offering same-sex civil marriage only because of *Obergefell v. Hodges.*[5]

How should the law address these situations? You might think that protection for employees would be *stronger* than protection for customers and clients. After all, most people depend on their jobs for their subsistence, and they would suffer even greater harm from discriminatory conduct on the part of their employers than they would from discrimination by providers of goods or services. Recall that the purposes of antidiscrimination law include promoting equality of opportunity and preserving equal standing in society for all citizens. Especially economic opportunity, but also social standing, could be impacted by discrimination in employment.[6]

And yet, employment discrimination law actually provides *weaker* protection for workers, and stronger exemptions for religious actors (in certain areas), than does public accommodations law. Presumably that is because the employment relationship can be critically important from the perspective of the employer as well. Federal law recognizes those religious interests in ways this chapter reviews. For example, congregations can hire and fire clergy for almost any reason, and they may favor people of the same faith in much other employment. So religion exemptions in the employment context are different from, and sometimes even more powerful than, the exemptions afforded to religious actors in other areas of civil rights law.

It is important to reiterate that religion exemptions from employment law affect not just LGBT citizens, or people in same-sex marriages, but a wider variety of protected groups. Think of Emily Herx, the teacher who tried to use reproductive technology, or Coty Richardson, the employee who became pregnant, or the teachers in San Francisco who face termination because of their speech. Existing federal exemptions allow religious employers to exclude various types of workers. And many of the new proposals have an even wider range of potential applications. Although occasioned by political mobilizations for LGBT rights, some of the current disputes nevertheless cover various forms of selectivity among workers.

Take for example Arkansas's Religious Freedom Restoration Act (RFRA), which was enacted in April 2015; it does not mention LGBT citizens or same-sex marriage, and it applies generally. So it could protect religious employers not just in hiring and firing, but also in decisions about employment benefits. And Mississippi passed a statute in 2016 that protects employers who, for religious reasons, take actions against workers based on a view that marriage is between one man and one woman, that sexual relations should be confined to marriage, or that gender identity should be fixed by biological characteristics at birth.[7]

Arkansas's law was modeled on the federal RFRA, which the Supreme Court used in *Hobby Lobby* to exempt a business corporation from an employee benefit requirement. And the court's previous decision on religious freedom and employment law, *Hosanna-Tabor Evangelical Lutheran Church and School v. Equal Employment Opportunity Commission*, concerned an employee's claim that she was retaliated against for filing a federal complaint of disability discrimination. So religious objections to employment law have extended beyond LGBT rights, and they can be expected to continue to apply to antidiscrimination provisions regarding reproductive freedom for women, disability, and retaliation for workers' speech, at least to some degree.

This chapter addresses such tensions. It argues that here, too, the best guide for how to resolve such disputes comes from broader employment discrimination law and from civil rights law generally. Unlike public accommodations law, however, employment law *does* provide significant exemptions for religious employers. The chapter assesses those exemptions and their applicability to current controversies.

The main work of the chapter is to describe and defend the paradigm cases and abstract principles that should guide our analysis and application of religious freedom in the context of employment law. That is the task of the first section. Because employment disputes are proliferating, and because they present permutations that are unpredictable, the chapter avoids detailed discussion of today's controversies. That said, it does offer some tentative applications of the framework to several examples, including the "Utah compromise," the Employment Non-Discrimination Act, and the San Francisco question about the public speech of teachers in religious schools.

Paradigms and Principles

A useful framework for understanding conflicts between religious freedom and employment law should include both paradigmatic judgments about concrete cases that have some stability and support, on the one hand, and principles that account for them and have withstood reflection and testing, on the other. Let us start with paradigm judgments, and then move to principles.

First, it is virtually uncontroverted among Americans that Roman Catholic congregations ought to be able to exclude women from clergy positions because of the parishes' theological commitment to an all-male priesthood, even though employment law normally prohibits sex discrimination. The Supreme Court recognized a general "ministerial exception" as constitutional law in *Hosanna-Tabor*, though it left the exact shape and scope of that rule unspecified, as Chapter 5 described. Whatever its contours, the principle that clergy members can be hired and fired with some significant degree of protection from employment law is enduring.[8]

Second, there is *fairly* widespread agreement that houses of worship ought to be able to favor coreligionists in employment, including for nonclergy jobs, even though employment discrimination on the basis of religion is normally prohibited. As Chapter 5 also explained, that commitment is written into a provision of the Civil Rights Act of 1964 known as Section 702. The idea is that local parishes and congregations should be able to define their associations according to religion, at least insofar as that means favoring members of the same faith, and that such freedom extends to employment as well as membership.[9]

Here again, however, there is some lack of clarity about the proper scope of the exemption, as described further below. Questions include whether it ought to apply beyond houses of worship to religiously affiliated nonprofits that are not close associations; whether it should extend to religiously objectionable *conduct* that is associated with protected groups, such as pregnancy or same-sex marriage; and whether it should apply to religious organizations that receive government funding. Despite these lingering issues, however, the core conviction is stable. Its foundation seems to be a conviction that congregations ought to enjoy the same ability as secular associations to choose employees who share, and thus can help shape, the organization's beliefs.[10]

Third, American civil rights law has consistently reflected a concern that very small employers with intimate workplaces ought to be able to make hiring and firing decisions freely, even on discriminatory grounds. Thus, federal employment discrimination laws exempt those with fewer than fifteen employees (twenty in cases of age discrimination). State laws are often more protective of employees, but they, too, recognize some leeway for the associational interests of small employers. For example, New York's human rights law exempts those with fewer than four employees. Regardless of the exact number, the value reflected by these laws is that intimate workplaces may have acceptable reasons to be exempt from government regulation of associational decisions.[11]

Fourth, some of the protections for religious organizations have secular analogues, even under existing law. While agreement around this jurisprudence is less common, it is reflected in constitutional law. So Boy Scout troops may exclude gay scoutmasters on a showing that such discrimination is required by their organization's mission. While the case that established that proposition, *Boy Scouts of America v. Dale,* involved a volunteer, it has been taken to cover hiring decisions as well.[12]

Finally, antidiscrimination provisions here apply to both business entities and nonprofit employers. Large hospitals and universities, for example, can be just as significant to worker opportunities as business corporations can be. In other words, employment discrimination law does not treat employers as categorically different in kind depending on whether they are sole proprietors or corporations, for-profit or nonprofit enterprises, partnerships, or associations. All of these can have associational interests, on the one hand, and all of them can have serious impacts on employees, on the other. Even private clubs, which are usually exempt from public accommodations law, must abide by civil rights protections in employment on the same terms as other employers.

What principles can be abstracted from these judgments? To begin, freedom of association appears to be implicated by several of them. Chapter 5 argued for a disaggregation of associational rights. First, intimate associations draw significant protections, which generally do not intersect with employment law at all. Second, though, community groups form bonds of trust and friendship that are essential to the formation of citizens' interests and ideals. Freedom of association therefore demands fairly robust protection from government regulation for these groups, as argued in Chapter 5.

That said, civic and community organizations should not enjoy exactly the same freedom in employment as they do in volunteer leadership and membership. Clear thinking here requires distinguishing not only between membership and employment but also between policy leadership and other positions. At root, the guiding conviction should be that employment relationships that are essential to the shaping of wills and worldviews may need to be shielded from antidiscrimination law, but in a tailored way. Policy leaders of these small groups can be chosen, presumptively, without significant government intervention. And workers generally can be hired or fired on the basis of ideology, a freedom that Section 702 makes available to religious congregations as well. But beyond those basic scenarios, decisions must be made by reference to the varied purposes of freedom of association. Most probably, civic and community organizations will not need (or enjoy) latitude to discriminate in employment of people not involved in policy formation and communication, beyond selectivity on the basis of religion or ideology as such. Excluding laypeople as workers on the basis of a protected characteristic will continue to violate employment discrimination laws, even for civic and community groups.[13]

Third, values organizations whose scope extends beyond the locality, and whose organizational structures have been bureaucratically rationalized, receive more limited protection. They may select policy leaders with some freedom from employment discrimination law, but only insofar as that is required by their articulated missions. Any immunity from civil rights law must be closely justified by the need for robust diversity in democratic deliberation on questions of public consequence. Most employment decisions by such entities will not have any impact on their ability to fulfill that important function in a thriving constitutional democracy.

Alongside freedom of association is the principle of avoiding harm to others. Accommodations cannot shift burdens from religious citizens to other private citizens without raising constitutional difficulties. As Chapter 3 described, the principle has limits: it allows religion accommodations where the cost to others does not amount to undue hardship. Yet overall it prevents the government from imposing the cost of private observance on other citizens.

And the impact of exemptions from employment discrimination laws can be serious. Recall *Corporation of the Presiding Bishop of the Church of Jesus Christ of Latter-Day Saints v. Amos*, where the court upheld Section 702 even though it meant that a janitor in a religiously affiliated gymnasium could be fired because he let his membership in the Mormon Church lapse. Cheryl Perich paid a similarly high price when she was fired for bringing her complaint of discrimination on the basis of disability to civil rights officials. She was required to bear the cost of religious convictions that she did not share.

Durable convictions hold that those costs can be justifiable when they are necessary to protect basic freedom of association. But the principle of avoiding harm to others still does important work. Exempting religious organizations from the prohibition on employment discrimination on grounds *other* than religion, for instance, trenches on equality of opportunity and citizenship in unwarranted ways, at least when it comes to hiring laypeople. So too does allowing values organizations to shape employment policy for leaders in ways not connected to theological mandates. So the principle of avoiding harm to others plays a powerful disciplining role in this context as elsewhere.

Fairness to others can come into play too. Accommodating religious employers but not secular employers who hold similarly sincere and profound objections to antidiscrimination law can work injustice. Chapter 4 called to mind Supreme Court precedents that embody a similar conviction across divergent areas of government regulation and funding. And scholars like Christopher Eisgruber and Lawrence Sager have reinforced the conviction that singling out religion for special relief from employment discrimination laws can violate basic fairness.[14]

Finally, government nonendorsement sets limits as well. Were a government to exempt religious employers from antidiscrimination laws solely with respect to LGBT status and conduct, for instance, it would risk communicating a message of unequal importance, as compared to more familiar forms of employment exclusion. And that could place the government's imprimatur on political contentions that LGBT discrimination is somehow more understandable than other forms of prohibited exclusion. In this way and others, government nonendorsement may be relevant to religion accommodations in the employment context.

How will these paradigms and principles play out in contemporary debates? The following sections provide some direction in answering that question. Although they cannot hope to keep pace with evolving disputes, and although their conclusions are meant to be illustrative rather than programmatic, they do demonstrate a *method* of thinking through the problems capable of generating answers that are warranted or justified.

The "Utah Compromise"

In 2015 Utah passed a law that extended antidiscrimination protection to LGBT people in employment and housing. Although Utah has politically conservative policies in many areas, it became one of the first twenty-five states to prohibit employment discrimination against gay men and lesbians. What came to be known as the "Utah compromise" was rightly cheered by both the Mormon Church and advocates for LGBT rights.[15]

Notably, the law contains significant religion accommodations. In particular, it exempts broad categories of religious entities. It defines the term *employer* like this, in part:

> (ii) "Employer" does not include:
> (A) a religious organization, a religious corporation sole, a religious association, a religious society, a religious educational institution, or a religious leader, when that individual is acting in the capacity of a religious leader;
> (B) any corporation or association constituting an affiliate, a wholly owned subsidiary, or an agency of any religious organization, religious corporation sole, religious association, or religious society; or
> (C) the Boy Scouts of America or its councils, chapters, or subsidiaries.[16]

Under this definition, large institutions with significant impact in Utah may discriminate in employment because they are church affiliated. Presumably this exemption would apply to universities, newspapers, and social service agencies that have a religious affiliation.

Especially in a state like Utah, where the Church of Jesus Christ of Latter-Day Saints (LDS) runs organizations that employ many people, this is a significant exemption. Not only is it not required by the principles reviewed in the previous section of this chapter, and defended in Chapter 5, but it tests other convictions about the proper balance between religious freedom and equality law. Most obviously, the imperative of avoiding harm to others is implicated by the accommodation. Both economic opportunity and equal social standing—two of the values driving antidiscrimination law—are impaired when large employers are made categorically exempt from basic civil rights laws.

Also relevant is fairness to others. No obvious reason exists to accommodate religious employers but not similarly affected secular organizations. Perhaps that is why the Utah law specifically exempts the Boy Scouts of America from its prohibition on employment discrimination against LGBT people. Yet the oddity of that exemption only highlights a potential injustice to other non-religious groups that might also like the freedom to make conscience-based employment decisions without government interference. Fairness to others suggests that Utah's exclusion of them may be problematic.

Comparison to paradigm cases intensifies that concern. After all, existing civil rights laws concerning employment do not wholly exempt religious employers from their protections. Even houses of worship must refrain from employment discrimination on the basis of race, sex, and ethnicity under federal law, for example (except when they are hiring clergy). Utah's categorical exemption therefore lacks precedent in most other jurisdictions. And because federal law applies in Utah, religious organizations must adhere to basic employment discrimination rules even there. Therefore, the conclusion that Utah was not justified in carving out such a wide accommodation for religious employers seems to comport with the paradigms and principles articulated in this chapter.

But it would be misleading to leave matters there. If the Utah compromise was unwarranted, why was it so widely embraced, including by LGBT advocates? The best explanation is that preexisting state employment law protecting other groups was equally narrow—the exemptions for religious employers predated the 2015 amendments. So compared to longstanding Utah employment law, those amendments were an improvement. They added LGBT status to the list of prohibited forms of discrimination without doing much more.[17]

Admittedly, and notably, the religion exemptions probably mattered less for racial minorities and women than they did for LGBT people. Because those other groups had long been protected by federal employment law, even against religious employers, they relied less on state law. And LDS doctrine prohibited racial discrimination in employment. LGBT people, by contrast, are still not protected by federal employment law, and they are sometimes treated differently by religious traditionalists. Still, the Utah compromise could have been seen—and was widely received—as an advance.[18]

Moreover, Utah's exemption is not misguided in every application or every respect. With regard to values organizations, it may be necessary to hire and fire policy leaders on prohibited grounds in order to preserve the ability of the organization to convey distinctive views—including perspectives that challenge liberalism itself. A church-run news outlet, for instance, may well need protection from civil rights laws so it can hire an editor who reflects its values.

Overall, then, a coherence approach can support a conclusion that Utah's categorical exemption of religious organizations from its employment discrimination laws, including crucial state protections for LGBT workers, creates *some* dissonance with other civil rights regimes in which Americans have come to have confidence. It can be supported on pragmatic grounds, as a kind of modus vivendi, and partly for moral reasons, but in other ways it sits uncomfortably with mediating principles that account for our judgments in civil rights law. If that is right, how might the analysis differ for narrower employment accommodations, such as the proposed federal exemption for religious employers who hold traditional views on same-sex marriage and gender identity?

The Employment Non-Discrimination Act and Section 702

If the Utah exemption for religious employers is too broad, there might be greater reason to support proposals for a narrower religion exemption on the federal level. As it turns out, however, those proposals also sometimes go too far.

You might wonder why the question of religion exemptions on the federal level is even relevant considering that federal employment law does not prohibit discrimination against LGBT people in the first place. Although that is true, in 2015 the EEOC interpreted the federal ban on *sex* discrimination in the workplace to prohibit discrimination on the basis of *sexual orientation*. That follows a respected theory in legal scholarship—namely, that discrimination on the basis of sexual orientation qualifies as sex stereotyping because it trades on outdated and overbroad judgments about the sexual behaviors that men and women should exhibit. In particular, discrimination against gay and lesbian people reinforces the stereotype that men should partner only with women, and vice versa. If the EEOC's interpretation is not overturned, either by the next presidential administration or the courts, then federal religion accommodations in employment will remain an issue even with respect to LGBT status and conduct.[19]

Another reason the question may be relevant is that Congress has been considering proposals that would add LGBT people to the list of protected groups under its main employment law, the Civil Rights Act of 1964. Currently, Title VII of the Civil Rights Act only guarantees nondiscrimination on the basis of race, sex, religion, and national origin. The Americans with Disabilities Act protects disabled people, and the Age Discrimination in Employment Act provides some assurance against employment actions on that ground. But no federal statute explicitly covers LGBT people in employment. A bill called the Employment Non-Discrimination Act (ENDA) would have remedied that situation.[20]

Yet some versions of ENDA contained one important difference from existing employment protections. They would have exempted broad categories of religious employers. For instance, a 2013 version of ENDA provided that it would not apply to any religious congregation, association, educational association, or society. Those entities could have continued to turn away LGBT workers, even though other employers could no longer refuse them work.[21]

Such an exemption would have been unusual in federal employment law. After all, religious employers enjoy no special relief from discrimination on the basis of race, gender, or national origin (except when they are hiring clergy). So it would have been difficult to fit the ENDA accommodation together with other long-standing judgments about the proper relationship between religious freedom and equality in employment. The religion exemption in ENDA seemed best explained by a political calculation—that it was necessary to ensure passage—rather than because it was justifiable.[22]

Perhaps because of that difficulty, ENDA *as a whole* began to lose support among civil rights advocates. How that came about is pertinent to the ongoing American experiment with religious freedom and equality. By 2014, the Obama administration had apparently become frustrated with Congress's failure to pass ENDA. The president indicated that he was prepared to take whatever action he could to protect LGBT workers without congressional approval. Accordingly, the administration moved toward an executive order designed to prohibit federal contractors from discriminating in employment against LGBT people. Because the action only applied to federal contractors it could be taken without Congress, according to the administration.[23]

But the administration's proposal raised the question of whether its executive order would contain the same broad religion accommodation that appeared in these particular ENDA bills. Certain religious actors urged the administration to include a generous exemption. They wrote a letter to the president and argued, among other things, that it would be wrong to exclude religious organizations from federal contracts because of their religious convictions about hiring LGBT workers, and also that doing so would impair the administration's "commitment to having 'all hands on deck' in the fight against poverty and other dire social problems."[24]

While the administration was considering those arguments, the Supreme Court handed down *Hobby Lobby.* Both sides immediately asked themselves whether and how the decision, although itself about reproductive freedom, could affect the struggle for LGBT rights in employment. In particular, arguments about *Hobby Lobby* were brought to bear on the proposed executive order. Only one day after the Supreme Court announced its decision, religious groups sent a second letter to President Obama, again asking him to include a substantial religion accommodation in the executive order. Although the letter did not mention *Hobby Lobby*, it was connected to the decision in news accounts.[25]

On the other side, the connection was even clearer. Letters from progressive religious leaders and legal scholars encouraged the president to retain only the narrower religion exemption already contained in Section 702 of the main federal employment law. The scholars emphasized that nothing in *Hobby Lobby* compelled the administration to include a broader exemption in the executive order, since that decision was limited to contraception coverage, and they emphasized that the court had premised its opinion on its belief that employees would not be harmed. The letter also pointed out that an existing executive order, promulgated by former president Bush, had already allowed religious contractors to prefer only coreligionists in employment, in the manner of Section 702. Those precedents, it argued, set the correct standard for accommodating religious belief in the context of civil rights laws that prohibit invidious discrimination in employment.[26]

All this discussion of the executive order, conducted against the backdrop of *Hobby Lobby*, may have caused LGBT advocates to rethink their support for ENDA. Shortly after the decision came down, a group of LGBT advocates and civil rights organizations announced that they were withdrawing support for the act because its religion provision was overly broad. Notably, their statement plainly invoked the principle of government nonendorsement, as defended in Chapter 6: a concern that the broader accommodation would send a message that religious opposition to hiring LGBT workers was more understandable than religious opposition to other forms of employment discrimination.[27]

Shortly after civil rights groups withdrew their support from ENDA, the administration issued the executive order, which retained only the narrower religion exemption patterned on Section 702 and contained in earlier executive orders. Subsequently, ENDA has not regained significant political momentum in Congress. Attempts to include LGBT citizens in civil rights laws, such as a bill called the Equality Act, do not seem designed to draw support from Republican members of Congress. Drafts of the Equality Act even exempt its provisions from RFRA—a provision that is unlikely to win bipartisan support. Rather, the Equality Act charts a future course for comprehensive federal antidiscrimination protection for LGBT citizens.[28]

In any event, President Obama's decision was justifiable. Exempting employers with religious objections to hiring LGBT workers would have been unusual—again, other federal employment discrimination laws have not done that for other forms of discrimination in hiring. Moreover, the most direct precedent—President Bush's executive order—followed the familiar exemption under Section 702, which again allowed congregations to favor employees of the same religion. So it would have been difficult, if not perhaps impossible, to make a broader accommodation fit together with other tested judgments about the role of religious freedom in employment.

Moreover, the broader ENDA exemption would have implicated the principle of avoiding harm to others. Employees would have had to face the prospect of bearing the costs of their employers' religious beliefs. Those costs would have come in at least two forms, tracking the purposes of antidiscrimination law: diminished economic opportunity, and impaired standing in the social and political community. And because that second harm would have been accompanied by a *government* message of approval for *private* decisions to exclude LGBT employees, it could also conceivably have implicated the principle of government nonendorsement, as the statement from LGBT groups indicated.

Finally, freedom of association *arguably* was not violated by rejection of a broader accommodation for religious employers. Here's why. It is true that narrow classes of community groups need latitude from government intervention to engage in the formation of citizens' interests and ideologies, as Chapter 5 argued, and that means they should have significant freedom to choose members and leaders. When it comes to employment, however, not every decision will impact that essential function. Close associations should have the ability to select employees who share their basic commitments, meaning environmental groups can hire only environmentalists, even outside policy roles. And Section 702 allows religious groups similar leeway by letting them choose workers of the same faith. It treats religion more like a belief system and less like an identity characteristic. When a congregation hires people of the same faith, it acts similarly to a nonreligious community organization that prefers employees who share its beliefs.

Moreover, Section 702 only applies to organizations that are primarily religious in their purpose and activities—not to nonprofits that provide nonreligious services but are incidentally affiliated with a religious organization. This limitation, while looser than the definition of community groups outlined in Chapter 5, nevertheless does separate out some purely nonreligious employers.[29]

When the Supreme Court upheld Section 702 in the *Amos* decision, it allowed a religious organization to fire a janitor whose membership in the denomination had lapsed. The best reading of that decision was that it allowed Congress to protect local organizations in their ability to form wills and worldviews. That reflected the value of freedom of association. Although the janitor was not in a policy-making role, his membership in the faith conceivably could have affected the group's core function. Moreover, a general policy of requiring employees to be members of the denomination could further that function overall, even if it did not do so in an obvious way in the particular case.

But beyond favoring their own beliefs, community groups would have to show that an employee has significant involvement in policy making and pedagogy to win constitutional exemptions from civil rights laws. The *Boy Scouts v. Dale* case allows nonreligious groups that latitude when it comes to selecting leaders, and *Hosanna-Tabor* does something similar for clergy.

Freedom of association gives no good reason, however, why civic or community organizations should be able to discriminate on other protected grounds when they hire for positions that have limited impact on their formation of wills and worldviews but significant impact on the equality rights of workers. The church in *Amos* could not have fired a janitor for being a woman, or for being a racial minority, when those characteristics could have only attenuated impact on the underlying reasons why we allow community groups to enjoy freedom of association in the first place. Nor should a nonreligious association have that ability.

So while Section 702's accommodation for hiring coreligionists is acceptable for a defined class of religious organizations, a broader exemption is unwarranted. This matters today, even if Congress makes no headway on ENDA. That is partly because of the EEOC's new policy banning discrimination on the basis of sexual orientation. Shoud it hold up, that move would make the question of religion exemptions pertinent, even without additional legislation. And if this chapter's arguments are correct, those religion exemptions should take the familiar form of allowing only selection of employees of the same faith by close associations. Any broader approach would be anomalous, and it would violate principles of avoiding harm to others and government nonendorsement.[30]

Should considerations be different for teachers in religious schools? What if they are fired not for their identity, but for opposing church teachings?

What if they have responsibility for actually communicating those teachings in school? These are thorny questions.

Teachers in Religious Schools

Among the more difficult issues in the employment context concerns teachers at religious schools. Think back to Flint Dollar, the music teacher who was fired when he announced on Facebook that he intended to marry his same-sex partner. Or consider the Catholic diocese of San Francisco, which now requires teachers to refrain from publicly challenging the church's teachings on matters like homosexuality, contraception, and stem-cell research. It also designates them part of the "ministry." Archbishop Salvatore Cordileone, who made the changes, said they would not apply to "private" communications—he also said he knew that many teachers in the schools were not themselves Catholic.[31]

Let's start with the relatively straightforward case of Flint Dollar. He was fired from his job simply because of his intent to marry another man. Nothing suggests that retaining him as a music teacher would have impaired the school's communication of church teachings to children—allegedly, Dollar simply announced his engagement on Facebook, not at school. Terminating him should count as prohibited discrimination on the basis of sex and sexual orientation. And the school would not qualify for constitutional protection. On the contrary, exempting the church from general employment rules would raise concerns under the principle of avoiding harm to others.

The situation in San Francisco is more complicated; a tentative conclusion is that the church probably ought to enjoy some protection under the freedom of association, but some applications of its new policy ought to be sanctionable under civil rights laws.

Assume first that there are difficulties with the church's new policy under state law; although establishing that claim is beyond the scope of the discussion here, it seems reasonable to assume that employment law in California does protect workers against being fired because of lawful expression outside the workplace. While administrators may regulate the speech of teachers when they are "on the job," of course—they can direct teachers to adopt a particular curriculum, for instance—employers have limited ability to control what workers say in their private lives. Conceivably, then, teachers in Catholic schools would have a retaliation claim if they were punished for speech they engaged in on their own time, away from the school.[32]

If employees are protected under state law in this manner, then the question becomes whether the schools can claim a religion exemption. One possibility, obviously contemplated by the archbishop's new policy, is that all teachers in parochial schools could be considered clergy for purposes of the ministerial exception announced in *Hosanna-Tabor.* If that argument succeeds, the schools would be constitutionally protected from many employment regulations. Cheryl Perich, the employee in *Hosanna-Tabor,* was herself a teacher in a religious school. She brought a retaliation claim and lost because the Supreme Court found her to be a minister.[33]

But that argument is weak in many cases. Perich had been "called" under church doctrine, and she taught at least some theological subjects. Even that mix of status and duties occasioned some controversy over the question of whether she was a minister. By contrast, some teachers in San Francisco's Catholic schools presumably teach only secular subjects. And we know that many of them are not even Roman Catholic, much less ordained in any sense. It would be exceedingly difficult to argue that they should be considered ministers for purposes of the ministerial exception.[34]

What about the freedom of association more generally, however? Chapter 5 argued that close associations should be able to choose their leaders and members without interference from the government—that doing so could be essential to their function of citizen formation. Earlier sections of this chapter have argued that such groups need latitude to hire workers who share the same beliefs, but they ordinarily do not require latitude to discriminate on other prohibited grounds outside leadership positions.

But what about employees who formulate policy? Can community groups show that discrimination in hiring those people is necessary for the group to fulfill its function of will formation? Conceivably, yes. Imagine that the troop leader in the Boy Scouts case had been an employee rather than the volunteer he was. Little in the analysis would have changed—he likely could have been excluded because of the group's freedom of association. (That is why the solicitor general could argue in *Hosanna-Tabor* that the case could have been resolved on freedom of association grounds, even though it concerned employment, rather than volunteering.) That thought experiment suggests that tightly knit community groups enjoy some latitude to employ leaders under the freedom of association. That is an uncomfortable conclusion for progressives, but it is arguably demanded by a coherent approach.[35]

Moreover, the same conclusion would follow for employees who do not head the organization but nevertheless guide the formation of policy. A group may need freedom to take employment actions against such people for the same reasons they need to freely hire and fire the leader of the organization.

Values organizations present a different case. There is no apparent reason to allow a bureaucratized organization to hire and fire all employees on protected grounds. Leaders and other policy makers within the organization *can* be hired and fired for reasons that otherwise would be considered discriminatory and impermissible, but only if the organization can show that those decisions are required by their theology or belief system.

Where in this scheme do parochial school teachers fit? That is the difficult question, and the one that needs to be answered. Are they comparable to the heads of civic or community groups, who can be employed without interference from antidiscrimination law? Or are they like those groups' other employees, who can be required to be members of the faith but otherwise are protected? Or are they like policy makers in bureaucratic expressive organizations, who can be hired and fired only for reasons connected to mission or ideology?

Answering these questions requires thinking back to the purposes of extending freedom of association to such groups in the first place. For civic and community groups that are characterized by close ties, the main imperative is to preserve sites where citizens can engage in the personal, trustful, and unstructured interactions that shape interests and ideas. For larger and looser organizations, the main commitment is to preserve their ability to influence debate on issues of democratic governance in a diverse way. These reviews of the arguments in Chapter 5 are telescoped—but they should serve to remind us of the main points.

Teachers share features with both protected and unprotected classes of workers. On the one hand, they do communicate ideas and methods of thinking that are essential to the growth of members of society and the political community. They make substantive choices about pedagogy that have an undoubted effect on developing participants in democratic life. And in so doing, they produce and perpetuate the values of the group itself—the church or the organization running the school.

On the other hand, teachers are workers. They do not have unfettered control over the curriculum, for instance. In the case of the San Francisco parochial schools, again, they are often not even members of the church. Oftentimes they teach subject matters that have little to do with the group's values, at least in their content—think of disciplines like math or physics.

And traditionally, the notion of academic freedom has meant they have some *insulation* from ideological control by the group.

Finally, teachers work in settings that are in some ways similar to local congregations and community organizations, but in many other ways look more like bureaucratized expressive organizations. Although schools undoubtedly can be sites of will formation, they also can be less intimate than paradigmatic voluntary associations. Parochial schools can cater to all students, not just members of the religious organization; they convey complex ideas, not just the tenets of the group; and they employ teachers from diverse backgrounds and with varying commitments—to say nothing of nonprofessional staff.[36]

Does freedom of association take on a different aspect when it involves children and their education? Seana Shiffrin has argued that children have an interest in developing independence of mind, potentially apart from their parents' conceptions. That consideration cuts against the court's ruling in favor of the Boy Scouts—because the state has an interest in exposing children to identities and ideologies that differ from those of their homes and churches. Processes of will formation should be protected for adults, who are figuring out *what* they think, but not necessarily in the same way for children, who are figuring out *how* to think as well. This is a critical and complex question that should be kept in mind wherever children are involved. No position is taken on it here.[37]

Several conclusions can be drawn from this analysis, if only provisionally. First, religious schools have the ability to require their teachers to communicate only ideas approved by the organization in the classroom and in their other roles as employees. Second, the heads and policy leaders of schools enjoy fewer protections against certain forms of selectivity that are necessary to ensure that they can shape the curriculum and steer other activities of the school in a way that reflects the group's values. They should not be subject to forms of discrimination that are unconnected to the group's mission.[38]

Third, teachers in close associations who are engaged in theological pedagogy or comparable ideological education may be subject to a requirement that they share the group's beliefs, and that they be members.

Fourth, and even more tentatively, teachers of nonreligious subjects enjoy the protection of employment discrimination law. Like security staff or maintenance workers, they perform functions that are not directly connected to belief formation or maintenance according to the group's ideology. If that is right, then they should not be subject to termination because of their membership in a protected group, including the LGBT community. At most, they can be required to be members of the faith like the janitor in *Amos*.[39]

Relatedly, teachers of nonreligious subjects should probably be protected against discipline for statements they make outside the classroom—including statements that are made publicly. Although schools have the power to require teachers to convey particular perspectives in school, they cannot police speech that occurs outside the workplace and in their capacity as ordinary citizens rather than as employees. Listeners should be able to distinguish between their social roles as teachers and employees, on the one hand, and individual citizens, on the other. California law may well embody that conviction in its prohibition on retaliation. Any other conclusion would allow employers to leverage their economic influence over workers to affect their ability to participate in democratic governance and personal expression outside their place of employment. That ought to be a matter of concern in a constitutional democracy.

Of course, there is a cost, and it is a serious one. Religious schools and other private institutions may worry that teachers' speech outside the workplace can undermine their messages on the job—communications that the church shapes. If students see their teachers criticizing the church's teachings in social media, that could change the way those students receive those teachings in the classroom. Apparently that was one concern of the archdiocese in San Francisco, and it is understandable. Likely the best response is to say that teachers of *religious* subjects can be required to refrain from undermining those teachings publicly, even outside the classroom. That protection for the church dovetails with its ability to require those particular instructors to be members of the faith where that applies. While under that kind of contract provision they still would have the right to engage in *nonpublic* speech, even if it contradicts church teachings, they would not be able to undercut the group's messages in open statements.

This tentative solution arguably does as much as possible to protect freedom of association for the church (and families) while minimizing harm to employees. People who elect to become teachers of religious doctrine are unlikely to actually disagree with the church's teachings, but nevertheless they can be required not to flout them publicly. But religious schools—like other ideological schools—cannot exclude teachers who are not engaged in conveying group doctrine directly to students. Questions will arise about teachers who teach a mix of religious and nonreligious courses, like Cheryl Perich, but those questions can be resolved on a case-by-case basis through ordinary adjudication.

Notably, Utah enacted a worker speech provision that broadly tracks these conclusions, as part of its LGBT workplace discrimination law analyzed earlier in this chapter. The law does two things. First, it gives workers the right to engage in speech *inside* the workplace, but only so long as that speech does not conflict with the core business purposes of the workplace. Conceivably, teachers of all stripes could be required to refrain from criticizing church teachings under that qualification, as suggested above.[40]

Second, the Utah law also protects the ability of workers to engage in speech *outside* the workplace. It says that employees cannot be retaliated against for engaging in speech outside the workplace, except when that speech directly conflicts with the business of the employer: "An employer may not discharge, demote, terminate, or refuse to hire any person, or retaliate against, harass, or discriminate in matters of compensation or in terms, privileges, and conditions of employment against any person otherwise qualified, for lawful expression or expressive activity outside of the workplace regarding the person's religious, political, or personal convictions, including convictions about marriage, family, or sexuality, unless the expression or expressive activity is in direct conflict with the essential business-related interests of the employer." This provision resonates with the conclusions reached above. That is, teachers of religious doctrine could well directly undermine their classroom effectiveness by making contradictory statements outside the workplace, at least in public. But teachers of nondoctrinal subjects run that risk to a lesser degree. Students and parents will be able to distinguish their personal views from those of the school or church, and nothing they say outside the school—in support of LGBT rights or contraception, for instance—will eliminate their effectiveness as teachers of math or gymnastics.[41]

Also, it is notable that the Utah provision, like the judgments reached in this section, is symmetrical. Not only will LGBT teachers be protected if they speak openly about their convictions outside of school, but traditionalist teachers likewise may not be fired if they take positions outside the classroom that contradict the egalitarian messages of a progressive school so long as their statements do not undermine the school's core educational mission.

In sum, the fairest resolution of the dispute in San Francisco begins with a recognition that teachers can be both policy makers and ordinary workers, and that schools can have aspects of both community groups and bureaucratic expressive associations. Solutions to the conflicts between associational and religious freedom, on the one hand, and equality protections for teachers, on the other, should reflect those complexities. Even if the conclusions explored here are not adopted, the method of exploration should be.

Conclusion

Employment law presents puzzles for religious freedom, and for equality law, that are different from those of public accommodations law (discussed in Chapter 7), and from debates over public officials (discussed in Chapter 9). Nevertheless, the best method for working through them is similar: to look at our considered convictions about analogous problems, and at the principles that abstract from them, and work to find solutions that fit together with those convictions. Moreover, the three situations involve principles that overlap, especially freedom of association and avoiding harm to others.

Even if that process is followed by others, however, the particular proposals in this chapter will very likely be criticized or rejected. A conversation will follow, with each person seeking to convince others that his or her interpretation is more convincing, while reexamining that interpretation in light of arguments offered by interlocutors. While the outcome is uncertain, the process of critically examining them in light of other perspectives can ensure that they are warranted.

NINE

PUBLIC OFFICIALS

HOW DO THE METHODS and principles set out in this book illuminate the problem of public officials who have religious objections to same-sex marriage? Think not only of judges, magistrates, and justices of the peace but also local clerks, registrars, and other government employees. Must they issue marriage licenses, or solemnize marriages, if they have sincere religious objections to same-sex marriage? The answer may surprise some egalitarians: in fact, public officials may well be eligible for certain protection.

One reason this conclusion might be surprising is that government employees are often thought to have the *weakest* claims for religion accommodations. For example, none of the states that enacted marriage equality by statute exempted public employees, even though all of them contained other religion exemptions. And that was not because the issue was not on the table—advocates had explicitly asked the states to accommodate public officials.[1]

In a public talk at Harvard University in 2015, justice Anthony Kennedy suggested that public officials with religious objections to implementing *Obergefell v. Hodges* should consider resigning. "Great respect, it seems to me, has to be given to people who resign rather than do something they view as morally wrong, in order to make a point," he remarked, before adding that "the rule of law is that, as a public official in performing your legal duties, you are bound to enforce the law." Many Americans share the conviction that public officials must either administer the law or find another line of work.[2]

Despite the apparent weakness of their claims, however, government officials were among the first to press for exemptions after *Obergefell*. Texas's attorney general issued an opinion two days after the Supreme Court's decision came down, saying that clerks and judicial officials retain religious freedom rights that allow them to refuse to process or perform same-sex marriages, but recognizing that legal concerns may arise if no official is willing.[3]

Even before *Obergefell*, the North Carolina legislature passed a law that accommodated public officials who had religious objections to administering weddings. Lawmakers were reacting to a lower court decision that had brought marriage equality to the state. The governor vetoed the measure, arguing that "no public official who voluntarily swears to support and defend the Constitution and to discharge all duties of their office should be exempt from upholding that oath." But the legislature overrode the veto and enacted the law.[4]

North Carolina's law had a specific structure: magistrates or clerks could refrain from processing or performing marriages because of a religious objection. But officials who invoked this accommodation were prohibited from licensing or solemnizing *all* marriages for a six-month period. They simply needed to notify a designated senior administrator, who was required to ensure that someone was available to perform the service. That law left McDowell County without any local magistrate judges willing to perform marriages—meaning that judges had to be transferred from neighboring counties to perform that service.[5]

Earlier in 2015, Utah also passed a provision regarding public officials, at the same time that it passed legislation adding lesbian, gay, bisexual, and transgender (LGBT) protection to some of its civil rights laws. First, the Utah law imposed a duty on county clerks to establish policies to ensure that all couples wishing to marry would be issued marriage licenses and would have access to a ceremony solemnizing their marriage. Apparently, LGBT couples had been having difficulty finding officials willing to process and perform their marriages at all, at least in some parts of the state. Utah's new legislation seemed to protect them. Second, however, the law allowed county clerks to delegate their responsibility to someone who was "willing" to perform the ceremony. Although the text of the law was somewhat ambiguous, it appeared to both obligate officials to ensure that someone was available to administer all weddings and give officials the option to recuse themselves for any reason.[6]

Finally and most prominently, Kim Davis, a county clerk in Kentucky, ordered her office to stop issuing marriage licenses after *Obergefell* because of her religious opposition to implementing that decision. After she refused a federal judge's order to comply with the Supreme Court's ruling, Kim Davis spent a few days in jail. She was released after her deputies started issuing licenses on a nondiscriminatory basis. Davis allegedly then ordered her deputies to remove her name from the licenses, to omit any reference to the office she holds, and to issue the licenses in their capacities as notaries rather than deputy clerks. The couples argued that the modified form was not legally sufficient. Kentucky's legislature resolved the dispute by setting out a uniform marriage license that contains no necessary reference to the county clerk's name.[7]

Although Kim Davis is in a minority among county clerks in her refusal to process same-sex marriages, she is not alone. An Indiana clerk brought a religious freedom suit after she was terminated for refusing to issue marriage licenses to same-sex couples. And Roy Moore, chief justice of the Supreme Court of Alabama, ordered state officials not to issue marriage licenses to same-sex couples.[8]

In one way, the fact that accommodations for public officials have appeared so early is intriguing. Again, many people assumed that public officials would be the last actors to receive religion accommodations, since they are government agents with a duty to serve everyone equally.

Yet in another way, the appearance of accommodations for public officials is predictable. That is because public officials were among the religious actors affected most directly and immediately by *Obergefell.* After all, private actors like businesses and nonprofits are governed by civil rights statutes, which did not change as a direct consequence of the court's decision. Public officials, by contrast, were immediately affected by it.

How should constitutional law respond to their requests for accommodations? Answering that question is difficult, in part because religion exemptions for public officials are rare in the law, while at the same time being somewhat understandable and, under some arrangements, relatively harmless to same-sex couples. Should they be allowed? The answer is yes, although that conclusion is rather narrowly limited to certain measures, as this chapter will explain. Moreover, it only supports that the government is *permitted* to accommodate public officials, not that it is legally *required* to do so.

Arguments of Law and Political Morality

Let's start with the background principle of avoiding harm to others, as that commitment is described in Chapter 3. Accommodating officials' religious observances cannot mean shifting meaningful harm to third parties.

Yet government agents interact with that principle in a different way from others. After all, the ordinary concern is that an exemption will work to impose the beliefs of one private citizen upon another private citizen. People like Kim Davis, however, are not ordinary private citizens. They are representatives of the state—at least in part. That circumstance raises special concerns.

There is a common conviction that government officials must serve everyone impartially. Public officials interpret and enforce the law regardless of any disagreement with its policies and regardless of the identity of citizens they serve. That idea is embodied in codes of conduct for judges and other government figures, as well as in the oaths of office that many public employees are required to take. Such oaths typically require faithful application of the Constitution and all other laws without partiality. Moreover, of course, the Constitution itself guarantees equal protection of the laws. And with respect to judges, the American Bar Association's model rules for judges say, "Judges must be available to decide the matters that come before the court. Although there are times when disqualification is necessary [e.g., to avoid conflicts of interest] . . . [t]he dignity of the court, the judge's respect for fulfillment of judicial duties, and a proper concern for the burdens that may be imposed upon the judge's colleagues require that a judge not use disqualification to avoid cases that present difficult, controversial, or unpopular issues." In other words, recusal may be necessary to preserve impartiality itself, but it should not be used to excuse oneself from difficult cases, presumably including those that present moral difficulties—a use that could interfere with impartiality. So there is a norm, both for judges and for other public officials, that government actors should be available to apply the law and serve all members of the public without exception.[9]

After marriage equality was established, some jurisdictions directed their officials to administer same-sex marriages despite any objections. Citing sources like the Equal Protection Clause and the judicial oath of office, North Carolina's court administrator issued a letter requiring all officials to process same-sex marriages, and ruling that the reasons for any objections were irrelevant.[10]

Courts have recognized this general duty as well. In a case concerning a police officer who had a religious objection to protecting abortion clinics, judge Richard A. Posner explained, "The public knows that its protectors have a private agenda; everyone does. But it would like to think that they leave that agenda at home when they are on duty . . . [consider] the loss of public confidence in governmental protective services if the public knows that its protectors are at liberty to pick and choose whom to protect."[11]

And in another case concerning a police officer with religious objections to protecting a casino, judge Frank A. Easterbrook emphasized "the need to hold police officers to their promise to enforce the law without favoritism—as judges take an oath to enforce all laws, without regard to their (or the litigants') social, political, or religious beliefs. Firefighters must extinguish all fires. . . . Just so with police." So requiring police officers to serve everyone impartially not only promotes equal status among citizens but also reassures the public that it will have evenhanded access to government services.[12]

But, of course, establishing this basic commitment does not alone answer the question of whether and when religion exemptions should be granted. In other words, stating the background norm shows that there is a general law or expectation of uniform government service, but it does not resolve the issue of whether an exception ought to be granted when it comes to religious objectors. How should we think about that?

One obvious tenet is that religious objections by public officials cannot be allowed to cause discriminatory loss of services. Because officials are acting as agents for the government, their actions cannot contravene the Constitution or other laws. Violation of that principle is what made Kim Davis's initial actions unsympathetic—and unconstitutional. After Davis directed her entire office to stop issuing marriage licenses because of her religious objection to same-sex marriage, a federal court promptly and properly declared her actions illegal and ordered her office to resume issuing licenses. Similarly, judge Vance Day was found to have violated rules of judicial impartiality when he directed same-sex couples to other judges while continuing to solemnize marriages for opposite-sex couples.[13]

Those rulings were straightforwardly correct, because the Supreme Court in *Obergefell* established a constitutional right of equal access to civil marriage for same-sex couples. Equal protection would have been infringed if Kim Davis had been permitted to order her office to deny licenses only to same-sex couples while continuing to issue them to different-sex couples. That would have had both material and expressive impact on the couples: they would have had to travel to another county to obtain a license, and they would have faced the indignity of being turned away at the point of service because of their status. Yet the couples' constitutional rights were also violated by Davis's decision to stop issuing licenses altogether. They faced the same material impediment to getting married—the need to travel to another county—and much the same expressive harm, since the motivation behind Davis's decision was evident.

Recall from Chapter 6 that the government can work a constitutional violation by its messaging alone. For example, when it expresses sentiments such as "America is a Christian nation" or "This is a white town" it constitutes excluded members as subordinate in their citizenship status. This has nothing to do with feelings; it effects a change in the legal relationship between government and members of the political community, who now stand before it not in a uniform way but as members of castes. And the principle that government expression can work constitutional harm holds not only for equal protection but for other rights as well. Moreover, it applies not only to explicit government expression, but also to purposive government action that telegraphs unconstitutional messages.[14]

Thus, government officials cannot be accommodated if that works an unlawful deprivation of services to the public. Proposals that marriage license clerks should be accommodated so long as same-sex couples can still be served "promptly" therefore do not do enough to protect couples against the indignity of being told to wait while a willing clerk is found, at least under circumstances where the meaning of the delay is manifest to any informed observer. For example, a 2016 Mississippi law exempts public officials who have religious objections to administering same-sex marriages, so long as couples are not "impeded or delayed" in their ability to obtain marriage licenses. Such an exception does not sufficiently protect against dignitary harm because a couple that is not delayed nevertheless may be impermissibly differentiated by an official's refusal. That follows from an uncomplicated application of the commitment to avoiding harm to others described and defended in Chapter 3.[15]

The same principle also prohibits accommodations of religious employees that would impose undue hardship on the government office or on other employees. While in many situations public servants can be accommodated without shifting meaningful harm onto their offices or coworkers, that may not be possible in all situations. And where it is not, an accommodation of a religious employee is inappropriate and unconstitutional.[16]

But what if an official's objections can be accommodated without any harm to colleagues and in a way that is invisible to applicants for marriage licenses? Usually that will mean there is no material harm to couples, who face neither deprivation nor inconvenience. Can such an accommodation be structured to avoid expressive harm as well?

In thinking through the answer, it may be helpful to distinguish between informal and formal accommodations. Imagine that a county clerk has no objection to same-sex marriage, but is approached by one of her deputies, who shares that he has religious qualms with issuing the licenses. Suppose that the clerk quietly assigns that deputy to other duties, so that he is not put in the position of issuing any licenses, and suppose further that there are enough other deputies (who do not have qualms) that services can be provided without discontinuation or delay. Few people would probably object to that kind of arrangement, even though it means government actors are not observing strict impartiality. Informal arrangements might also accommodate government employees with objections to administration of the death penalty, terminations of pregnancies, gambling or gaming, and military conscription.

Yet informal arrangements should be distinguished because they do not constitute law. They are arranged without reference to any kind of authority—that is precisely what makes them informal. And it is also what makes them invisible to the public. No one outside a clerk's office will know, or has a way of knowing absent some investigative reporting, whether a deputy has been accommodated in this way. For both reasons, the expressive impact is negligible or even nonexistent. But that solution also does little to answer the legal question that is the subject of this chapter, because it exists outside of law. That is, it leaves open the question of what happens when a religion accommodation is refused or challenged through legal channels.

As long as there is no harm to same-sex couples in the form of refusal or delay of service, the answer to this question turns on the expressive impact of government action. And there are at least two paradigms available to guide our thinking on the question of expressive harm.

First, there is government endorsement of a message of disapproval of same-sex civil marriage. It is possible to imagine a regime that sent such a message, even if it had no material impact on access to civil marriage. A state decision to get out of the business of civil marriage altogether in the wake of *Obergefell*, as some state lawmakers have proposed, would carry a message of disapproval of same-sex marriage. And that would be true even though the action would affect all couples, same-sex and different-sex alike, because the government's objective would be plain from historical context. Such a law would render same-sex couples, as well as LGBT citizens more generally, disfavored within the political community in violation of equal protection.[17]

An objection to this way of thinking is that the Supreme Court seemed to permit a similar policy in a case called *Palmer v. Thompson*. During the civil rights struggle in the 1950s and 1960s, the city of Jackson, Mississippi, operated racially segregated parks and swimming pools. After a court ruled that the segregation violated equal protection, the city decided to close (or renounce ownership of) the swimming pools rather than integrate them, citing fears of public disorder as well as financial concerns. Nonwhite citizens challenged the closings in court. The Supreme Court ruled against them, holding that the city could elect to close the pools rather than integrate them. The court in *Palmer* reasoned the closings left all the citizens of Jackson in the same position—without swimming pools—and therefore they did not violate equal protection.[18]

Palmer should not be taken as support for the proposition that purposive discrimination by the government is constitutional, so long as it affects everyone equally. If closing the swimming pools did communicate opposition to integration, as seems likely, the court's holding should be reconsidered. A reading of the case that upholds government action with a discriminatory social meaning contravenes equal protection law, which provides that government action that conveys a racialized message is unconstitutional, even absent a disparate effect on nonwhites. Recall that a government proclamation to the effect of "This Town Is for Whites" would be unconstitutional. A reading that takes the City of Jackson's decision to shutter the swimming pools to have the same purpose and expressive effect should lead to the same outcome. Jackson's actions would be unconstitutional because they constitute nonwhite citizens as subordinate.[19]

Let's return now to a state attempt to get out of the marriage business altogether. Today that action would signal disapproval of same-sex marriage in violation of the *Obergefell* opinion. After all, *Obergefell* could be understood to rest on a concern with expressive harm. Several states had extended all the material rights and benefits to same-sex couples through civil union or domestic partnership statutes—so the only remaining harm to these couples was withholding the status of marriage. And that expressive harm alone was enough to doom the laws, according to *Obergefell*. Similarly, a state's decision to end civil marriage because of antipathy to same-sex marriage would be sufficient to defeat the law, assuming the social meaning of the action was clear. Incidentally, that would be true whether or not the right at issue was conceptualized as equal protection or as a fundamental right to civil marriage under due process.

A second paradigm is available for thinking about the expressive impact of exemptions for public officials, however. Under this alternative template, the social meaning of an accommodation is connected to the importance of religious freedom rather than disapproval of the official activity itself. Government would be marking its recognition of the significance of individual rights of religion and conscience by crafting special arrangements for officials with deep objections, in the manner of familiar religion exceptions that appear in many statutes. No couple need be inconvenienced in any material way, and none would be relegated to a subordinate status.[20]

As examples of this sort of solution in the context of public officials, think of judges who oppose the death penalty and seek to be relieved from implementing it. Or think of judges who object to presiding over cases concerning the right to terminate a pregnancy, such as judicial bypass hearings where minors seek permission to end a pregnancy without notifying their parents. As long as another judge is available to preside, courts typically allow those judges to step aside. That practice does not appear to be wildly controversial. Certainly a concern in such cases is that the judge will not be able to maintain impartiality, but concerns unconnected to bias also are thought to justify relief in these situations. After all, government employees other than judges can be excused from involvement with the death penalty as well.[21]

Of course, in many jurisdictions judicial officers are not required to perform marriages at all—they can opt out, so long as they do not do so in a discriminatory way. But judicial recusal in situations where they *do* have a duty to serve can provide a powerful analogy for clerks and other officials whose duties involve processing marriages. And where a judicial officer's reason for not solemnizing marriages is widely understood to be religious opposition to same-sex weddings, the question of a religion accommodation is nevertheless squarely presented.

It could be argued that *any* provision for religious beliefs held by public officials is inappropriate, and therefore that this second paradigm simply does not exist. Perhaps the strongest form of this objection is the one described at the outset: that government officials and offices have a duty to apply the law impartially to everyone, and that employees with religious objections should simply resign.

But that extreme position cannot be squared with our considered convictions in this area. After all, the duty of employers to provide religion accommodations that is imposed by Title VII of the Civil Rights Act of 1964 does apply to government employees (outside of elected officials and political appointees). And remember also that judges are accommodated in certain situations. And again, federal law excuses government employees who hold moral or religious objections to the death penalty from attending or participating in capital prosecutions or actual executions. So a blanket objection to all accommodations for public officials does not comport with attractive judgments in analogous situations. Judges Posner and Easterbrook, in the passages quoted above, were writing in the context of police officers and firefighters, where considerations may well be distinct, as the next section will explain.[22]

Moreover, the interests of some public officials are understandable in an era of swift legal change toward greater equality. Some officials have been in their jobs for decades, and could not have anticipated that they would be called upon to administer marriages to which they have a profound religious objection.[23]

What if a clerk were objecting to *interracial* marriages? Many surely have an intuition that such an official would not be permitted to withdraw from issuing marriage licenses, even if deputies could assume her duties in a seamless way. And many people will find that analogy dispositive here. Yet it should be tested against other analogies that cut the other way. Public officials who have religious objections to processing civil marriages because of other theological qualms likely could be accommodated. Think of officials who object to interfaith couples or couples who seek to remarry in contravention of theological teachings. Comparisons to those situations suggest that the refusal to accommodate theological objections to interracial marriage may be an outlier in this particular circumstance, and that other religion exemptions are tolerable, if not legally required—again, in this particular scenario. If that is right, then relieving clerks who have religious objections to same-sex marriage has an *available* social meaning of regard for religious freedom rather than denigration of LGBT citizens.

Which of the two paradigmatic social understandings should control will depend on the particularities of an actual case. By carefully examining those circumstances, we can draw justified conclusions about whether exempting a public official on religious grounds should be seen to impugn public values—marriage equality for LGBT citizens, for instance—or whether it simply effectuates a government policy of solicitude for the conscientious objections of individuals apart from the public offices they hold. To see how this works, it is helpful to consider more carefully the Kim Davis situation.

Kim Davis and the Office of the County Clerk

While Kim Davis's initial case was relatively easy to resolve because of the way the affair unfolded, that initial story masked difficult questions surrounding how she *might* be accommodated, and whether the ultimate arrangement was constitutionally permissible.[24]

Here the focus will be on whether any accommodations for Davis were constitutionally permissible rather than legally required. So the matter of whether Kentucky's religious freedom law required her to be protected will be bracketed and the question instead will be whether any state accommodations, including the ones she crafted for herself and the one implemented by the legislature, were constitutionally permissible under the principles we have been tracking. This section's conclusion will be that some but not all of those allowances were valid.

Davis was the elected clerk for Rowan County, Kentucky. That made her the head of the Rowan County Clerk's Office, directing its deputy clerks and all its operations. Although she had held the position for a relatively brief period of time before 2015, she had worked for years as a deputy before she was elected. She was also a committed Christian with theological objections to same-sex marriage.

After *Obergefell* came down, those objections became relevant because a function of her office was to process marriage licenses for the county. In response to the decision, Davis announced that her office would no longer process *any* licenses for civil marriage. Same-sex couples brought suit in federal court, arguing that her refusal violated the Fourteenth Amendment as interpreted in *Obergefell*. Davis defended her action by citing religious freedom protections afforded by the Free Exercise Clause and the Kentucky Religious Freedom Restoration Act (RFRA).[25]

A federal trial court quickly ruled against Davis and ordered her to issue the licenses. The judge reasoned that the Supreme Court had definitively found in favor of marriage equality in *Obergefell*, and the Free Exercise Clause provided no relief from that rule of general applicability. Moreover, the state RFRA could not help her against a federal constitutional provision. That ruling was obviously correct on the facts as they stood at the beginning of the story. When Davis nevertheless refused to obey the order, the judge found her in contempt and ordered that she be jailed.[26]

While Davis was imprisoned, her deputies began issuing licenses themselves, at the suggestion of the judge. At least one of her deputies had no religious objection to doing so. A few days later, the judge released Davis from federal custody and ordered her not to interfere with the issuance of marriage licenses from her office.

By the summer of 2016, a gay or lesbian couple could obtain a marriage license from the Rowan County Clerk's Office. Because Davis objected to any personal involvement, her name did not appear on the license. After being released, she also apparently objected to having the name of her *office* listed on the document. Moreover, Davis ordered her deputies to include a statement that the license was being issued pursuant to a federal court order, and she directed them to issue the licenses in their capacities as notary publics rather than members of the Rowan County Clerk's Office. (This was all according to the American Civil Liberties Union, which was representing the plaintiffs.) Finally, the state legislature passed a law that seemed designed to accommodate Davis, along with others in her position. It established a uniform marriage license form—one that allowed deputies to sign, and required only their name to be included, not the name of the county clerk—but it did not go further and insist that marriage licenses include disclaimers that referred to federal court orders, and it did not provide for deputies to issue licenses in another capacity.[27]

Could something like this arrangement satisfy both Kim Davis's religious freedom concerns and the constitutional rights of the couples? Perhaps, but only with important conditions. Seeing exactly why and how requires distinguishing between the officeholder and the office. While Kim Davis the individual has deeply held beliefs for which she can claim some protection, Davis the elected Rowan County clerk can have no such beliefs because she acts for a government office. Douglas Laycock has persuasively drawn this distinction in his comments on the Davis controversy. Exempting Davis in her capacity as officeholder would raise serious Establishment Clause issues, because it would align a public entity—a state office—with a particular religion. Moreover, any official objections to same-sex marriage would work constitutional harm to the couples seeking equal access to civil marriage. Therefore, distinguishing between a private individual and the public office she holds can help navigate the solution.[28]

First, consider arguments for accommodating Davis. As long as no couple experiences a difference in service, there should be no tangible impact. In fact, the accommodation should be invisible to anyone applying for a license. Moreover, the purpose and expressive impact of the arrangement could be limited to protecting religious freedom, and need not extend further to expressing opposition to *Obergefell* as long as the accommodation extends only as far as the personal objections of Davis the individual and not to Davis the officeholder. That means Davis herself need not be involved in the process of issuing marriage licenses as long as one of her deputies is available to process them in a seamless way, and it means that Davis's name need not appear on the document. Moreover, undue hardship on colleagues can be avoided if enough of them are available to issue marriage licenses.[29]

Second, however, removing references to the clerk of Rowan County, while other marriage licenses retain references to clerks' offices, would risk communicating official resistance to marriage equality. And that would alter the legal relationship between the government and LGBT citizens, in violation of the Fourteenth Amendment as interpreted in *Obergefell.* Moreover, asking deputies to issue the licenses in anything other than their official capacities as deputies risks rendering same-sex couples subordinate in their relationship to the government as well as in their standing with respect to other citizens. Licenses issued outside the aegis of the County Clerk's Office, while licenses in other counties retained such references, would have signaled disapproval of same-sex marriage in violation of federal law. As the couples who are suing Davis said in one of their court filings, "The marriage licenses currently issued by the Rowan County Clerk's Office are so materially altered that they create a two-tier system of marriage licenses throughout the state. The adulterated marriage licenses received by Rowan County couples will effectively feature a stamp of animus against the LGBT community, signaling that, in Rowan County, the government's position is that LGBT couples are second-class citizens unworthy of official recognition."[30] The couples were surely correct that the altered licenses worked a degradation of citizenship status. Nothing in that conclusion was changed by the fact that any altered licenses would be used for all couples in the county, different-sex and same-sex alike. In context, the social meaning of the altered form was obvious. Davis's impetus was theological disapproval of marriage between anyone other than one man and one woman, and that purpose could not constitutionally be endorsed by the government. That two-tiered situation was remedied by the statute, which established a uniform marriage license throughout the state.

But Davis's decision to remove her own name from the license had a different social meaning. To see why, notice that the problem with the licenses she created was that they associated *the government* with a message of subordinate citizenship status, as the couples said, because they removed any reference to the Rowan County Clerk's Office, an official entity, while other counties retained those references. But exempting Davis from personal involvement by removing her name was different. Arguably, it was analogous to other situations in which public officials have been allowed to avoid direct involvement in public functions to which they have a profound conscientious objection. A judge who is relieved from involvement in death penalty cases need not have his or her name associated with those rulings. It was concern for Davis's religious beliefs that was signified—not antipathy on the part of the government that would have altered the legal relationship between same-sex couples and the state, and among members of the political community.[31]

Another complication was that Davis was an *elected* official rather than an ordinary government employee. Some might argue that accommodating unelected employees is markedly different from exempting elected representatives because of their religious objections. On this view, elected officials have a duty to carry out the will of the people regardless of their personal convictions, whereas civil servants can be accommodated as long as their functions continue to be performed by others. Once elected, officials who find that their duties run up against personal beliefs have only one alternative, and that is to resign. Some support for this distinction comes from Title VII's religion accommodation provision, which applies to government employees but not to elected officials, as noted above.[32]

This argument, while serious, should not defeat any and all accommodations for clerks. Although elected as a formal matter, county clerks are arguably closer to bureaucratic managers than they are to legislators or other policy makers; they have limited power to make new policy. Moreover, it is possible to imagine other government officials who would be eligible for religion accommodations even though elected. Judges, for example, would seem to be able to be relieved from cases to which they are conscientiously opposed even if they are elected. If that is right, then there are reasons to think, however tentatively, that the fact of election alone should not automatically defeat a claim for accommodation.

Even putting aside the complication that Kim Davis was an elected official, there was precedent that might have supported a requirement that she serve everyone impartially or resign. Consider the police officer cases quoted earlier in this chapter. Adjudicated under Title VII, these decisions concerned officers who asked to be relieved of the duty to protect certain citizens because of theological disagreement with their activities. Judges in those cases expressed concern about the idea of letting officers pick and choose which citizens to protect.

Judge Easterbrook, a prominent jurist and longtime professor at the University of Chicago Law School, explained his reasons for denying an exemption to a police officer with religious objections to protecting gambling casinos:

> Many officers have religious scruples about particular activities: to give just a few examples, Baptists oppose liquor as well as gambling, Roman Catholics oppose abortion, Jews and Muslims oppose the consumption of pork, and a few faiths . . . include hallucinogenic drugs in their worship and thus oppose legal prohibitions of those drugs. If [the officer] is right, all of these faiths, and more, must be accommodated by assigning believers to duties compatible with their principles. Does [religious freedom law] require the State Police to assign Unitarians to guard the abortion clinic, Catholics to prevent thefts from liquor stores, and Baptists to investigate claims that supermarkets mis-weigh bacon and shellfish? Must prostitutes be left exposed to slavery or murder at the hands of pimps because protecting them from crime would encourage them to ply their trade and thus offend almost every religious faith?[33]

And in the second major case, Judge Posner, another leading member of the judiciary, voted to deny the claim of an officer who objected to serving outside abortion clinics. Citing Judge Easterbrook's opinion, he expressed concern that the public would lose confidence in the police if they knew that officers could pick and choose which people they would protect.[34]

On the other hand, there may be meaningful differences between police officers and county clerks. Law enforcement organizations serve the public in an essential way, often with regard to situations involving serious risks to life and property, and therefore they impact public confidence powerfully. Moreover, paramilitary organizations like the police may require stricter discipline and obedience than other government operations. Both of those considerations figured into the reasoning of Judges Posner and Easterbrook. And even in those cases, accommodations were offered to the police officers.[35]

Concerns about public safety and confidence in the government had weaker application to situations like Kim Davis's. Evidently her functions were more routine and administrative: certainly issuing marriage licenses itself did not involve risks to life and property. Perhaps for that reason, among others, public confidence in the local clerk's evenhandedness was not as critical as public confidence in the police force. So opposition to any and all accommodations for Davis based on analogy to the police cases did not seem dispositive, even if it was perfectly understandable. Her situation seemed closer to cases concerning administrative officials, where public confidence is not an overriding concern.[36]

What about the analogy to discrimination on the basis of race? Would we accommodate a county clerk with a religious objection to interracial marriage, even in the limited way proposed here? Again, American law would not offer an accommodation in those circumstances. And if that were the only possible analogy to Davis's suggestion, we might conclude that she could not be accommodated.[37]

There are, however, countervailing analogies. As mentioned above, public officials can be relieved from personal involvement with death penalty cases for reasons of conscience. And it is possible to imagine accommodations in the marriage context for clerks with theological qualms about remarriage or interfaith unions. So here relieving burdens on religious objectors is not the anomaly it would be in areas of public accommodations law, as discussed in Chapter 7. On balance, analogies to remarriages and interfaith marriages therefore could be understood to work in favor of allowing someone like Kim Davis to opt out of personal involvement with same-sex marriage. Accommodating her was not obviously an anomaly and it did not necessarily constitute a government message of disapproval or denigration of LGBT people. It should also be recognized, however, that the objection based on an analogy to racial discrimination is serious, and it is a matter about which reasonable people can and will disagree.

Ultimately, then, it was possible to provide to Davis something like the accommodation she eventually received, although certain aspects of the earlier exemption she fashioned for herself risked violating the Fourteenth Amendment—it was especially worrisome that the improvised marriage licenses avoided all mention of Rowan County alone and were issued by her deputies in their capacities as notaries. The subsequent statute establishing uniform licenses addressed these issues. Progressives may be surprised by this conclusion because they might expect public officials to enjoy the smallest degree of leeway because of the public nature of their responsibilities. Yet careful consideration of the interests on both sides—religious freedom on the part of the official, and equal citizenship for LGBT couples, along with the full exercise of fundamental freedoms—suggests that some room for accommodation exists. And consideration of other situations involving religious objections by public officials reinforces that conclusion, even if contrary convictions on racial discrimination make it somewhat complicated.

Conclusion

Intriguingly, the upshot is that even public officials can claim exemptions on the basis of their religious convictions, if only in limited circumstances. Like other government employees, and employees more generally, there are places where people like Kim Davis can be accommodated without harm. Material cost to LGBT couples must be avoided, including not only overt point-of-service denials but also delays.

Beyond those tangible harms, however, the intangible or expressive impact of accommodations causes the greatest concern. And to avoid that sort of harm, exemptions must be tailored closely enough so that they communicate official concern for the religious freedom of individual government employees and not endorsement of opposition to *Obergefell* or other elements of civil rights law. Where they accommodate government employees in an anomalous manner, an impermissible message of endorsement may be difficult to avoid. But where they run alongside commonly recognized grounds for accommodation and principles supporting them, exemptions may violate no constitutional law or principle.

Of course, the Kim Davis scenario provides only one test of this approach. Others include the North Carolina law that allows judges to opt out of processing all marriages, subject to certain notices and safeguards, and Utah's similar system. How these cases should be resolved will depend on the particular facts. But the considerations offered in this chapter, and in this book more generally, should provide a useful framework for resolving them in a justified way.

TEN

GOVERNMENT SUBSIDY AND SUPPORT

SO FAR, government regulation has been the focus of Part III: the issue has been whether civil rights laws can restrict religious actors in public accommodations or employment. But sometimes the government acts not as regulator but as funder. Countless government programs support religious actors in their activities, both religious and nonreligious. For example, religious organizations have long been exempt from taxation, alongside other nonprofits.

That government subsidizes many religious activities will surprise readers who assume that the separation of church and state prohibits most kinds of state support. In recent decades, however, the Supreme Court has loosened restrictions on government funding under the Establishment Clause, and that change in constitutional law has permitted public money to flow to a variety of religious activities in a variety of ways.

Think, for instance, of school vouchers, which allow tax dollars to support even quintessential sectarian activities such as worship and proselytizing. A Supreme Court decision in 2002 approved that sort of indirect funding for the first time. Another Supreme Court decision in 2000 upheld a federal program that provided certain educational materials directly to schools, including religious schools; the court overruled two precedents to reach that result. Or think more generally of the federal government's Office of Faith-Based Initiatives, which underwrites religious social service programs. Or consider local development projects that subsidize the restoration of building facades, including the exteriors of churches. Courts have turned away challenges to such projects. Under this newly permissive approach, much government support of religion is allowed so long as it is neutral as among beliefs, and between belief and unbelief. Cash aid is still thought to present constitutional difficulties when given directly to religious organizations, but that barrier might not last for long.[1]

Court relaxation of Establishment Clause restrictions on funding has brought a new question to the foreground. Now that the government *may* fund sectarian groups, *must* it do so? That is, can the government decide that it would rather not allow tax dollars to flow to religious groups as a matter of policy, even if it is now permitted to do so as a matter of constitutional law? That turns out to be a difficult, complicated question. And the general issue is now before the Supreme Court in a case concerning funding for school playgrounds. Missouri declined to extend the funding to religious schools, citing a commitment to the separation of church and state, and the schools brought suit.[2]

Though many policies that defund religious actors do not involve equality law, some of them do. After all, one of the reasons that officials may wish to withdraw support is to discourage discriminatory practices. In a canonical case, the Internal Revenue Service (IRS) denied tax-exempt status to Bob Jones University, a school with a religious policy against interracial dating among students. The IRS invoked a policy that prohibited tax exemptions from benefiting discriminatory groups. The Supreme Court upheld the IRS decision in *Bob Jones University v. United States*. Regardless of whether the government-as-regulator could *prohibit* the school's dating policy without violating the Free Exercise Clause, the government-as-funder could *defund* the policy. That case did not raise the issue of selective defunding, since the IRS's antidiscrimination policy applied to religious and nonreligious institutions alike, but it nevertheless illustrated the general connection between state subsidies and equality concerns.[3]

Recall too that federal and state governments have long defunded the decision to terminate a pregnancy, among other exercises of reproductive freedom, even though those practices are constitutionally protected from regulation, and even though protecting them is largely driven by a commitment to full and equal citizenship for women. So the question of government funding is important to the conflict between religious freedom and equality law across a range of rights.[4]

On the one hand, some have warned that private actors could lose public support because of their opposition to same-sex marriage or contraception. During oral argument in *Obergefell v. Hodges*, for example, justice Samuel

Alito invoked the *Bob Jones* case and asked the government's lawyer whether a university that opposed same-sex marriage could lose its tax-exempt status in a similar way. The solicitor general of the United States, who was arguing for the government, replied, "You know, I—I don't think I can answer that question without knowing more specifics, but it's certainly going to be an issue. I—I don't deny that. I don't deny that, Justice Alito. It is—it is going to be an issue." That was a notable answer.[5]

And indeed, the justices took note. In his dissent, chief justice John Roberts recalled this remark by the solicitor general, and he warned that tax exemptions may be at risk for religious institutions that oppose same-sex marriage.[6]

Stoking these fears and going even farther, some commentators have called for the government to pull financial support for groups that continue to adhere to traditional views on lesbian, gay, bisexual, and transgender (LGBT) rights, including religious organizations.[7]

On the opposite end of the debate, some commentators have begun to question not only the propriety of defunding groups that defend traditional sexual mores but the *Bob Jones* decision itself. They are unsettling the long-standing assumption that the *Bob Jones* decision is a permanent part of the constitutional canon.[8]

Positions in between these two poles exist as well, of course. Several commentators have pointed out that tax-exempt status has never been revoked because of discrimination on any ground other than race. In fact, the mainstream liberal position on defunding seems to be that government will not move to withdraw support to traditional groups unless and until there is a social consensus that such views are abhorrent. And at that point, groups that oppose same-sex marriage or contraception will be in the tiny minority everywhere in the country, just as groups that discriminate on the basis of race currently are.[9]

Such assurances have not placated everyone, however. Some have pointed out that nothing in the *logic* of *Bob Jones* limits defunding to cases of racial discrimination. Where the law's letter allows defunding, they worry that mere politics will not provide sufficient protection. Leaders of religious colleges and universities wrote to Congress, quoting the remarks by the solicitor general and expressing grave concern about a loss of tax-exempt status.[10]

Republican lawmakers reacted to these developments by introducing the First Amendment Defense Act (FADA). That bill that quotes the remarks of the solicitor general and expresses serious concern. It responds by protecting any person or entity from loss of federal tax exemptions or other support because of a position, "in accordance with a religious belief or moral conviction," that marriage should be limited to one man and one woman. Beyond funding, FADA may also protect such entities against a range of federal "penalties." And the FADA idea is no longer hypothetical. Mississippi became the first jurisdiction to enact a FADA law, which protects religious actors with traditional views on sexuality from defunding, among other repercussions.[11]

Apparently some religious universities have even preemptively declined federal support out of a fear that the funding could be used as leverage to press for recognition of same-sex marriage or tolerance of contraception use. Wyoming Catholic College, for example, decided to decline federal student aid, saying it would safeguard its ability to "practice [the] Catholic faith without qualifying it," according to the president of the college. Other schools have taken similar steps, or are considering doing so, out of fear that they could be required to provide benefits to the same-sex spouses of employees or bathrooms to transgender students.[12]

Note too that government support can take the form not just of funding but of speech. Officials can endorse or condemn private activities, including activities that are constitutionally protected. In fact, the two practices are closely related: government often expresses approval through funding and disapproval through defunding. Think, for instance, of the many laws that prohibit government subsidies of a woman's decision to terminate a pregnancy. Or recall the long-standing tax exemption for charitable activities. In these situations and others, government spending and speech work together.

How should we think about the possibility that government could defund groups that adhere to traditional views on questions such as LGBT rights and reproductive freedom for women? The question is particularly pointed where the government lacks the ability to prohibit discrimination through regulation, either because the groups are protected by religious freedom laws or because the legislature simply has not yet enacted civil rights for LGBT citizens, but it nevertheless wishes to defund or disapprove of such groups. This chapter focuses on those situations.

It offers the argument that, generally, government has latitude to decline to support discriminatory groups, according to the most attractive interpretation of political theory and constitutional law. Of course, that does not mean that government will or should choose to do so; that remains a matter of policy that is within its discretion to consider. It also does not mean that real constitutional limits on defunding do not exist. But, generally, religious freedom law does not—and should not, under the most compelling understanding—require the government to extend support to actors that engage in discriminatory practices.

The chapter first sets out the moral and legal case for government discretion over funding. It then qualifies that position by noting important limits on the government's ability to deny support to discriminatory practices. Limitations include the prohibition on discrimination among sects, a ban on irrational animus against religious actors, and a bar on what the court has called "unconstitutional conditions" on government spending. Finally, the chapter applies the approach to a few conflicts that are currently unfolding on the ground, and it suggests places where defunding, although constitutional, would be unwise or counterproductive.

Government Defunding and Disapproval in Law and Political Morality

According to common understandings, there is a basic distinction between government regulation and funding—especially with respect to liberty rights. If you think of liberty in a simple way, as the ability of private actors to engage in practices free of government control, then you can see how regulation would affect the right differently from defunding. Whereas regulation determines whether and how a liberty right can be exercised, funding determines whether state resources are available to support the activity. According to this commonplace distinction, citizen activity can be constitutionally protected from regulation but still defunded or discouraged. On this view, people are no less free to exercise their rights because they lose subsidies; they simply may find it more expensive to do so.

Take an example from a distinct—but politically related—area of law and morality. A woman's right to terminate a pregnancy has been constitutionally protected ever since the Supreme Court's 1973 decision in *Roe v. Wade*. Yet, soon after that decision was announced, Congress passed legislation prohibiting certain forms of government funding for abortion. Additional defunding laws followed, both on the federal level and in the states. Since then, the trend toward defunding reproductive freedom has only strengthened.[13]

In a line of decisions, the Supreme Court upheld such laws. It reasoned that a woman's right to terminate her pregnancy was not impaired by government decisions to deny subsidies for that practice. Moreover—and this is the government speech point—policy makers could send a message of disapproval to women seeking to end a pregnancy, not only through denials of material support but also by requiring "informed consent," meaning information that could be designed to persuade a woman to continue the pregnancy to term. With regard to both material and expressive support, the court reasoned that liberty rights are not denied simply because the government refused to endorse or facilitate them. Even though some of these cases went too far, they nevertheless illustrated the basic doctrinal distinction between regulatory prohibitions and denials of support.[14]

Notably, the distinction between regulation and funding does not work in the same way for equality rights. Even government funding that is completely discretionary is subject to the Equal Protection Clause and other guarantees of government evenhandedness. So equality rights apply just as strongly to government decisions to deny benefits, whereas liberty rights are only sometimes violated when the government decides to defund activity, even if that activity is constitutionally protected.[15]

All of this applies to the free exercise of religion, which is largely understood as a liberty provision. Because removing a government subsidy does not impair the ability of citizens to practice their religion, it cannot violate this aspect of free exercise.

This argument works most simply when the government policy of withholding funds is not specific to religion, but applies across a broader category. For example, the IRS's rule against tax exemptions for discriminatory groups did not just apply to Bob Jones University and other religious organizations; it applied to all nonprofits. Similarly, Congress's decision to defund abortions applied evenhandedly to women who felt that a decision to terminate a pregnancy was religiously permitted or required. Loss of a subsidy that affects religious actors alongside others does not normally raise free exercise concerns.

Yet even when a decision to defund is specific to religion, it can be permissible. Again, to the extent that free exercise is understood as a liberty right, withdrawing support can leave citizens just as free to observe their faith, even if the withdrawal is specific to religion.

Notably, free exercise does have an equality component that prohibits invidious discrimination on the basis of faith. And that component applies fully to defunding. However, it can be counterbalanced by Establishment Clause values, even absent an Establishment Clause violation. After all, nonestablishment is thought to *require* targeted disabilities for religion. According to this understanding, excluding religious actors from funding schemes can therefore promote Establishment Clause values even where it is not required by them.

Consider Joshua Davey. He was a student in Washington State, where he attended a religiously affiliated college. Because he had done well in high school, he won a state scholarship that he could use to offset some college expenses. (He also met certain income criteria.) However, he lost the scholarship when he decided to major in the study of religion from a faith perspective, with the goal of becoming a minister. Washington had a strong commitment to the separation of church and state, and accordingly it provided that its scholarship could not be used to major in theology, even though it could be used at religious colleges and even though it could be used for coursework that included the study of religion from a faith perspective.

In *Locke v. Davey*, the Supreme Court upheld the funding exclusion. Chief Justice William Rehnquist, writing for the court, analogized implicitly to abortion funding cases, saying that the loss of a subsidy cannot constitute a burden on the right. He also argued that Davey could in fact retain the scholarship for the study of secular subjects if he pursued ordination at a different institution, using his own money. Finally, he wrote that the state had an interest in avoiding direct subsidy of intense observance, such as training for the clergy, under the state's own conception of nonestablishment. Washington State, like several others, had a provision in its state constitution that required strict separation of church and state. That separation promoted nonestablishment commitments, even if it wasn't required by the federal Establishment Clause itself.[16]

So, at least under the Religion Clauses, it seems that observance can be defunded without raising constitutional concerns, even when the withdrawal of support is specific to religion. But the doctrine here is somewhat complicated, and even contradictory. Justice Antonin Scalia strongly dissented in *Locke v. Davey*, arguing that discrimination on the basis of religion violates free exercise even when it appears in funding schemes. For him, free exercise includes an equality component that, like equal protection itself, fully applies to government funding. So far, the court has not agreed with that perspective, but it has issued few decisions on the matter.[17]

Another complication comes from the Free Speech Clause. In that area of law, defunding religious actors sometimes has been prohibited. The idea is that government subsidies of speech cannot discriminate based on viewpoint. So while a state could subsidize speech only on certain subjects, it cannot defund particular viewpoints within a general topic. Although a state could elect not to support political speech, for instance, it could not exclude only political speech by Democrats. If you think about religious speech as presenting a viewpoint, then defunding only that speech is prohibited.

That is exactly how the court saw the matter in a case called *Rosenberger v. Rectors of the University of Virginia.* The University of Virginia had a student activity fund that it used to support undergraduate groups, and one part of that program supported student newspapers by paying printing costs. But the University of Virginia was worried about the separation of church and state, so it excluded religious student newspapers from the program. That drew a lawsuit by a Christian student publication called *Wide Awake,* which argued that its freedom of speech had been denied. The Supreme Court agreed. It ruled that Virginia had established a forum for speech but had excluded only religious perspectives, in violation of the rule against viewpoint discrimination. In that case, a funding denial that was specific to religion was found to be unconstitutional, even though it did not prevent the students from publishing their newspaper—it only denied government support.[18]

How does *Rosenberger* fit together with *Locke v. Davey?* Not very well; the decisions are contradictory. In a footnote, Chief Justice Rehnquist attempted to distinguish *Rosenberger* by saying that Joshua Davey's suit did not involve freedom of speech. But that was unsatisfying, because studying religion in college obviously had an expressive dimension. And denying funds for that study seemed to be viewpoint discriminatory. How should we think about the doctrine in view of this contradiction?

The best resolution combines commitments to freedom of religious exercise, equality on the basis of religion, freedom of speech, and nonestablishment. Government presumptively has latitude to deny funding for religious activities, because withholding a subsidy does not impose the same kind of constitutional harm as regulating free exercise. Religion can be targeted for defunding in the interest of vindicating nonestablishment commitments, which give the government good reason to treat observance differently. On this view, *Rosenberger* was wrongly decided because Virginia ought to have had discretion to implement its convictions about the importance of nonestablishment, just as the State of Washington did.[19]

There are, however, important limits on the ability of governments to defund religious speech and practice. First, it is unconstitutional to single out specific faiths for withdrawals of support. Discrimination on the basis of denomination is impossible to connect to legitimate government objectives and ought to, presumptively, be prohibited. Moreover, this boundary also applies to what the government can *say* about religious people and practices. In other words, there are limits not only on government withdrawal of material support but also on withdrawal of expressive support. And the prohibition on singling out particular denominations is one important boundary.

Second, public officials cannot deny support simply because of hostility toward, or moral disapproval of, religion. Acting out of concern for antiestablishment values is one thing, but targeting religion simply out of animus is another. A good way to tell the difference is to ask whether the government has denied support for religion for reasons that are connected to nonestablishment concerns regarding the particular program. If not, that is an indication that officials are acting out of hostility. Imagine, for instance, a law that denied basic services—police and fire protection, access to public utilities for water and electricity, or town garbage removal—to houses of worship. No antiestablishment concerns demand that kind of exclusion, which appears to be driven solely by condemnation. Or think of a state university that denied funding to *religious* student organizations that excluded members of protected groups from membership, but not to discriminatory student organizations more generally. There, too, the mismatch between the program's purposes and the exclusion would signal prohibited hostility toward religion.[20]

Third, the so-called unconstitutional conditions doctrine ought to be observed. Although that legal rule is notoriously difficult to rationalize at the margins, it has a core that prohibits government from denying funds to citizens just because they engage in some unrelated protected activity with their own resources. In other words, officials can decline to subsidize *activities*, but they cannot defund *persons* just because they engage in some other activity using private funds. So while Washington could deny support to Joshua Davey when he declared a theology major, it could not have withdrawn, say, welfare support or health care coverage because of that decision.[21]

What should not continue to limit government withdrawal of support is the rule against viewpoint discrimination, where the denial is rooted in Establishment Clause values like protecting religion from the state and vice versa, avoiding conflict along religious lines, and preserving individual autonomy. Denials of support for religious speech, like denials of support for religious practices, can leave religious actors free to pursue their beliefs. And the differentiation itself can be explained by commitments to the separation of church and state.

Overall, law and political morality supports government discretion over how to spend taxpayer dollars, and whether to endorse citizen practices, within certain limits. That latitude includes the ability to single out religion for denials of support—again, within limits—and it allows government to defund or disapprove of categories of practices that happen to include religion. For example, government disapproval of private discrimination does not target religion as such, but encompasses all groups that engage in exclusion of protected classes. The following sections take a closer look at some concrete examples.

Tax Exemptions

Today, the central concern over government funding pertains to tax exemptions, and whether religious organizations that exclude LGBT people could lose their tax-exempt status. Although almost completely hypothetical, withdrawal of tax exemptions could have a significant impact on the balance sheets of many affiliated organizations, including schools and universities, social service organizations, and even hospitals. In theory, at least, the stakes are quite high. And, as already noted, some commentators have called for a denial of tax-exempt status for groups that discriminate against LGBT people, though people who take this position are not in the mainstream.

Advocates for the religious freedom of traditional groups have responded to such calls by seeking to protect against the loss of tax exemptions. Recall FADA, the bill to protect against funding denials and perhaps other penalties, as well as the Mississippi version that has been enacted into law. Or consider that the governor of Kansas issued an executive order providing, in part, that no "discriminatory action" could be taken by the state against any religious organization that declines goods or services for any purpose related to the "solemnization, formation, celebration or recognition of any marriage" because of a conviction that marriage should be limited to one man and one woman. The term "discriminatory action" is defined specifically to protect against the withdrawal of "an exemption from taxation."[22]

On the understanding defended in this chapter, it is *constitutionally permissible* for the government to deny tax benefits to groups that engage in certain forms of discrimination that conflict with public policy. Any such denial would apply to all exclusionary groups, not just religious ones. Just as tax exemption itself applies to broad categories of charitable and educational nonprofits, including religious ones but not limited to them, so too a decision that government does not wish to subsidize nonprofits that exclude protected groups would apply broadly. Groups that lose benefits under such a policy may continue to operate in an exclusionary way. In fact, they are substantially protected in their ability to do so by the Constitution. They simply cannot do so with government support.

Even though that conclusion is relatively straightforward as a matter of constitutional law, it does not mean that policy makers must, should, or will deny tax exemptions to groups with traditional views on sexual morality and gender identity. Governments may well be wise to stay their hand out of recognition that groups may need time to deliberate over rapid changes in social mores on questions like marriage equality and transgender inclusion. Decisions like *Obergefell* send a clear message of constitutional commitments on such questions, and private organizations can be expected to respond over time.

Moreover, tax exemptions for religious organizations have a long history in the United States, and that has been true even when such groups have engaged in illiberal behavior. True, the IRS did defund Bob Jones University, and the court's decision to uphold that action is properly seen as basic to American constitutional law. But that case only stands for the principle that government has discretion to defund illiberal groups in this way, not that it must. And the government has not moved to deny tax exemptions to groups that discriminate on any other ground, such as gender or religion itself, thus making the IRS action in *Bob Jones* somewhat exceptional.

Although the court was right to say in *Locke v. Davey* that loss of benefits is more like losing a carrot than being subjected to a stick, lawmakers nevertheless may be wise to avoid either tactic for a time. Eventually, defunding might be appropriate as a response to persistent intransigence. But in the meantime, a more temperate approach is appropriate in order to avoid social conflict that could be damaging and perhaps even counterproductive. That is why most commentators are predicting that a loss of tax-exempt status is not imminent for groups that continue to adhere to traditional views on sexual morality.[23]

This is not even a question of constitutional underenforcement if no constitutional rule *requires* nonprofits to avoid exclusionary practices. It is a matter of policy making, even if policy on civil rights carries constitutional significance.[24]

In sum, withholding tax-exempt status from groups that discriminate against LGBT people is permissible as a matter of constitutional law, even when it affects groups that are following sincere religious convictions. Nevertheless, governments would do well to hesitate before taking that strong step, at least during the period of transition to full equality.

Accommodation of Adoption Agencies

Recall that some marriage equality laws accommodate only adoption agencies that do not receive public funding. Connecticut's statute provides that its same-sex marriage statute shall not "affect the manner in which a religious organization may provide adoption, foster care or social services," but only "if such religious organization does not receive state or federal funds." That is, religious child placement agencies may continue to turn away same-sex couples after marriage equality—without being held liable for discriminating on the basis of marital status, say—but only if they receive no support from taxpayer dollars. Minnesota has a similar provision, and we can expect additional jurisdictions to follow the model now that marriage equality is required everywhere in the United States.[25]

Chapters 5 and 7 contributed to an argument that religious social services agencies that are open to the public should be required to serve LGBT people, including same-sex spouses, on the same terms as others with fairly narrow exceptions. Yet a jurisdiction that rejects that argument and exempts a broader category of organizations with traditional religious commitments may wish to limit that exemption to groups that do not receive public support.

One way of thinking about that kind of provision is as a condition on funding. Essentially, the state is saying to an adoption agency, "You may continue to exclude members of same-sex marriages—in fact, we are creating an exemption that will protect your ability to do so—but if you wish to receive state funding, you must give up that practice." Or, conversely, "The state will support your activities, but only if you agree to refrain from refusing to serve people married to someone of the same sex."

Viewed this way, Connecticut's law is a decision about what to fund. The state is saying that it wishes to support adoption agencies, but not ones that refuse service to LGBT people who are legally married. And that provision is permissible as a government decision to deny funding without interfering with religious freedom or freedom of association.

That the state statutes also deny exemptions to groups that receive *federal* funds is somewhat more complicated. There Connecticut is limiting the religion accommodation to adoption agencies that are funded by some other government. That kind of law cannot be understood as a condition on funding, nor is it a decision about what kinds of activities the state wishes to support—because the state's own money is not in play.

That part of the statute, then, is not like a funding denial at all; it is more like a strong commitment to the separation of church and state. Connecticut is saying that religious exclusions of service to members of same-sex weddings should not be supported with public money, even if that money comes from the federal government rather than the state. After all, taxpayers within Connecticut will be contributing to those funds. And regardless, Connecticut has a commitment to nonestablishment that leads it to conclude that public accommodation provisions of civil rights laws should apply to religious organizations that receive government support. That seems permissible, tentatively, even if it cannot be conceptualized as a funding decision.

Faith-Based Organizations

A visible issue concerning government funding of religious organizations has been the constitutionality and policy wisdom of the federal program variously referred to as "faith-based initiatives" or "charitable choice." The impetus behind the program has been the sense that religious social service organizations should be eligible for federal contracts and funding on equal terms as secular providers, without being required to forfeit too much of their religious character. In fact, many supporters of the program believe that these organizations provide effective social services precisely because their mission is religious. Aside from the basic question of whether federal funds should be directed to such organizations at all, the main issue the program has raised is how it can be structured to avoid harm to others—chiefly, employees and members of the public who benefit from social services the organizations provide.

Worries concerning faith-based organizations (FBOs), as they will be referred to in this chapter, could be seen to concern employment or public accommodations, addressed in previous parts of this book. But because the precise question here is whether FBOs should receive government support, not whether they can exist using their own funds, it makes sense to consider them as part of this chapter's discussion. As it turns out, the distinction between regulation and funding figures centrally in any nuanced evaluation of the FBO program.

President Clinton signed the law creating charitable choice in 1996, as part of his welfare reform efforts. That original law clarified that FBOs were eligible for social service contracts made in connection with certain block grants from the federal government to the states, and the statute prohibited discrimination against religious organizations in such contracting. It specified that FBOs could retain their religious character, including their practice of displaying religious symbols in their buildings and their control over internal governance. However, the statute also placed limits on FBOs. Although they could continue to favor employees of their own religion, in accordance with Section 702 of the Civil Rights Act described in Chapters 5 and 8, they were not given the ability to discriminate against workers on other protected grounds. And FBOs were prohibited from discriminating against beneficiaries of their services, even if such exclusion was required by their religion or their beliefs. Finally, FBOs were prohibited from using the funds for theological instruction, worship, or proselytizing.[26]

Subsequently, presidents of both parties continued or expanded the FBO program through executive orders, and Congress passed additional regulations from time to time. Mostly, these laws upheld the compromise between religious freedom and equality law contained in the 1996 statute. Centrally, they allowed FBOs to favor workers of the same religion, but they prohibited discrimination against beneficiaries.

Yet there were exceptions. Congress has passed a few laws that prohibit grant recipients from preferring members of their own faith in hiring. For instance, the Juvenile Justice and Delinquency Prevention Act authorizes federal funding for children's services, including "the prevention, control, or reduction of juvenile delinquency." It is subject to another law, the Safe Streets Act, which prohibits grantees from favoring coreligionists in employment. Other funding programs likewise seem to prohibit religious discrimination in hiring.[27]

Such statutes raise the question of whether religious freedom law overrides such nondiscrimination statutes and protects the ability of FBOs to favor employees of the same faith. In particular, the issue is whether the Religious Freedom Restoration Act (RFRA) provides that protection. In 2007, the Office of Legal Counsel issued an opinion on the matter. World

Vision was an FBO that won a federal contract to provide services to at-risk youth. It wanted to continue to favor members of its faith when hiring workers. The Bush administration's Office of Legal Counsel (OLC) decided that the federal agency could allow World Vision to continue its hiring exclusion, despite Congress's prohibition, because of RFRA. Given that the federal government often does allow FBOs to employ only coreligionists in its other grant programs, the OLC concluded that Congress did not have a compelling interest in requiring nondiscrimination in this particular program. World Vision therefore could be given a religion exemption under RFRA.[28]

That decision has since returned to the foreground of public attention. In 2015 a group of about 130 progressive organizations wrote to President Obama asking his administration to withdraw the World Vision memo. Their argument was brief, but it seemed to feature the claim that federal funding should not support religious discrimination in hiring. Whatever the justification behind allowing religious organizations to prefer coreligionists in employment discrimination law, the letter seemed to say, it should not extend to supporting such selectivity with federal funds.[29]

Even more recently, the question has arisen whether FBOs might have a right to refuse to *provide services* because of religious objections. Does the Religious Freedom Restoration Act protect FBOs' ability to exclude beneficiaries, in addition to employees, because of theological beliefs about their identities or conduct? For example, World Vision and the United States Conference of Catholic Bishops, together with other groups, wrote to the Obama administration, arguing that RFRA protected the right of their social service agencies to refuse to provide services in connection with emergency contraception and referrals for abortion. Even federal funding programs addressing sexual abuse of unaccompanied children could not require FBOs to provide such services, according to the group.[30]

The intersection between religious freedom and federal grant programs may present difficult questions for equality law. Whether *defunding* religious groups that exclude employees who are not members of the faith should be understood in the same way as *regulating* on that question, for example, is an issue that implicates freedom of association, avoiding harm to others, and government nonendorsement, among other principles.

Whatever the result of that analysis, however, the question of whether FBOs can exclude beneficiaries is simpler to answer. Government must have leeway to decide what kinds of services it wishes to provide for unaccompanied minors who have been subject to sexual assault or abuse, for instance. Religious organizations have recognized interests in controlling who they employ, possibly even when they are providing social services funded by the government. But they have no similarly strong associational interests in deciding whom to serve and how to serve them. And the government has a legitimate concern over how its social services are provided to vulnerable populations. Of course, religious agencies may design their programs in any way they like, subject only to civil rights laws. They can still provide valuable help to people in serious need, but they cannot demand that the government fund them without taking into account their willingness to serve the public evenhandedly.

Notably, this is an area where the most consequential legal decisions will be made outside the courts. Presidential administrations will decide whether RFRA overrides any congressional requirement of equality in hiring, or toward beneficiaries, when they determine who gets federal contracts or grants. That means policy organizations, commentators, and citizens have an opportunity to shape the law by influencing presidential administrations directly.

Conclusion

Use of the social coherence method to harmonize the Constitution's approach to public funding across doctrines and subject matters has led to the conclusion that government has significant latitude to decide whether and how to decline support to private actors that engage in discriminatory or exclusionary practices. Because those actors can continue to engage in activity that is constitutionally protected without government funding, and to the extent that they can, political morality and constitutional law both grant officials discretion. That said, this chapter has also identified important limits on their ability to defund.

Similarly, and relatedly, this chapter has suggested that government has broad ability to decide what to say about discrimination by private groups, including religious groups, even when that conduct is constitutionally protected. That is, government may decline not only material support, but also expressive support. But again, that ability is subject to limits designed to protect the religious and associational rights of religious and moral actors to dissent from liberal orthodoxy on equality matters.[31]

AFTERWORD

HOW SHOULD WE THINK about the current impasse between religious freedom and equality law? This book has argued first that we *can* think through the questions it raises, and argue about them, without devolving into rank conflict. Ideas can play a role, even if that role is overshadowed by interests and ideologies. This is critical for the health of the constitutional culture.

On the substance of these questions, existing legal arrangements can provide a guide—by suggesting precedents or the principles that explain them—even though the inherited settlements must constantly be critically examined. Part of the examination involves identifying principles that account for our considered convictions about concrete cases while also rejecting those judgments that cannot comport with higher-order commitments. When all that is done, answers emerge that are relatively clear in some areas. For example, public accommodations laws provide fairly narrow exemptions for religious actors. That such solutions nevertheless draw heated disagreement is not necessarily an indication that they are incorrect—though in theory they, too, can be unsettled through sustained critique.

Answers in other areas leave plenty of room for reasonable disagreement. Think of employment law or accommodations for government officials; in those areas, solutions can be offered, but they must be subjected to ongoing debate in the public arena.

In a moment of intense divisiveness on such deep questions of law and policy, it is tempting to see in these debates a trade-off between peace and justice. Some will ask whether it would not be wiser to settle on a modus vivendi, not necessarily because we have no alternative but because the alternative sets citizens against one another. Justice is thought to carry an unacceptable price in the form of increased civil resentment and even unrest. And if our attempts to identify just solutions are themselves untrustworthy or duplicitous, the cost to civic unity is even more concerning.

Yet one promise of coherence is to diminish or dissolve the apparent tension between peace and justice. Starting with judgments and principles that have common appeal, it is possible to make arguments for solutions to current disputes. That is, reasons can be given for outcomes, including outcomes that are enforced by state coercion; it is not necessary to simply impose government solutions on dissenters without giving an explanation that is accessible to them. And giving accessible reasons should ameliorate the divisiveness that follows from unreasoned impositions of state power.

Of course, that people can understand the reasons the government has for regulating or defunding them does not guarantee they will accept those reasons. But that is not the ambition. Reasonable disagreement will persist, and should persist in any constitutional democracy. Civil peace is not the same thing as civil agreement, which should never be the goal of a polity such as the one in the United States. Robust dissent is vital to the health of the democracy, not just for reaching right outcomes but also for cultivating the full realization of citizens' capacities.

True peace then comes not from striking compromises that settle disputes without explanations. In fact, governing that way can be counterproductive for unity—it can paper over resentments and allow them to fester. Striving for outcomes that are backed by reasons can be more controversial in the short term, because the losers of a particular fight are not merely accommodated but told they are on the wrong side of justice. But over time the hope is that governing with reasons can promote a more lasting unity not only because citizens who experience government regulation can understand why their arguments have been rejected but also because they know that their arguments matter and someday may prevail.

That is not a recipe for the end of disagreement, which should not be the aspiration anyway. But it may promote the only kind of civic harmony that democracies ought to seek—one that presumes deep respect for the inherent capacities and worth of every citizen, without exception. Giving citizens reasons, grounded in justice, may intensify dissent in the short term, but it also sets the conditions for a more enduring and respectful form of political and social unity.

NOTES

Introduction

1. Obergefell v. Hodges, 135 S.Ct. 2584 (2015).
2. Burwell v. Hobby Lobby Stores, Inc., 134 S.Ct. 2751 (2014); Zubik v. Burwell, 136 S.Ct. 1557 (2016) (remanding).
3. On one side, for example, Mary Sanchez accuses religious actors of being disingenuous, pretending to seek religious freedom protections when in fact what they hope to obtain is a "right to discriminate." Mary Sanchez, "'Religious Freedom' Laws Are about the Freedom to Discriminate," *Chicago Tribune,* March 28, 2016, http://www.chicagotribune.com/news/opinion/commentary/ct-transgender-bathrooms-north-carolina-20160328-story.html. On the other side, David Harsanyi notes, "If you admit . . . that millions of Christians hold some form of a genuine, long-standing religious conviction that prohibits them from celebrating gay marriages but you still support state coercion against them, then you might as well just concede that religious freedom isn't compatible with your conception of a contemporary society." David Harsanyi, "The Beginning of the End of Religious Freedom: Compelling Bakers to Bake Cakes Part of a Broader Drive to Limit Faith-Based Decisions by Private Businesses," Reason.com, August 21, 2015, https://reason.com/archives/2015/08/21/the-beginning-of-the-end-of-religious-fr.
4. Elane Photography v. Willock, 309 P. 3d 53 (N.M. 2013).
5. Examples of court decisions in the Kim Davis case include Miller v. Davis, No. 15-CV-44-DLB, 2015 WL 9461520 (E.D.K.Y. Sept. 11, 2015) (denying Davis's motion for emergency injunctive relief pending appeal), and Miller v. Davis, No. 15-5880, 2015 WL 10692640 (6th Cir. Aug. 26, 2015) (denying Davis's motion for a stay pending appeal). Ultimately, the state legislature

resolved the controversy by passing a law that provides for a uniform marriage license, which need not include the name of the county clerk. Ky. Rev. Stat. Ann. § 402.100 (2016).

6. Zubik v. Burwell; Robert Pear, "Health Law's Contraceptive Coverage Isn't Burden on Religion, Court Rules," *New York Times,* July 14, 2015.
7. Steve Barnes, "Arkansas, Indiana Enact Fixes to Measures Seen as Targeting Gays," Reuters, April 2, 2015, http://www.reuters.com/article/usa-religion-idUSL2N0WZ0Q020150402.
8. Hosanna-Tabor Evangelical Lutheran Church and School v. Equal Employment Opportunity Commission, 132 S.Ct. 694 (2012); Carol Pogash, "Morals Clause in Catholic Schools Roils Bay Area: Archbishop Cordileone of San Francisco Defends Changes," *New York Times,* February 26, 2015, A13.
9. Christian Legal Society Chapter of the University of California, Hastings College of the Law v. Martinez, 561 U.S. 661 (2010).
10. For examples of skeptical approaches to religion clause jurisprudence, see Steven D. Smith, *Getting Over Equality: A Critical Diagnosis of Religious Freedom in America* (New York: New York University Press, 2001), 45–57; Steven D. Smith, *The Rise and Decline of American Religious Freedom* (Cambridge, MA: Harvard University Press, 2014), 1–13; Winnifred Fallers Sullivan, *The Impossibility of Religious Freedom* (Princeton, NJ: Princeton University Press, 2005), 8; Stanley Fish, *The Trouble with Principle* (Cambridge, MA: Harvard University Press, 2001), 10–15; Frederick Mark Gedicks, *The Rhetoric of Church and State: A Critical Analysis of Religion Clause Jurisprudence* (Durham, NC: Duke University Press, 1995), 123; and Stanley Fish, "Where's the Beef?," *San Diego Law Review* 51 (2014): 1043 ("cases involving free exercise exemptions and the danger of establishment continue to arise and must be dealt with, and there is no satisfactorily rational way of dealing with them"). Smith is particularly prominent in the religious freedom literature; another respected academic called him "the most penetrating and thoughtful scholar of religious freedom of our generation." See Marc DeGirolami, "Review of Steve Smith's *Rise and Decline of American Religious Freedom,*" *Mirror of Justice,* July 21, 2014, http://mirrorofjustice.blogs.com/mirrorofjustice/2014/07/review-of-steve-smiths-rise-and-decline-of-american-religious-freedom.html. For an example of a skeptical view not focused on religious freedom disputes, but presumably including them, see Richard A. Posner, *The Problematics of Moral and Legal Theory* (Cambridge, MA: Belknap Press, 1999).
11. For a prominent religious freedom skeptic whose substantive positions are left of center, see Sullivan, *Impossibility of Religious Freedom,* 8. As for the political right, Paul Horwitz compares Steven Smith's brand of traditional religious skepticism to a politically conservative version of critical legal

studies. Paul Horwitz, "More 'Vitiating Paradoxes': A Response to Steven D. Smith," *Pepperdine Law Review* 41 (2014): 945–946. Another example, arguably, is Posner, *Problematics*.

12. An elegant version of this narrative can be found in Smith, *Getting Over Equality*, 45–57. For a view that religious liberty can only sensibly be defended on religious grounds, see Michael Stokes Paulsen, "Is Religious Freedom Irrational?," *Michigan Law Review* 112 (2014): 1043. Michael Perry asks whether a nonreligious ground is available for human rights, including freedom of religion. Michael J. Perry, "The Morality of Human Rights: A Nonreligious Ground?," *Emory Law Journal* 54 (2005): 126, 129. An important new defense of the specialness of religious freedom, based largely on theological grounds, is Kathleen A. Brady, *The Distinctiveness of Religion in American Law* (Cambridge: Cambridge University Press, 2015).
13. The argument that courts should avoid religious freedom decisions, at least to a greater extent than they currently do, can be found in Smith, *Getting Over Equality*, 6, 68. See also Posner, *Problematics*, x ("the limitations of moral and constitutional theory provide a compelling argument for judicial self-restraint").
14. The suggestion that constitutional arguments on religious freedom might not be appropriate in *any* forum is made in Smith, *Getting Over Equality*, 79.
15. For an argument that judicial review should be avoided because it homogenizes local community norms on questions of religious freedom, see Richard W. Garnett, "Judicial Review, Local Values, and Pluralism," *Harvard Journal of Law and Public Policy* 32 (2009): 6. For an argument that the Roberts Court has been comparatively restrained in religion-clause cases, both through its use of standing doctrine and because it interprets the substance of both clauses narrowly, see Marc O. DeGirolami, "Constitutional Contraction: Religion and the Roberts Court," *Stanford Law and Policy Review* 26 (2015): 388–390.
16. Patricia Marino argues that our moral life is pluralistic in two senses. First, our values are plural. Second (and related), people prioritize and harmonize those cares differently, leading to moral diversity. Patricia Marino, *Moral Reasoning in a Pluralistic World* (Montreal: McGill-Queens University Press, 2015), 16.
17. Approaches to religious freedom that incorporate plural values include Kent Greenawalt, *Religion and the Constitution*, vol. 1, *Free Exercise and Fairness* (Princeton, NJ: Princeton University Press, 2006), 6–7; Kent Greenawalt, *Religion and the Constitution*, vol. 2, *Establishment and Fairness* (Princeton, NJ: Princeton University Press, 2008), 1; Marc O. DeGirolami, *The Tragedy of Religious Freedom* (Cambridge, MA: Harvard University Press, 2013), 3, 11–12; Paul Horwitz, *The Agnostic Age: Law, Religion,*

and the Constitution (New York: Oxford University Press, 2011), xxvii; Steven H. Shiffrin, *The Religious Left and Church-State Relations* (Princeton, NJ: Princeton University Press, 2009), 2–3; and Alan Brownstein, "Why Conservatives, and Others, Have Trouble Supporting the Meaningful Enforcement of Free Exercise Rights," *Harvard Journal of Law and Public Policy* 33 (2010): 929. Kent Greenawalt has responded to the skeptics' critique by saying only that at a certain point in the analysis of hard cases, reasons simply run out. Kent Greenawalt, "Fundamental Questions about the Religion Clauses: Reflections on Some Critiques," *San Diego Law Review* 47 (2010): 1144. For a powerful argument that the term *religion* has variegated meanings, and that the rationales for state treatment of religion and its analogues should also be differentiated, see Cécile Laborde, "Religion in the Law: The Disaggregation Approach," *Law and Philosophy* 34 (2015): 581–600; see also Cécile Laborde, *Liberalism's Religion* (Cambridge, MA: Harvard University Press, forthcoming).

18. This comparison between the actual interpretive practices of skeptics and pluralists is made and supported in greater detail in Nelson Tebbe, "Religion and Social Coherentism," *Notre Dame Law Review* 91 (2015): 374–376, 375n64.
19. For citations to the work of John Rawls, Ronald Dworkin, and other political theorists whose work is important to the argument, see Chapter 1.
20. At root, there is nothing special about the application of social coherence to religious freedom jurisprudence. It works in other areas of constitutional interpretation as well. But the method does respond to a skeptical critique that seems to have particular force in that field today. Partly, this is because of the argument that religious freedom requires theological justifications. See Paulsen, "Is Religious Freedom Irrational?" And partly it is because of political polarization around the relationship between religion and government; see Paul Horwitz and Nelson Tebbe, "Religious Institutionalism—Why Now?," in *The Rise of Corporate Religious Liberty:* Hobby Lobby *and the New Law of Religion in America*, ed. Micah Schwartzman, Chad Flanders, and Zöe Robinson (New York: Oxford University Press, 2016), 209.
21. See, for instance, Ronald Dworkin, *Law's Empire* (Cambridge, MA: Belknap Press, 1986), 52, 65–68, 96–98.
22. See, for instance, Posner, *Problematics*, 6–11.
23. For an early statement of support for free exercise accommodations, although without a compelling interest test, see Nelson Tebbe, "Free Exercise and the Problem of Symmetry," *Hastings Law Journal* 56 (2005): 702, 704–705, 730–733.
24. Holt v. Hobbs, 135 S.Ct. 853 (2015). Some do take issue with RFRA and its state analogues. For example, see Ira C. Lupu and Robert W. Tuttle, *Sec-*

ular Government, Religious People (Grand Rapids, MI: Eerdmans, 2014), 198–201.

25. Even strong critics of the ministerial exception are willing to contemplate the possibility that Roman Catholic parishes can hire only men as priests, if only because of the Free Speech Clause and only insofar as their mission requires that kind of exclusion. See Caroline Mala Corbin, "Above the Law? The Constitutionality of the Ministerial Exemption from Antidiscrimination Law," *Fordham Law Review* 75 (2007): 1972.
26. For background on such clauses, as well as treatment of their relevance for debates over religious freedom exemptions, see Douglas NeJaime and Reva Siegel, "Conscience Wars: Complicity-Based Conscience Claims in Religion and Politics," *Yale Law Journal* 124 (2015): 2534–2542; and Elizabeth Sepper, "Doctoring Discrimination in the Same-Sex Marriage Debates," *Indiana Law Journal* 89 (2014): 722–723.
27. The exception to employment discrimination law for religious employers who only hire coreligionists is codified at 42 U.S.C.A. § 2000e-1(a). It is known as Section 702 because of its original placement in Title VII of the Civil Rights Act of 1964. The Fair Housing Act also allows religious organizations to prefer tenants of the same religion, though only if the dwellings are operated "for other than a commercial purpose," 42 U.S.C. § 3607(a). The Americans with Disabilities Act has an exemption analogous to Section 702, 42 U.S.C. § 12113(d)(1). The "Mrs. Murphy" exemption for small landlords can be found at 42 U.S.C. § 3603(b). However, the Federal Housing Administration prohibits discriminatory landlords from advertising, 42 U.S.C. § 3604(c).
28. Burwell v. Hobby Lobby Stores, Inc.
29. Ibid., 2786–2787 (Kennedy, J., concurring).
30. For decisions extending conscientious objector status to claimants who were arguably nonbelievers, despite language in the statute that limited that status to religious pacifists, see United States v. Seeger, 380 U.S. 163 (1965), and Welsh v. United States, 398 U.S. 333 (1970). Although the court did not explicitly ground those decisions in the Constitution, justice John Marshal Harlan II did. Welsh v. United States, 344–345 (Harlan, J., concurring in the judgment). For a decision finding a constitutional violation when a prison refused to allow a nonbeliever to access meeting rooms on the same terms as religious inmates, see Kaufman v. McCaughtry, 419 F.3d 678, 683–684 (7th Cir. 2005). However, the court reached that result after finding that atheism constituted a religion for purposes of Kaufman's religious claim. Ibid., 682–683.
31. Elane Photography v. Willock.
32. Pogash, "Morals Clause in Catholic Schools Roils Bay Area." In what may be the first such decision, a court has ruled against a claimant in a civil

rights case because the employer was protected by RFRA. EEOC v. R.G. & G.R. Funeral Homes, Inc., __ F. Supp. 3d __, 2016 WL 4396083 (E.D. Mich. 2016).

33. Bob Jones University v. United States, 461 U.S. 574 (1983). John Inazu, for example, suggests that although *Bob Jones* may have been rightly decided in the historical context of the civil rights era, it should not come down the same way if it were decided today. John D. Inazu, *Confident Pluralism: Surviving and Thriving through Deep Difference* (Chicago: University of Chicago Press, 2016), 74–80.
34. Christian Legal Society v. Martinez. For a critique, see Inazu, *Confident Pluralism,* 79–80.

1. Social Coherence

1. Elane Photography v. Willock, 309 P. 3d 53 (N.M. 2013).
2. John Rawls, *A Theory of Justice* (Cambridge, MA: Belknap Press, 1971), 20, 46–53; John Rawls, "The Independence of Moral Theory," in *Collected Papers* (Cambridge, MA: Harvard University Press, 1999), 286, 288; John Rawls, "Outline of a Decision Procedure for Ethics," *Philosophical Review* 60 (1951): 177, 187–189. See also Norman Daniels, "Reflective Equilibrium," in *The Stanford Encyclopedia of Philosophy,* spring 2011 ed., ed. Edward N. Zalta, http://plato.stanford.edu/archives/spr2011/entries/reflective-equilibrium/.

   For more on coherence approaches, see Patricia Marino, *Moral Reasoning in a Pluralistic World* (Montreal: McGill-Queens University Press, 2015), 7; Geoffrey Sayre-McCord, "Coherentist Epistemology and Moral Theory," in *Moral Knowledge? New Readings in Moral Epistemology,* ed. Walter Sinnott-Armstrong and Mark Timmons (Oxford: Oxford University Press, 1996), 141; David Lyons, "Nature and Soundness of the Contract and Coherence Arguments," in *Reading Rawls: Critical Studies on Rawls' "A Theory of Justice,"* ed. Norman Daniels (Palo Alto, CA: Stanford University Press, 1989), 144–146; and Tom L. Beauchamp and James F. Childress, *Principles of Biomedical Ethics,* 6th ed. (New York: Oxford University Press, 2009), 381–387.

   Marino, following Sayre-McCord, uses the term *conviction ethics* to describe approaches that take "considered moral judgments as the proper starting points for moral reflection." She elaborates her coherence method from the perspective of conviction ethics. Marino, *Moral Reasoning,* 21.
3. T. M. Scanlon, *Being Realistic about Reasons* (Oxford: Oxford University Press, 2014), 78.
4. Ibid.

5. Joseph Raz, "The Relevance of Coherence," *Boston University Law Review* 72 (1992): 277–278.
6. Compare Rawls, "Independence," 289–290 ("the procedure of reflective equilibrium . . . does not presuppose the existence of objective moral truths"); and Daniels, "Reflective Equilibrium," 24–25.

   Another issue is whether the coherence method has implications not just for justification but also for epistemology. That depends on how the term *epistemology* is understood. Quite possibly, coherence could have implications for knowledge about certain matters, such as the meaning of constitutional provisions. The discussion here leaves this interesting issue to one side. For an argument for distinguishing between coherence approaches to justification and epistemology, see Marino, *Moral Reasoning*, 69.

   Relatedly, the argument here has no implications for the debate between coherence and correspondence theories of truth because it brackets truth claims altogether. For background on that debate, see Marian David, "The Correspondence Theory of Truth," in *The Stanford Encyclopedia of Philosophy*, fall 2015 ed., ed. Edward N. Zalta, http://plato.stanford.edu/archives/fall2015/entries/truth-correspondence/; James O. Young, "The Coherence Theory of Truth," in *The Stanford Encyclopedia of Philosophy*, fall 2015 ed., ed. Edward N. Zalta, http://plato.stanford.edu/archives/fall2015/entries/truth-coherence/.
7. Marino points out that the method should only require coherence at a given point in time. A coherence approach that required harmony with all previously settled cases would make change difficult or impossible. Marino, *Moral Reasoning*, 87.
8. Rawls, "Independence," 289; Scanlon, *Being Realistic*, 76–77, 77n13.
9. John Rawls, *Political Liberalism*, expanded ed. (New York: Columbia University Press, 2005), 97, 385; Scanlon, *Being Realistic*, 77, 77n14.
10. Rawls, "Independence," 288–289 ("It may seem that the procedure of reflective equilibrium is conservative. . . . But several things prevent this."); see also Ronald Dworkin, *Law's Empire* (Cambridge, MA: Belknap Press, 1986), 99 (a conception "like any interpretation, can condemn some of its data as a mistake, as inconsistent with the justification it offers for the rest, and perhaps propose that this mistake be abandoned"). Beauchamp and Childress also defend their approach against a charge of conservatism, noting, "This outlook may seem to introduce an unwarranted conservative bias into the account, but this worry is not a problem because of the close connection to reflective equilibrium, which allows—indeed encourages—many sorts of development of moral belief. Almost all criticisms of social practices proceed by appeal to entrenched and well-considered moral judgments, which are extended in new ways." Beauchamp and Childress, *Principles of Biomedical Ethics*, 385–386.

11. J. M. Balkin, "Understanding Legal Understanding: The Legal Subject and the Problem of Legal Coherence," *Yale Law Journal* 103 (1993): 105, 106; Raz, "The Relevance of Coherence," 273–274.
12. Dworkin argues that morality plays a role in legal interpretation throughout his work, notably in *Law's Empire,* 47, 52, 65–68, 96–98. Dworkin's criterion of fit resembles the requirement here that interpretations must harmonize with legal authorities that are accepted and authoritative, even just as a matter of historical contingency. Ibid., 66–68. And his criterion of justification resembles—though it is not identical to—the emphasis here on the *quality* of reasoning, as well as the conviction that there is room for freestanding moral argument in legal interpretation. Ibid., 66–68, 96.

    There is a debate about whether Dworkin is best viewed as a coherence theorist. On the one hand, there are similarities that the discussion here has drawn out. For a view that Dworkin was a coherentist, see Mike Dorf, "Requiem for a Hedgehog: Ronald Dworkin R.I.P.," Dorf on Law, February 15, 2013, http://www.dorfonlaw.org/2013/02/requiem-for-hedgehog.html. On the other hand, Dworkin goes further in certain respects, particularly when he argues that there is at least in principle one best interpretation of law that can be shared by the entire interpretive community. Dworkin, *Law's Empire,* 225. For a view that he was not a coherentist, or not exactly, see Raz, "The Relevance of Coherence," 317. Other treatments of Dworkin's relationship to coherence theory include S. L. Hurley, "Coherence, Hypothetical Cases, and Precedent," *Oxford Journal of Legal Studies* 10 (1990): 221; and Kenneth J. Kress, "Legal Reasoning and Coherence Theories: Dworkin's Rights Thesis, Retroactivity, and the Linear Order of Decisions," *California Law Review* 72 (1984): 369, 398–402.
13. For examples of such condemnations of religious freedom law as contradictory or confused, see Paul Horwitz, *The Agnostic Age: Law, Religion, and the Constitution* (New York: Oxford University Press, 2011), xiii; Andrew Koppelman, *Defending American Religious Neutrality* (Cambridge, MA: Harvard University Press, 2013), 1; and Steven D. Smith, *The Rise and Decline of American Religious Freedom* (Cambridge, MA: Harvard University Press, 2014), 10.
14. On singularism and pluralism in religious freedom theory, see Nelson Tebbe, "Nonbelievers," *Virginia Law Review* 97 (2011): 1128–1129.
15. Marino, *Moral Reasoning,* 16.
16. Micah Schwartzman, following Gerold Gaus, distinguishes between intrapersonal "indeterminacy," which coherence denies is inevitable, and "inconclusiveness" understood as interpersonal disagreement, which coherence recognizes as an unavoidable source of unpredictability in legal outcomes. Micah Schwartzman, "The Completeness of Public Reason,"

Politics, Philosophy, and Economics 3 (2004): 192–193. Marino identifies different ways of prioritizing values as a source of reasonable disagreement. Marino, *Moral Reasoning*, 16.

Of course, it is also possible for people to criticize the law itself as unjust, but at that point they are moving beyond interpretation of what the law is to freestanding argument about what it should be.

17. Scanlon, *Being Realistic*, 79.
18. Dworkin, *Law's Empire*, 88. He goes on to explain that "the general intellectual environment, as well as the common language that reflects and protects that environment, exercises practical constraints on idiosyncrasy and conceptual constraints on imagination" (88).
19. Marino, *Moral Reasoning*, 158.
20. This aspect of the approach draws on modern constitutional theory, and particularly accounts that emphasize the democratic responsiveness of legal interpretation. The actors who shape constitutional thinking are located in a variety of institutional settings (not just the courts), and they are influenced by information and arguments that are sourced not just from judicial opinions but from a wide range of individuals, institutions, and organizations. This is one of the central insights of a loose family of theories that have been grouped under the term *popular constitutionalism*. Constitutional interpretation—and change—happens in courts but also in legislatures, administrative agencies, political party offices, movement headquarters, media outlets, universities, and so forth. For a definition of popular constitutionalism and an overview of its several varieties, see Larry D. Kramer, "Popular Constitutionalism, circa 2004," *California Law Review* 92 (2004): 959–1011. See also Jack M. Balkin, *Living Originalism* (Cambridge, MA: Belknap Press, 2011), 277–282; and Robert C. Post and Reva B. Siegel, "Democratic Constitutionalism," in *The Constitution in 2020*, ed. Jack M. Balkin and Reva B. Siegel (New York: Oxford University Press, 2009), 25.
21. David Brooks, "Religious Liberty and Equality," *New York Times*, March 31, 2015. As Andrew Koppelman comments, "The gay rights movement has won. It will not be stopped by a few exemptions. It should be magnanimous in victory." Andrew Koppelman, "Gay Rights, Religious Accommodations, and the Purposes of Antidiscrimination Law," *Southern California Law Review* 88 (2015): 628. Elizabeth Sepper, on the other hand, warns against "marriage triumphalism." Elizabeth Sepper, "Gays in the Moralized Marketplace," *Alabama Civil Rights and Civil Liberties Law Review* 7 (2015): 160–169.
22. Newman v. Piggie Park Enterprises, Inc., 390 U.S. 400, 402n5 (1968).
23. Koppelman usefully (and expertly) describes the core purposes of antidiscrimination law this way: "Antidiscrimination law has multiple purposes. Canonically, they are the amelioration of economic inequality, the prevention

of dignitary harm, and the stigmatization of discrimination." Koppelman, "Gay Rights," 627. Sepper makes the argument that civil rights laws are not just about economic opportunity, and therefore that they apply even where market alternatives exist. Sepper, "Gays in the Moralized Marketplace," 153–160.

24. On the current state of civil rights protections for LGBT people, see Erik Eckholm, "The Next Fight for Gay Rights: Bias in Jobs and Housing," *New York Times*, June 27, 2015.

2. The Skeptics' Objections

1. For examples of skeptical approaches to religious freedom jurisprudence, see Stanley Fish, *The Trouble with Principle* (Cambridge, MA: Harvard University Press, 2001), 10–15; Frederick Mark Gedicks, *The Rhetoric of Church and State: A Critical Analysis of Religion Clause Jurisprudence* (Durham, NC: Duke University Press, 1995), 123; Steven D. Smith, *Getting Over Equality: A Critical Diagnosis of Religious Freedom in America* (New York: New York University Press, 2001), 45–57; Steven D. Smith, *The Rise and Decline of American Religious Freedom* (Cambridge, MA: Harvard University Press, 2014), 1–13; Steven D. Smith, "Discourse in the Dusk: The Twilight of Religious Freedom?," *Harvard Law Review* 122 (2009): 1895, 1906; and Winnifred Fallers Sullivan, *The Impossibility of Religious Freedom* (Princeton, NJ: Princeton University Press, 2005), 8. Richard Posner calls himself a "pragmatic moral skeptic" on questions of both law and morality, though he believes that social science can help lawyers and judges resolve cases. Richard A. Posner, *The Problematics of Moral and Legal Theory* (Cambridge, MA: Belknap Press, 1998), 8. Posner suggests that moral pluralism means that moral reasoning is impossible or at least ineffectual. Ibid., 7, 9–10, 22. Patricia Marino reads Posner as a kind of skeptic. Patricia Marino, *Moral Reasoning in a Pluralistic World* (Montreal: McGill-Queens University Press, 2015), 151. Finally, Rick Hills believes that conflicts over cases like *Hobby Lobby* are so intractable that they can only be managed by giving them to states and localities. Roderick M. Hills, "Decentralizing Religious and Secular Accommodations," in *Institutionalizing Rights and Religion: Competing Supremacies*, ed. Leora F. Batnitzky and Hanoch Dagan (Cambridge: Cambridge University Press, forthcoming), 9–10.
2. A related group of thinkers think religious freedom law is inevitably tragic. They essentially agree with the skeptics that First Amendment jurisprudence incorporates multiple values that are irreconcilable or incommensurate. They think this means that constitutional actors will regularly find them-

selves in situations where they must simply sacrifice one value for the sake of another, without justification and therefore with regret. See Marc O. DeGirolami, *The Tragedy of Religious Freedom* (Cambridge, MA: Harvard University Press, 2013), 6; and Paul Horwitz, *The Agnostic Age: Law, Religion, and the Constitution* (New York: Oxford University Press, 2011), xxv.

3. Scanlon agrees with Dworkin that external skepticism does not pose a serious challenge. T. M. Scanlon, *Being Realistic about Reasons* (Oxford: Oxford University Press, 2014), 86n27; see also Ronald Dworkin, *Law's Empire* (Cambridge, MA: Belknap Press, 1986), 78–83.
4. Dworkin, *Law's Empire,* 78–83.
5. As Dworkin, *Law's Empire,* 83, puts it, "The practices of interpretation and morality give these claims all the meaning they need or could have."
6. Compare Marino, *Moral Reasoning,* 7.
7. Compare Micah Schwartzman, "The Completeness of Public Reason," *Politics, Philosophy, and Economics* 3 (2004): 192–193, which distinguishes between the inconclusiveness of individual reason and the indeterminacy of public outcomes. *Indeterminacy* means that any individual cannot resolve competing value claims. *Inconclusiveness* arises because different people have conflicting reasonable arguments about the proper resolution to a problem. Using that language, indeterminacy is avoidable, but inconclusiveness, or rational disagreement, is a fixed feature of a healthy democracy.
8. Ibid., 196 (delineating problems of vagueness, equal value, and incomparability). On indeterminacy more generally, see the essays collected in *Incommensurability, Incomparability, and Practical Reason,* ed. Ruth Chang (Cambridge, MA: Harvard University Press, 1997).
9. Good News Club v. Milford Central School, 533 U.S. 98 (2001).
10. Kent Greenawalt, *Religion and the Constitution,* vol. 2, *Establishment and Fairness* (Princeton, NJ: Princeton University Press, 2008), 206.
11. Smith, "Discourse in the Dusk," 1893.
12. Tom L. Beauchamp and James F. Childress, who adopt a coherence approach for bioethics, also argue that disagreement is no reason for skepticism about moral thinking. Tom L. Beauchamp and James F. Childress, *Principles of Biomedical Ethics,* 6th ed. (New York: Oxford University Press, 2009), 25.
13. For versions of the individualism critique generally, including the worry that a racist's coherent views could not be critiqued, see Joseph Raz, "The Relevance of Coherence," *Boston University Law Review* 72 (1992): 280; and Geoffrey Sayre-McCord, "Coherentist Epistemology and Moral Theory," in *Moral Knowledge? New Readings in Moral Epistemology,* ed. Walter Sinnott-Armstrong and Mark Timmons (Oxford: Oxford University Press, 1996), 170. For the worry that coherence lacks a "base" and therefore is inappropriate for legal decision making, see Raz, "Relevance of Coherence," 284. Jack M.

Balkin responds to this point. Jack M. Balkin, "Understanding Legal Understanding: The Legal Subject and the Problem of Legal Coherence," *Yale Law Journal* 103 (1993): 120–121. And Marino's critique can be found in *Moral Reasoning,* 104–105.

14. Beauchamp and Childress argue that the possibility of individualistic views that are internally coherent but plainly immoral—they use the example of a pirate's creed—suggests that coherence approaches must be grounded in what they call the "common morality." Put differently, the problem is that "we cannot justify every moral judgment in terms of another moral judgment without generating an infinite regress or vicious circle of justification in which no judgment is justified. The way to escape this regress is to accept some judgments as justified without dependence on other judgments." They accept and address that this approach is usually characteristic of foundationalism and that it sets them apart from most coherence approaches. They believe their combination of reflective equilibrium with the common morality escapes easy classification as either foundationalist or coherentist. Beauchamp and Childress, *Principles of Biomedical Ethics,* 384–385.

    Here the method of social coherence connects a coherence method with shared legal understandings for the narrow purposes of constitutional interpretation without accepting that internally consistent views cannot be criticized using a coherence method and without arguing that the method requires an external source of morality in order to avoid infinite regress. Constitutional interpretation, disagreement, and change can all be understood without saying that legal understandings must receive external justification. But in many other respects social coherence shares much with the proposals of Beauchamp and Childress, as well as Marino.
15. Brown v. Board of Education of Topeka, 347 U.S. 483 (1954).
16. Scanlon, *Being Realistic,* 77–78.
17. For more on singularism and pluralism, as well as a critique of the typology itself, see Nelson Tebbe, "Nonbelievers," *Virginia Law Review* 97 (2011): 1128–1129.
18. On the relationship between reflective equilibrium and epistemology, see Norman Daniels, "Reflective Equilibrium," in *The Stanford Encyclopedia of Philosophy,* spring 2011 ed., ed. Edward N. Zalta, http://plato.stanford.edu /archives/spr2011/entries/reflective-equilibrium/.

3. Avoiding Harm to Others

1. The leading article on third-party harms is Frederick Mark Gedicks and Rebecca G. Van Tassell, "RFRA Exemptions from the Contraception Mandate:

An Unconstitutional Accommodation of Religion," *Harvard Civil Rights–Civil Liberties Law Review* 49 (2014): 343–384. For representative work developing the idea, see Micah Schwartzman, Richard Schragger, and Nelson Tebbe, "The Establishment Clause and the Contraception Mandate," November 27, 2013, http://balkin.blogspot.com/2013/11/the-establishment-clause-and.html; Nelson Tebbe, Richard Schragger, and Micah Schwartzman, "Hobby Lobby and the Establishment Clause, Part II: What Counts as a Burden on Employees?," December 4, 2013, http://balkin.blogspot.com/2013/12/hobby-lobby-and-establishment-clause.html; Micah Schwartzman, Richard Schragger, and Nelson Tebbe, "Hobby Lobby and the Establishment Clause, Part III: Reconciling Amos and Cutter," December 9, 2013, http://balkin.blogspot.com/2013/12/hobby-lobby-and-establishment-clause_9.html; Nelson Tebbe, Richard Schragger, and Micah Schwartzman, "Hobby Lobby's Bitter Anniversary," June 30, 2015, http://balkin.blogspot.com/2015/06/hobby-lobbys-bitter-anniversary.html; Nelson Tebbe, Micah Schwartzman, and Richard Schragger, "When Do Religious Accommodations Burden Others?," in *The Conscience Wars: Rethinking the Balance between Religion, Identity, and Equality,* ed. Susanna Mancini and Michel Rosenfeld (Cambridge: Cambridge University Press, forthcoming); and Nelson Tebbe, Micah Schwartzman, and Richard Schragger, "How Much May Religious Acommodations Burden Others?," in *Law, Religion, and Health in the United States,* ed. Elizabeth Sepper, Holly Fernandez Lynch, and I. Glenn Cohen (Cambridge: Cambridge University Press, forthcoming).

2. Burwell v. Hobby Lobby Stores, Inc., 134 S.Ct. 2751, 2760 (2014).
3. University of Notre Dame v. Burwell, 786 F.3d 606, 607–608 (7th Cir. 2015) (Posner, J.) (examining empirical medical findings that cost-free contraception coverage promotes women's health); Priests for Life v. U.S. Department of Health and Human Services, 772 F.3d 229, 259–262 (D.C. Cir. 2015) (Pillard, J.) (examining similar evidence).
4. Gedicks and Van Tassell, "RFRA Exemptions," 362–363.
5. James Madison, Letter to Edward Livingston, July 10, 1822, in *Writings* (New York: Library of America, 1999), 787–788; Thomas Jefferson, "Notes on the State of Virginia," in *Writings* (New York: Library of America, 1984), 285. Although Jefferson may not have been talking about exemptions but rather about discrimination on the basis of religion, his words are taken to also refer to the limits of religious freedom more generally. Thomas C. Berg, "Religious Accommodation and the Welfare State," *Harvard Journal on Law and Gender* 48 (2015): 131.
6. Prince v. Massachusetts, 321 U.S. 158, 177 (1944) (Jackson, J., concurring). Jackson continues, "Religious activities which concern only members of the faith are and ought to be free—as nearly absolutely free as anything can be."

But nonreligious activities, such as when religious organizations engage in secular businesses to raise money from nonbelievers, are "Caesar's affairs, and may be regulated by the state so long as it does not discriminate against one because he is doing them for a religious purpose and the regulation is not arbitrary and capricious, in violation of other provisions of the Constitution."

7. Burwell v. Hobby Lobby, 2786–2787 (Kennedy, J., concurring).
8. Ibid., 2801–2802 and 2802n25 (Ginsburg, J., dissenting). Justice Ginsburg later reiterated the importance of avoiding third-party harms. Holt v. Hobbs, 135 S.Ct. 853, 867 (2015) (Ginsburg, J., concurring). For the majority's doubts about the third-party harm doctrine, see Burwell v. Hobby Lobby, 2781n37. For a critique of that footnote, see Tebbe, Schwartzman, and Schragger, "When Do Religious Accommodations Burden Others?," 9–13.
9. See generally, Micah Schwartzman, "Conscience, Speech, and Money," *Virginia Law Review* 97 (2011): 317–384.
10. Christopher L. Eisgruber and Lawrence G. Sager, *Religious Freedom and the Constitution* (Cambridge, MA: Harvard University Press, 2007), 124–128. This means the principle of avoiding harm to others may well extend to nonreligious commitments that are comprehensive and about which government has no legitimate interest in taking sides. But it also means that coerced support of nonreligious, noncomprehensive speech raises different constitutional concerns. Compare Schwartzman, "Conscience, Speech, and Money," 325.
11. Holt v. Hobbs. That unequal citizenship is a matter of legal and political status, not subjective feelings, is well established in the literature on the expressive functions of law, though it is often overlooked. See, for instance, Elizabeth S. Anderson and Richard H. Pildes, "Expressive Theories of Law: A General Restatement," *University of Pennsylvania Law Review* 148 (2000): 1524, 1528, 1548; and Deborah Hellman, "The Expressive Dimension of Equal Protection," *Minnesota Law Review* 85 (2000): 10.
12. Estate of Thornton v. Caldor, Inc., 472 U.S. 703, 709 (1985).
13. Ibid., 710 (quoting judge Learned Hand in Otten v. Baltimore & Ohio R. Co., 205 F.2d 58, 61 [2d Cir. 1953]). For the narrow reading of *Caldor*—limiting it to situations in which the government places "unyielding" weight on religious freedom interests—see Marc O. DeGirolami, "Free Exercise by Moonlight," *San Diego Law Review* 52 (forthcoming), http://ssrn.com/abstract=2587216, 23–24.

Texas Monthly v. Bullock arguably involved a concern for third parties too. There the court struck down a law that exempted religious publications from the state sales tax without also exempting secular publications. The justices held that "when government directs a subsidy exclusively to religious organizations that . . . burdens nonbeneficiaries markedly," its actions violate the Establishment Clause. Texas Monthly, Inc. v. Bullock, 489 U.S. 1, 6 (1989). The court's exact reasoning was somewhat unclear; it might have invoked unfairness to others as well as burdens on taxpayers. But an *available* reason for the decision, although perhaps not a decisive one, was that competing publications were disadvantaged, and they suffered that cost solely on the basis of religion. *Texas Monthly* was one such periodical—a nonreligious magazine that was disadvantaged in the marketplace. In that sense, it was a "nonbeneficiary" that was "burden[ed] . . . markedly" in violation of the principle against shifting the costs of a religion accommodation onto others. Gedicks and Van Tassell understandably reject the idea that shifting costs to taxpayers generally was enough to support the conclusion that the Texas exemption violated the Establishment Clause. Gedicks and Van Tassell, "RFRA Exemptions," 358, 367n114. But the opinion can be read to turn on the disadvantage imposed on competing publications.

14. Cutter v. Wilkinson, 544 U.S. 709, 720 (2004).
15. Marc DeGirolami argues that this language in *Cutter* is dicta. Marc DeGirolami, "On the Claim that Exemptions from the Mandate Violate the Establishment Clause," December 5, 2013, http://mirrorofjustice.blogs.com/mirrorofjustice/2013/12/exemptions-from-the-mandate-do-not-violate-the-establishment-clause.html. For the reasons given in the text, the better reading is that the warning about harm to nonbeneficiaries is part of the holding. And DeGirolami later joined a brief arguing that the language in *Cutter* prohibiting harm to "nonbeneficiaries" expressed what was required of the government, albeit by the statute itself, not the Establishment Clause. Brief of Constitutional Law Scholars as Amici Curiae in Support of Hobby Lobby and Conestoga, et al., Burwell v. Hobby Lobby Stores, Inc., Nos. 13-354, 13-356 (S.Ct. Jan. 28, 2014), 9. Rick Garnett also believes that avoiding harm to others is required by RFRA itself. Richard W. Garnett, "Accommodation, Establishment, and Freedom of Religion," *Vanderbilt Law Review En Banc* 67 (2014): 46.
16. Corporation of the Presiding Bishop of the Church of Jesus Christ of Latter-Day Saints v. Amos, 483 U.S. 327 (1987).
17. Ibid., 335–337, 337n14.
18. Ibid. These two paragraphs draw on Schwartzman, Schragger, and Tebbe, "Hobby Lobby and the Establishment Clause, Part III." Note that the argument here need not mean that religion is special; Chapter 5 sets out an understanding of associational interests that applies equally to religious and nonreligious groups.
19. Some have suggested that *Amos* came out the way it did because the government had merely lifted a burden on a private actor, the church, which

then harmed the employee Mayson of its own volition. On this reading, harm to others only presents constitutional concerns when the government itself shifts costs from religious citizens onto others, as in *Caldor*. Eugene Volokh, *Sebelius v. Hobby Lobby: Corporate Rights and Religious Liberties* (Washington, DC: Cato Institute Press, 2014), 64. There is some language in *Amos* that supports this reading. Corporation of the Presiding Bishop v. Amos, 337n15. But that understanding of the distinction between *Amos* and *Caldor* is illogical. There is no reason why the government should be any less constitutionally responsible when it lifts a burden on religious actors, knowing that harm to third parties will result. For that reason, Justice O'Connor rejected the court's attempt to distinguish *Caldor* that way. Ibid., 347 (O'Connor, J., concurring in the judgment). Moreover, that narrow reading of the third-party harm doctrine conflicts with precedent. The court's reliance on the rule against harming others in *Cutter* would make no sense if it was never relevant where the government merely lifted a burden on private actors. For a fuller response to this worry, see Tebbe, Schwartzman, and Schragger, "When Do Religious Accommodations Burden Others?," 8–10, 9n42.

20. Hosanna-Tabor Evangelical Lutheran Church and School v. Equal Employment Opportunity Commission, 132 S.Ct. 694 (2012).
21. United States v. Seeger, 380 U.S. 163 (1965); Welsh v. United States, 398 U.S. 333 (1970).
22. For more on why other cases do not cut against the commitment to avoiding harm to others, see Nelson Tebbe, Richard Schragger, and Micah Schwartzman, "Reply to McConnell on *Hobby Lobby* and the Establishment Clause," March 30, 2014, http://balkin.blogspot.com/2014/03/reply-to-mcconnell-on-hobby-lobby-and.html.
23. United States v. Lee, 455 U.S. 252, 261 (1982). Only Justice Stevens did not join this reasoning, though he concurred in the result.
24. 26 U.S.C.A. § 3127.
25. Tony and Susan Alamo Foundation v. Secretary of Labor, 471 U.S. 290 (1985). Frederick Gedicks and Rebecca Van Tassell, "Of Burdens and Baselines: Hobby Lobby's Puzzling Footnote 37," in *The Rise of Corporate Religious Liberty*, ed. Micah Schwartzman, Chad Flanders, and Zöe Robinson (New York: Oxford University Press, 2015), 326; Gedicks and Van Tassell, "RFRA Exemptions," 24. It should be acknowledged that Gedicks and Van Tassell call this reasoning dicta; see 24n71. Note also that the court does not explicitly invoke *United States v. Lee* in this passage, though it does cite the case elsewhere: Tony and Susan Alamo Foundation v. Secretary of Labor, 303.
26. For the contemporary argument, see Brief of Constitutional Law Scholars in Hobby Lobby, 9. The *Hobby Lobby* majority could be read to reinforce a

similar idea when it said, "It is certainly true that in applying RFRA 'courts must take adequate account of the burdens a requested accommodation may impose on nonbeneficiaries.' That consideration will often inform the analysis of the Government's compelling interest and the availability of a less restrictive means of advancing that interest." Burwell v. Hobby Lobby, 2781n37 (quoting Cutter v. Wilkinson, 720). In his concurrence, Justice Kennedy said, "Among the reasons the United States is so open, so tolerant, and so free is that no person may be restricted or demeaned by government in exercising his or her religion. Yet neither may that same exercise unduly restrict other persons, such as employees, in protecting their own interests, interests the law deems compelling." Ibid., 2786–2787.

27. See, for example, Brief of Amici Curiae Constitutional Law Scholars in Support of Petitioners, Zubik v. Burwell, Nos. 14-1418, 14-1453, 14-1505, 15-35, 15-105, 15-119, and 15-191, 2016 WL 183794 (S.Ct. January 11, 2016), 5; Garnett, "Accommodation and Establishment," 46–47; and Kevin C. Walsh, "A Baseline Problem for the 'Burden on Employees' Argument against RFRA-Based Exemptions from the Contraceptives Mandate," January 17, 2014, http://mirrorofjustice.blogs.com/mirrorofjustice/2014/01/a-baseline-problem-for-the-burden-on-employees-argument-against-rfra-based-exemptions-from-the-contr.html.
28. For more on the baseline problem, see Tebbe, Schwartzman, and Schragger, "When Do Religious Accommodations Burden Others?"
29. See Elizabeth Sepper, "Free Exercise Lochnerism," *Columbia Law Review* 115 (2015): 1453–1519; and Cass R. Sunstein, "Lochner's Legacy," *Columbia Law Review* 87 (1987): 873, 875.
30. Stinemetz v. Kansas Health Policy Authority, 252 P. 3d 141, 143–146 (Kan. App. 2011). Christopher C. Lund, "Keeping *Hobby Lobby* in Perspective," in Schwartzman, Flanders, and Robinson, eds., *The Rise of Corporate Religious Liberty*, 290.
31. Gedicks and Van Tassell, "Of Burdens and Baselines," 337–340.
32. The main antidiscrimination provision is 42 U.S.C. s 2000e-2(a)(1). Awkwardly, Congress passed the new provision as an amendment to Title VII's definition of religion. As amended, the definition of religion reads, "The term 'religion' includes all aspects of religious observance and practice, as well as belief, unless an employer demonstrates that he is unable to reasonably accommodate to an employee's or prospective employee's religious observance or practice without undue hardship on the conduct of the employer's business." 42 U.S.C. s 2000e(j).
33. Trans World Airlines, Inc. v. Hardison, 432 U.S. 63, 73–74 (1977).
34. Ibid., 81–83.
35. Ibid., 84.

36. Hardison v. Trans World Airlines, Inc., 375 F. Supp. 877, 883, 883n1 (W.D. Mo. 1974) (quoting Otten v. Baltimore & Ohio R.R., 205 F.2d 58, 61 [2d Cir. 1953] [Hand, J.]). See also Hardison v. Trans World Airlines, Inc., 527 F.2d 33, 43 (8th Cir. 1975) ("The view that it is constitutionally impermissible for a government to enforce accommodation of religious beliefs in a manner which results in privileges not available to a nonbeliever, or which result in inconvenience to the nonbeliever, is not without articulate support.").
37. See, for instance, Webb v. City of Philadelphia, 562 F.3d 256, 260 (3rd Cir. 2009) ("We focus on the specific context of each case, looking to both the fact as well as the magnitude of the alleged undue hardship."); and Anderson v. General Dynamics Convair Aerospace Division, 589 F.2d 397, 400 (9th Cir. 1978); Tooley v. Martin-Marietta Corporation, 648 F.2d 1239, 1243 (5th Cir. 1981).
38. Tooley v. Martin-Marietta, 1242–1243. See also O'Brien v. City of Springfield, 319 F. Supp. 2d 90, 109 (D. Mass. 2003) (holding that, even in the absence of a union surplus, "'The loss of one employee's dues . . . does not inflict undue hardship on a union'" [quoting International Association of Machinists and Aerospace Workers v. Boeing Co., 833 F.2d 165, 168 (9th Cir.1987)]).
39. Tooley v. Martin-Marietta, 1243; Protos v. Volkswagen of America, Inc., 797 F.2d 129, 137 (3rd Cir. 1986) (Adams, J.).
40. Tooley v. Martin-Marietta, 1246. Other courts have likewise ruled that the undue hardship standard is consistent with the Establishment Clause. See, e.g., Turpen v. Missouri-Kansas-Texas R. Co., 736 F.2d 1022 (5th Cir. 1984) ("courts must balance the prohibitions of the Establishment Clause of state-mandated favoritism in employment on the basis of religion and the respect for 'bona fide' seniority systems built into the statutory scheme of Title VII against Congress' intent . . . to correct discrimination on the basis of religion. [*Trans World Airlines v.*] *Hardison*, [432 U.S. 63 (1977),] held that the statute does not require an employer to deviate from its seniority system in order to give an employee shift preference for religious reasons, ibid., 81, and that accommodation that would require an employer to incur a greater than de minimis cost or would create a greater than de minimis imposition on co-workers constitutes undue hardship. Ibid., 84"); Protos v. Volkswagen of America, Inc., 136 ("Unlike the Connecticut statute [in Estate of Thornton v. Caldor, 472 U.S. 703 (1985)], Title VII does not require absolute deference to the religious practices of the employee, allows for consideration of the hardship to other employees and to the company, and permits an evaluation of whether the employer has attempted to accommodate the employee.").
41. Opuku-Boateng v. State of Cal., 95 F.3d 1461, 1473 (9th Cir. 1996); Crider v. Univ. of Tennessee, Knoxville, 492 F. App'x 609, 613 (6th Cir. 2012) (quoting

Draper v. United States Pipe and Foundry Co., 527 F.2d 515, 520 [6th Cir. 1975]); ibid., 614 (noting that *Draper,* although decided before *TWA v. Hardison,* survives that opinion). Brown v. General Motors Corporation, 601 F.2d 956, 961 (8th Cir. 1979) ("The district court's final concern was that accommodating Brown would in effect discriminate against all employees who did not adhere to Brown's religion. We cannot agree with this interpretation of *Hardison.* Such an application of *Hardison* would provide a per se proscription against any and all forms of differential treatment based on religion.").

42. For an application of the de minimis standard that appears to allow fewer religion accommodations, see Marci A. Hamilton, *God vs. the Gavel: Religion and the Rule of Law* (New York: Cambridge University Press, 2005), 275.
43. Burwell v. Hobby Lobby, 2781n37 (adequate account); ibid., 2760 ("precisely zero"); ibid. ("In any event, our decision in these cases need not result in any detrimental effect on any third party."). For reasons why footnote 37 was unconvincing and implausible, see Tebbe, Schwartzman, and Schragger, "When Do Religious Accommodations Burden Others?," 9–13.
44. Burwell v. Hobby Lobby, 2786–2787 (Kennedy, J., concurring).
45. Coverage of Certain Preventative Services under the Affordable Care Act, 80 Fed. Reg. 134, July 14, 2015; Nelson Tebbe, Richard Schragger, and Micah Schwartzman, "Update on the Establishment Clause and Third Party Harms: One Ongoing Violation and One Constitutional Accommodation," October 16, 2014, http://balkin.blogspot.com/2014/10/update-on-establishment-clause-and.html.
46. Notre Dame v. Burwell, 607–608; Priests for Life v. U.S. Department of Health and Human Services, 257–264.
47. Notre Dame v. Burwell, 607–608 (quoting Susan A. Cohen, "The Broad Benefits of Investing in Sexual and Reproductive Health," *Guttmacher Report on Public Policy* 7 [2004]: 5–6).
48. The dissenters in *Hobby Lobby* also took the court to task for allowing a business corporation to bring a religious freedom claim at all—an intuition that is shared among many progressives. Burwell v. Hobby Lobby, 2793–2797. Notably, however, Justices Stephen Breyer and Elena Kagan did not join that part of the dissent. Ibid., 2806. And in fact, the question of whether and when business corporations should enjoy constitutional rights (or their statutory cognates) is a difficult question of law and morality that this discussion will leave to one side.
49. Recall, for instance, DeGirolami's reasonable argument that *Caldor* prohibits only accommodations that place "unyielding" weight on others. DeGirolami, "Free Exercise By Moonlight," 24.
50. Holt v. Hobbs, 867 (Ginsburg, J., concurring).

51. For instance, Douglas Laycock argues that Indiana's RFRA, as originally proposed, would not have led to religion exemptions from antidiscrimination laws. Douglas Laycock, "The Campaign against Religious Liberty," in Schwartzman, Flanders, and Robinson, eds., *The Rise of Corporate Religious Liberty*, 248–249. For a bill preventing harm to others, see the Do No Harm Act, H.R. 5272, 114th Cong. (2015–2016).

4. Fairness to Others

1. For a paradigmatic law that accommodated secular as well as religious opposition to abortion, see the 1973 Church Amendment, 42 U.S.C. § 300a-7. For expert accounts of the development of "conscience clauses" or "refusal clauses" in the health care context, beginning with the Church Amendment, see Douglas NeJaime and Reva Siegel, "Conscience Wars: Complicity-Based Conscience Claims in Religion and Politics," *Yale Law Journal* 124 (2015): 2534–2542; and Elizabeth Sepper, "Doctoring Discrimination in the Same-Sex Marriage Debates," *Indiana Law Journal* 89 (2014): 722–724.

   For a fascinating example of a fairness argument in the context of abortion, see March for Life v. Burwell, 128 F.Supp.3d 116 (D.D.C. 2015). In that litigation, a secular pro-life organization argued that the religion exemption from the contraception mandate, imposed under the Affordable Care Act, was unconstitutional because it benefited only religious employers and not similarly situated secular employers. A trial court found for the secular pro-life organization, although under the Equal Protection Clause rather than the First Amendment. The court found that March for Life was similarly situated to employers with religious objections to contraception coverage and that it could not rationally be excluded from the accommodation that the government was offering them. Ibid., 125–126.
2. For a formulation of equal citizenship in the context of religious freedom claims, see Alan Patten, "Three Theories of Religious Liberty," unpublished manuscript, May 2015, 30.
3. The notion of profound and worthwhile reasons is loosely drawn from Christopher L. Eisgruber and Lawrence G. Sager, *Religious Freedom and the Constitution* (Cambridge, MA: Harvard University Press, 2010), 89. For a fascinating treatment of the secular analogue to religion for purposes of neutral treatment by the liberal state, see Cécile Laborde, *Liberalism's Religion* (Cambridge, MA: Harvard University Press, forthcoming). On the specialness of religion generally, see Brian Leiter, *Why Tolerate Religion?*

(Princeton, NJ: Princeton University Press, 2012); Micah Schwartzman, "What If Religion Is Not Special?," *University of Chicago Law Review* 79 (2013): 1351–1472.

4. United States v. Seeger, 380 U.S. 163 (1965); Welsh v. United States, 398 U.S. 333 (1970).
5. United States v. Seeger, 165–166.
6. Welsh v. United States, 345 (Harlan, J., concurring in the judgment) (finding that the rulings in favor of Welsh can only be justified on constitutional grounds—that is, that the statute as written conflicts with the religion clauses of the First Amendment).
7. Alternatively, as argued in Chapter 3, *Seeger* and *Welsh* did not implicate the principle against burden shifting because no identifiable draftee could attribute his assignment to a combat position to the government's accommodation of a conscientious objector. Too many factors influence that result to be able to identify a single cause.
8. On the definition of religion in both legal scholarship and the academic study of religion, see Nelson Tebbe, "Nonbelievers," *University of Virginia Law Review* 97 (2011): 1130–1149.
9. Texas Monthly, Inc. v. Bullock, 489 U.S. 1, 9, 15 (1989).
10. Ibid., 28 (Blackmun, J., joined by O'Connor, J., concurring in the judgment).
11. Cutter v. Wilkinson, 544 U.S. 709, 724 (2005) (quoting Corporation of the Presiding Bishop of the Church of Jesus Christ of Latter-day Saints v. Amos, 483 U.S. 327, 338 [1987]).
12. Kaufman v. McCaughtry, 419 F.3d 678 (7th Cir. 2005) (finding an Establishment Clause violation against an atheist inmate). *Cutter* comes close to recognizing this limitation on religion accommodations when it says that they must be "administered neutrally among different faiths." Cutter v. Wilkinson, 720. To the degree that requirement recognizes the unfairness of excluding nonbelievers, it captures the principle of fairness to others. To the degree that it does not also recognize the potential unfairness of failing to accommodate secular actors, like the magazine *Texas Monthly*, it misses some part of the principle defended in this chapter.
13. One way freedom of conscience can be implicated by an accommodation of a nonreligious commitment that is not profound is by undermining the government's argument that it has a strong interest in not extending a similar exemption to a religious actor. That is not *necessarily* a violation of fairness; it might just indicate that the government's interests in denying a religion accommodation are legitimate but not compelling.
14. See, for instance, 2016 Miss. Laws ch. 334 (H.B. 1523).
15. Texas Monthly v. Bullock, 28.

5. Freedom of Association

1. For example, Cécile Laborde likewise seeks to disaggregate values driving the freedom of association, but she identifies them somewhat differently. She isolates coherence interests, which refer to the ability of a group to live by its own commitments, and competence interests, which refer to the group's ability to interpret its own commitments. Cécile Laborde, *Liberalism's Religion* (Cambridge, MA: Harvard University Press, forthcoming), 114–115.
2. Roberts v. United States Jaycees, 468 U.S. 609, 618–619 (1984).
3. On personhood as a central concept for freedom of association, see James D. Nelson, "The Freedom of Business Association," *Columbia Law Review* 115 (2015): 491–496.
4. Seana Shiffrin, "What Is Really Wrong with Compelled Association?," *Northwestern Law Review* 99 (2005): 865–866; Lawrence Sager, "Why Churches (and, Possibly, the Tarpon Bay Women's Blue Water Fishing Club) Can Discriminate," in *The Rise of Corporate Religious Liberty:* Hobby Lobby *and the New Law of Religion in America,* ed. Micah Schwartzman, Chad Flanders, and Zöe Robinson (New York: Oxford University Press, 2016), 77–101. Community groups here are quite similar to what Sager calls "close associations." They also resemble the voluntary associations that James Nelson describes as essential to the formation and maintenance of personhood, in both its conceptual and emotional aspects; he calls these "constitutive associations." Nelson, "The Freedom of Business Association," 491–496. Like Nelson, the chapter here understands Shiffrin's associations as important not only for independent ideas but also for the development of independent will, motivation, or affect. Ibid., 492n166. It is useful to compare the typology offered in the text to Meir Dan-Cohen's distinction between communities and expressive associations. Meir Dan-Cohen, "Freedoms of Collective Speech: A Theory of Protected Communications by Organizations, Communities, and the State," *California Law Review* (1991): 1257–1258.
5. Nelson distinguishes between two functions that voluntary associations perform for a democracy: an educative function, including both individual development and production of social capital, and fostering political participation through membership in groups. Nelson, "The Freedom of Business Association," 477–484. Distinct from either of these, for Nelson, is the importance of voluntary associations for personhood. Ibid., 491–496. This chapter draws on those insights but separates out types of associations. With regard to intimate associations, it emphasizes personhood functions, and with respect to community groups it acknowledges both democratic and personhood dynamics.

On social capital and its relationship to associations that feature bonds of trust and mutual identification, see Robert D. Putnam, *Bowling Alone: The Collapse and Revival of American Community* (New York: Simon and Schuster, 2000), 22–24. For depictions of freedom of association that feature its importance for democratic deliberation see, for instance, Ashutosh Bhagwat, "Associational Speech," *Yale Law Journal* 120 (2011): 978–1030; and Paul Horwitz, *First Amendment Institutions* (Cambridge, MA: Harvard University Press, 2013).

Robert M. Cover developed his account of group meaning formation, along with several other groundbreaking ideas, in "The Supreme Court 1982 Term Foreword: Nomos and Narrative," *Harvard Law Review* 97 (1983): 4–68. He argues, "The narratives that any particular group associates with the law bespeak the range of the group's commitments. Those narratives also provide resources for justification, condemnation, and argument by actors within the group, who must struggle to live their law" (46). On voluntary associations as sites of independence from state and market power, see Nelson, "The Freedom of Business Association," 485; John D. Inazu, *Liberty's Refuge: The Forgotten Freedom of Assembly* (New Haven, CT: Yale University Press, 2012), 5; Richard W. Garnett, "Do Churches Matter? Toward an Institutional Understanding of the Religion Clauses," *Villanova Law Review* 53 (2008): 291–293 (arguing that the "special place, role and freedoms of groups, associations and institutions are often overlooked" in American discourse on freedom of religion).

6. Shiffrin, "Compelled Association."
7. Ibid., 874 (on trust and identification). Seana Shiffrin's project, though important to the ideas in this chapter, does not address groups that, though not commercial, are too large or loose to provide for identification and trust.
8. Compare Roberts v. Jaycees, 620 (noting several factors that may be relevant to determining whether an association receives First Amendment protection, including "size, purpose, policies, selectivity, congeniality, and other characteristics that in a particular case may be pertinent"). Here the text draws on the framework that courts have developed for determining when an organization qualifies for the commonplace exemption from public accommodations laws for private clubs. As Elizabeth Sepper explains,

> As distinguished from a public accommodation, a truly private club must: have machinery to carefully screen applicants for membership; limit the use of its facilities to members and bona fide guests; be controlled by the membership through meetings and elections; be operated on a non-profit basis solely for the benefit and pleasure of its members; and direct any publicity solely to its members. . . .

> Although disagreement arises at the margins between public and private, it has long been clear that characteristics of commercialism, profit, openness to the public, and lack of selectivity signal the public nature of an entity.
>
> The Supreme Court's analysis of constitutional freedom of association tracks this statutory distinction between private club and public accommodation.

Elizabeth Sepper, "The Role of Religion in State Public Accommodations Laws," *Saint Louis Law Journal*, forthcoming (citing Wright v. Cork Club, 315 F. Supp. 1143 [S.D. Tex. 1970] and other cases). Later, Sepper again makes a connection between public accommodations law and constitutional law, arguing that a "theory of close association should expressly incorporate attributes of exclusivity, selectivity, purpose, and size to allocate constitutional protection from antidiscrimination law." Ibid.

Note that no one of these factors is essential. It is possible to imagine groups that are large but qualify as community groups, such as megachurches. There also may be organizations that are highly bureaucratized but nevertheless serve as sites of will formation; the military may be one such institution. So these factors should be assessed together, without making any one of them dispositive.

9. Roberts v. Jaycees, 623.
10. Notably, the court in *Hosanna-Tabor* did insist on distinctive treatment for religion in the context of hiring leaders. It called "remarkable" the solicitor general's argument that the ministerial exception could be understood in terms of the doctrine of expressive association articulated and applied in *Boy Scouts v. Dale.* Hosanna-Tabor Evangelical Lutheran Church and School v. Equal Employment Opportunity Commission, 132 S.Ct. 694, 706 (2012).
11. Roberts v. Jaycees, 614–615.
12. James Nelson argues that nonprofit status, although imperfectly aligned with the understanding of an association as essential to personhood, nevertheless is a "reasonable proxy for the kinds of organizations that ought to be eligible for protection from state intrusion." Nelson, "Freedom of Business Association," 511.
13. Roberts v. Jaycees, 618–619. Since this ruling, courts have interpreted intimate association narrowly, seldom extending the category beyond the family. John Inazu, "The Unsettling 'Well-Settled' Law of Freedom of Association," *Connecticut Law Review* 43 (2010): 165n84 (citing cases holding that religious groups, civic organizations, cohabitants, and even brothers-in-law do not qualify as intimate associations). Compare Moore v. City of East Cleveland, 431 U.S. 494, 499 (1977) (striking down an ordinance that limited cohabitation

to members of a nuclear family and observing that "when the government intrudes on choices concerning family living arrangements, this Court must examine carefully the importance of the governmental interests advanced and the extent to which they are served by the challenged regulation."); Troxel v. Granville, 530 U.S. 57 (2000) (invalidating a lower court order awarding visitation rights to a grandparent over the custodial mother's objection).

14. Hosanna-Tabor v. EEOC, 706.
15. Boy Scouts of America v. Dale, 530 U.S. 640, 653 (2000) ("As we give deference to an association's assertions regarding the nature of its expression, we must also give deference to an association's view of what would impair its expression.")
16. Section 702 is codified at 42 U.S.C. § 2000e-1.
17. Corporation of the Presiding Bishop of the Church of Jesus Christ of Latter-Day Saints v. Amos, 483 U.S. 327, 330n3 (1987).
18. A more detailed discussion of ENDA and related developments, with citations, can be found in the section titled "The Employment Non-Discrimination Act and Section 702" in Chapter 8. For the letter from progressive groups, see "Request for Review and Reconsideration of June 29, 2007 Office of Legal Counsel Memorandum Re: RFRA," August 20, 2015, https://www.au.org/files/2015-08-20%20-%20OLC%20Memo%20Letter%20to%20President-FINAL_2.pdf.
19. For example, employers with fewer than fifteen employees need not comply with Title VII; see 42 U.S.C. § 2000e(b). In New York, employers with fewer than four employees need not comply with state antidiscrimination rules; see N.Y. Exec. Law § 292(5).
20. National Association for the Advancement of Colored People v. Alabama, 357 U.S. 449, 462 (1958). Somewhat related, the "Mrs. Murphy" exemption from federal housing law allows landlords who live in a building with five or fewer rental units to exclude tenants without any limitation from antidiscrimination requirements. 42 U.S.C. § 3603(b).
21. N.Y. City Admin. Code § 8-102; Amy Zimmer, "Men-Only Clubs in NYC: After Augusta National Allows Women, Will Big Apple Clubs Follow Suit?," *Huffington Post,* August 21, 2012, http://www.huffingtonpost.com/2012/08/21/augusta-national-now-accepts-women-all-male-nyc-clubs_n_1818998.html.
22. Boy Scouts of America v. Dale, 530 U.S. 640, 653 (2000).
23. Memorandum for William P. Marshall, Deputy Counsel to the President, Office of Legal Counsel, Department of Justice, October 12, 2000, 30–32 (concluding that Section 702 does not allow religious employers to prefer or exclude employees on protected grounds other than religion itself).
24. On the broad scope of the ministerial exemption, see Petruska v. Gannon University, 462 F.3d 294, 304–305, 304n7, 307 (3d Cir. 2006) (citing other

cases); and Caroline Mala Corbin, "Above the Law? The Constitutionality of the Ministerial Exemption from Antidiscrimination Law," *Fordham Law Review* 75 (2007): 1975. On preserving the intimate relationship between clergy and congregation as a rationale for the exemption, see Petruska v. Gannon University, 306–307.

25. See, for example, Kaufman v. McCaughtry, 419 F.3d 678, 682–683 (7th Cir. 2005) (determining that atheism constitutes a religion for purposes of the constitutional claims).
26. See Nelson, "Freedom of Business Association," 511 (proposing nonprofit status as a "reasonable proxy" for identifying the associations that deserve constitutional protection).
27. For thoughtful work bearing on the question of corporate constitutional rights, see Tamara Belinfanti and Lynn Stout, "Shareholder Value Theory and the Systems Alternative in Corporate Law," unpublished manuscript, April 24, 2016; Margaret M. Blair and Elizabeth Pollman, "The Derivative Nature of Corporate Constitutional Rights," *William and Mary Law Review* 56 (2015): 1673–1743; David Ciepley, "Neither Persons nor Associations: Against Constitutional Rights for Corporations," *Journal of Law and Courts* 1 (2013): 221–245; Kent Greenfield, "In Defense of Corporate Persons," *Constitutional Commentary* 30 (2015): 309–333; and Robert C. Hockett and Saule T. Omarova, "'Special,' Vestigial, or Visionary? What Bank Regulation Tells Us about the Corporation—and Vice Versa," *Seattle University Law Review* 39 (2016): 453–500.

6. Government Nonendorsement

1. Town of Greece v. Galloway, 134 S.Ct. 1811 (2014).
2. See, generally, Nelson Tebbe, "Government Nonendorsement," *Minnesota Law Review* 98 (2013): 648–712. For a thoughtful response, see Abner S. Greene, "Government Endorsement: A Reply to Nelson Tebbe's *Government Nonendorsement*," *Minnesota Law Review Headnotes* 98 (2014): 87–95. For a thoughtful treatment of the morality of what the government can say, see Corey Brettschneider, *When the State Speaks, What Should It Say?* (Princeton, NJ: Princeton University Press, 2012).
3. Obergefell v. Hodges, 135 S.Ct. 2584 (2015).
4. There are exceptions. See, for instance, McCreary County v. American Civil Liberties Union of Kentucky, 545 U.S. 844, 893–895 (2005) (Scalia, J., dissenting) (arguing that the government could constitutionally "acknowledg[e] a single creator" or endorse "monotheis[m]" and that the Establishment Clause "permits this disregard of polytheists and believers in unconcerned

deities, just as it permits the disregard of devout atheists"); Steven D. Smith, *Getting Over Equality: A Critical Diagnosis of Religious Freedom in America* (New York: New York University Press, 2001), 68–69, 72–75.

5. McCreary County v. American Civil Liberties Union; Lynch v. Donnelly, 465 U.S. 668 (1984).
6. Christopher C. Lund, "Leaving Disestablishment to the Political Process," *Duke Journal of Constitutional Law and Public Policy* 10 (2014): 56–57. Dissenting from the denial of certiorari in another case, justice Antonin Scalia, joined by justice Clarence Thomas, wrote that "*Town of Greece* abandoned the antiquated 'endorsement test.'" Elmbrook School District v. Doe, 134 S.Ct. 2283, 2284 (2014) (Scalia, J., dissenting from the denial of certiorari). Regarding the coercion test, he added, "*Town of Greece* made categorically clear that mere '[o]ffense . . . does not equate to coercion' in any manner relevant to the proper Establishment Clause analysis. '[A]n Establishment Clause violation is not made out any time a person experiences a sense of affront from the expression of contrary religious views.'" Ibid., 2284–2285 (citation omitted, alterations in the original).

   Moreover, the court has steadily been eroding the ability of ordinary citizens to challenge Establishment Clause violations. In a line of cases, the court has been narrowing the class of people who have "standing" to challenge government speech that endorses religion. Although the technical legal doctrine is not important here, the standing rule requires people who want to challenge government programs to show that they have suffered some concrete, individualized injury because of those programs. Although the standing doctrine is supposed to regulate only who can make it into court, not anything about the substance of the law, this development might mean that the court is questioning whether government speech without tangible effect really can violate the Establishment Clause. Combined with critique of the endorsement test, this development may signal doubt about the principle of government nonendorsement concerning the subject matter of religion. See, for example, Hein v. Freedom from Religion Foundation, 551 U.S. 587 (2007) (throwing out a challenge to an aspect of the White House's faith-based initiative on standing grounds); and Arizona Christian School Tuition Organization v. Winn, 563 U.S. 125 (2011).

   Yet the court's standing cases can and should be taken for what they say, at least for the moment—that they concern solely *who* may challenge a government program in court, not *whether* any such program actually violates the Establishment Clause. Regardless of standing requirements, policy makers in places like the Town of Greece can, should, and must evaluate practices like the legislative prayer program not only for policy desirability but also for constitutionality. Their oath of office requires that. And dissenting citizens may pressure officials to comply with the Constitution outside the courts as well as through litigation. When they do so, they should rely on the principle that bars government embrace of a particular religion.

7. Elk Grove Unified School District v. Newdow, 542 U.S. 1 (2004) (turning away a challenge to the Pledge of Allegiance on standing grounds).
8. Town of Greece v. Galloway, 1824 ("Absent a pattern of prayers that over time denigrate, proselytize, or betray an impermissible government purpose, a challenge based solely on the content of a prayer will not likely establish a constitutional violation.").
9. A well-known example of the American approach is Collin v. Smith, 578 F.2d 1197 (7th Cir. 1978), which struck down a "racial slur" ordinance in the Village of Skokie, Illinois, where a Nazi organization had planned to march.

    And in 2011, the Supreme Court ruled in favor of the Westboro Baptist Church, a hate group that protests outside the funerals of fallen American military members. A lower court found the group liable for intentional infliction of emotional distress—a tort—and imposed a significant monetary judgment. That was overturned on appeal because the group was found to be engaged in protected speech. Snyder v. Phelps, 562 U.S. 443 (2011). For an argument that legislative prohibitions on hate speech can work to protect the free speech of minorities, see Owen M. Fiss, *The Irony of Free Speech* (Cambridge, MA: Harvard University Press, 1996), 15–18.
10. Actual cases invalidating racialized government speech are hard to find, but one possible example is Anderson v. Martin, 375 U.S. 399, 400 (1964), in which the court invalidated a Louisiana requirement that ballots display the race of each candidate. That measure impermissibly sent an official message to voters that race should matter in their decision making. Ibid., 402 ("by directing the citizen's attention to the single consideration of race or color, the State indicates that a candidate's race or color is an important—perhaps paramount—consideration in the citizen's choice"). Even if *Anderson* came down the way it did partly because the law harmed the electoral chances of minority candidates, it nevertheless could be grounded independently on a concern for the racialized message.
11. Elizabeth S. Anderson and Richard H. Pildes, "Expressive Theories of Law: A General Restatement," *University of Pennsylvania Law Review* 148 (2000): 1524, 1528, 1548; Deborah Hellman, "The Expressive Dimension of Equal Protection," *Minnesota Law Review* 85 (2000): 10. Justice Kagan adopted a similar understanding of the harm of religious establishment in her seminal dissent in Town of Greece v. Galloway, 1844–1845, where she explained that government can effect an establishment when "a civic function of some kind brings religious differences to the fore: That public proceeding becomes (whether intentionally or not) an instrument for dividing [a religious dissenter]

from adherents to the community's majority religion, and for altering the very nature of her relationship with her government." In other words, the harm of such an establishment is that the government differentiates its legal relationships with citizens on the basis of religion. That infringes equal citizenship, and it does so entirely independent of subjective feelings. Later in the opinion, Justice Kagan reiterated, "In this country, when citizens go before the government, they go not as Christians or Muslims or Jews (or what have you), but just as Americans (or here, as Grecians). That is what it means to be an equal citizen, irrespective of religion. And that is what the Town of Greece precluded by so identifying itself with a single faith." Ibid., 1851.

12. Charles L. Black Jr., "The Lawfulness of the Segregation Decisions," *Yale Law Journal* 69 (1960): 426–427. See also Christopher L. Eisgruber and Lawrence G. Sager, *Religious Freedom and the Constitution* (Princeton, NJ: Princeton University Press, 2007): 302–303n11 (quoting Black); and Michael C. Dorf, "Same-Sex Marriage, Second-Class Citizenship, and Law's Social Meanings," *Virginia Law Review* 97 (2011): 1293 (citing Black).
13. Loving v. Virginia, 388 U.S. 1, 11 (1967) ("The fact that Virginia prohibits only interracial marriages involving white persons demonstrates that the racial classifications must stand on their own justification, as measures designed to maintain White Supremacy.").
14. Shaw v. Reno, 509 U.S. 630, 642 (1993); see also Miller v. Johnson, 515 U.S. 900, 916 (1995) (setting out the "predominant factor" test).
15. Richard H. Pildes and Richard G. Niemi, "Expressive Harms, 'Bizarre Districts,' and Voting Rights: Evaluating Election-District Appearances after *Shaw v. Reno*," *Michigan Law Review* 92 (1993): 494; Anderson and Pildes, "Expressive Theories of Law," 1538–1539; Dorf, "Same-Sex Marriage," 1294–1296; Hellman, "Expressive Dimension," 17–18, 26–27.
16. Most obviously, racialized government speech violates the Equal Protection Clause. But it also may interfere with the full exercise of the capacities of citizenship, in violation of the Free Speech Clause. Insofar as minority citizens are hampered in their political participation because the government's speech has constituted them as less able contributors to public life, they have suffered a violation of free speech as well. Tebbe, "Government Nonendorsement," 665–668. Yet here the focus will remain on the more straightforward equal protection understanding of the harm worked by racialized government speech.
17. When it guaranteed marriage equality in the *Goodridge* decision, the Massachusetts Supreme Court noted that the "benefits accessible only by way of a marriage license are enormous, touching nearly every aspect of life and death," and it listed many of those government benefits, citing specific laws. Goodridge v. Department of Public Health, 440 Mass. 309, 323–325 (2003).

18. Perry v. Schwarzenegger, 704 F.Supp.2d 921 (N.D. Cal. 2010); Baker v. Vermont, 744 A.2d 864 (Vt. 1999).
19. Obergefell v. Hodges, 135 S.Ct. 2584, 2597–2602 (2015).
20. Ibid., 2635–2636 (Thomas, J., dissenting); Nelson Tebbe and Deborah Widiss, "Equal Access and the Right to Marry," *University of Pennsylvania Law Review* 158 (2010): 1378–1379.
21. Obergefell v. Hodges, 2604.
22. Ibid., 2602.
23. Ibid., 2607. Micah Schwartzman, Richard Schragger, and Nelson Tebbe, "*Obergefell* and the End of Religious Reasons for Lawmaking," *Religion and Politics*, June 29, 2015, http://religionandpolitics.org/2015/06/29/obergefell-and-the-end-of-religious-reasons-for-lawmaking/.
24. Tebbe, "Government Nonendorsement," 672.
25. Robert C. Post, "Subsidized Speech," *Yale Law Journal* 106 (1996): 153–154.
26. Burt v. Blumenauer, 699 P. 2d 168, 175 (Or. 1985) (en banc) (relying on "principles of representative government enshrined in our constitutions" as well as the Free Speech Clause); Larry Alexander, *Is There a Right of Freedom of Expression?* (New York: Cambridge University Press, 2005), 90, 101–102 (locating the prohibition on government electioneering in the Speech Clause without considering alternatives); Steven Shiffrin, "Government Speech," *UCLA Law Review* 27 (1980): 620 (arguing that free speech, and not equal protection, should be the primary source of restrictions on government speech and noting that "a major concern with government speech is its impact on the total system of freedom of expression"). On the other hand, Justice Scalia has said that although it would be unconstitutional for the government to promote Republican candidates, "I do not think that unconstitutionality has anything to do with the First Amendment." National Endowment for the Arts v. Finley, 524 U.S. 569, 598n3 (1998) (Scalia, J., concurring in the judgment). His view seems to be that government funding for speech promotes expression, even if it is viewpoint discriminatory, so long as a public forum is not created. Ibid., 598–599.
27. Roe v. Wade, 410 U.S. 113 (1973); Planned Parenthood of Southeastern Pennsylvania v. Casey, 505 U.S. 833, 878 (1992) ("Unnecessary health regulations that have the purpose or effect of presenting a substantial obstacle to a woman seeking an abortion impose an undue burden on the right.").
28. Planned Parenthood v. Casey, 877–878 ("Regulations which do no more than create a structural mechanism by which the State, or the parent or guardian of a minor, may express profound respect for the life of the unborn are permitted, if they are not a substantial obstacle to the woman's exercise of the right to choose. Unless it has that effect on her right of choice, a state mea-

sure designed to persuade her to choose childbirth over abortion will be upheld if reasonably related to that goal.") (citations omitted); Harris v. McRae, 448 U.S. 297 (1980); Maher v. Roe, 432 U.S. 464 (1977).

7. Public Accommodations

1. The accepted terminology here is confusing, since the word *accommodation* is used both to describe the entities covered by these civil rights laws ("public accommodations") and the exemptions that religious actors claim ("religion accommodations"). Because it is standard, this terminology nevertheless is retained here, with clarifications where necessary.
2. Elane Photography v. Willock, 309 P. 3d 53, 61 (N.M. 2013); Washington v. Arlene's Flowers, 2015 WL 94248 (Wash. Super. 2015); In the Matter of Melissa Elaine Klein, dba Sweetcakes by Melissa, 2015 WL 4868796 (Or. Bureau of Labor and Indus. 2015); In the Matter of Todd Wathen and Mark Wathen, Nos. 2011SP2488, 2011SP2489 (Ill. Human Rights Comm., September 15, 2015), http://www.aclu-il.org/wp-content/uploads/2015/09/Wathen-liability-determination.pdf. In addition to *Elane Photography*, appellate decisions in wedding vendor cases include Craig v. Masterpiece Cakeshop, Inc., 370 P.3d 272 (Colo. App. 2015); Gifford v. McCarthy, 23 N.Y.S.3d 422 (App. Div. 2016).
3. Complaint at 23, Protect Fayetteville v. Fayetteville, No. CV-1510-1 (Cir. Ct. of Wash. Cty., Ark., Aug. 31, 2015). The ordinance applies not just to public accommodations but also to employment and housing. The Mississippi law is 2016 Miss. Laws H.B. 1523; for an analysis that shows how it would impact some local protections in cities like Jackson, see Public Rights/Private Conscience Project, Columbia Law School, "Memorandum: Mississippi H.B. 1523 and the Establishment Clause," April 5, 2016, http://web.law.columbia.edu/sites/default/files/microsites/gender-sexuality/files/memo_regarding_ms_hb1523.pdf, 3n10. H.B. 1523 has now been ruled unconstitutional. Barber v. Bryant, __ F. Supp. 3d __, 2016 WL 3562647 (S.D. Miss. 2016).
4. For an example of a law that seeks to protect religious adoption agencies against antidiscrimination requirements, see 2016 Miss. Laws H.B. 1523, Section 4(2).
5. Andrew Koppelman, "Justice for Large Earlobes! A Comment on Richard Arneson's 'What Is Wrongful Discrimination?,'" *San Diego Law Review* 43 (2006): 811–814. As Richard Epstein notes, "Ordinary businesses in competitive markets should be free to choose their customers and their employees by whatever test they see fit." Richard A. Epstein, "Forgotten No

More: A Review of *Liberty's Refuge: The Forgotten Freedom of Assembly* by John D. Inazu," *Engage* 13 (2012): 140.

6. Andrew Koppelman, *Antidiscrimination Law and Social Equality* (New Haven: Yale University Press, 1996), 1–114; Andrew Koppelman, "Gay Rights, Religious Accommodations, and the Purposes of Antidiscrimination Law," *Southern California Law Review* 88 (2015): 627–628. Compare Elane Photography v. Willock, 64 ("Antidiscrimination laws have important purposes that go beyond expressing government values: they ensure that services are freely available in the market, and they protect individuals from humiliation and dignitary harm."). On the question of whether exclusion by market actors needs to be systemic to be justifiably prohibited by civil rights laws, see Elizabeth Sepper, "Gays in the Moralized Marketplace," *Alabama Civil Rights and Civil Liberties Law Review* 7 (2015): 129–170. Sepper argues that even if discrimination by economic actors leaves adequate alternatives for members of protected classes, and even on the questionable assumption that such exclusion does not harm their economic opportunity in other ways, discrimination of that sort nevertheless impedes the other goals of antidiscrimination law. Ibid., 131–132.
7. See, for instance, Samuel R. Bagenstos, "'Rational Discrimination,' Accommodation, and the Politics of (Disability) Civil Rights," *Virginia Law Review* 89 (2003): 843–844 ("Antidiscrimination law also serves an important expressive purpose by offering to previously excluded groups a tangible invitation of admission as full members of society."). Partly for this reason, public accommodations laws often also prohibit businesses from advertising their exclusion of protected classes. For example, New York's law provides, in part,

> It shall be an unlawful discriminatory practice for any . . . place of public accommodation . . . directly or indirectly, to publish, circulate, issue, display, post or mail any written or printed communication, notice or advertisement, to the effect that any of the accommodations, advantages, facilities and privileges of any such place shall be refused, withheld from or denied to any person on account of race, creed, color, national origin, sexual orientation, military status, sex, or disability or marital status, or that the patronage or custom thereat of any person of or purporting to be of any particular race, creed, color, national origin, sexual orientation, military status, sex or marital status, or having a disability is unwelcome, objectionable or not acceptable, desired or solicited.

N.Y. Exec. Law § 296 (McKinney 2016). Accordingly, Sepper argues that "a requirement that businesses disclose their religious objections to serving same-sex couples facilitates the material goals of the law at the price of the equal dignity and citizenship of gays." Sepper, "Gays in the Moralized Marketplace," 158.

8. Koppelman, "Gay Rights," 627–628.
9. As Singer notes, "The baseline idea that most businesses have no duties to the public is a distinctly post–Civil War idea characteristic of the period of classical legal thought, a period that did not come into its own until the 1880s." Joseph W. Singer, "No Right to Exclude: Public Accommodations and Private Property," *Northwestern University Law Review* 90 (1996): 1300.

   Decisions adopting the equal access rule include Uston v. Resorts International Hotel, Inc., 445 A.2d 370, 375 (N.J. 1982) ("[W]hen property owners open their premises to the general public in the pursuit of their own property interests, they have no right to exclude people unreasonably. On the contrary, they have a duty not to act in an arbitrary or discriminatory manner toward persons who come on their premises. That duty applies not only to common carriers . . . but to all property owners who open their premises to the public."); Leach v. Drummond Medical Group, Inc., 144 Cal. App. 3d 362, 372 (Cal. Ct. App. 1983) (recognizing a common-law duty on all enterprises that hold themselves out as providing goods or services to the public "to serve all members of the public on reasonable terms without discrimination" and recognizing codification of that rule in California's Unruh Civil Rights Act); Harder v. Auberge Des Fougeres, Inc., 338 N.Y.S.2d 356, 358 (N.Y. App. Div. 1972) (rejecting the distinction between inns and "other places of public accommodation" under the common law and concluding, "In our view, a restaurant proprietor should be under the same duty as an innkeeper to receive all patrons who present themselves 'in a fit condition', unless reasonable cause exists for a refusal to do so"); Beech Grove Investment Company v. Civil Rights Commission, 157 N.W.2d 213, 226–227 (Mich. 1968) (discussing the common-law right against "unjust discrimination").
10. Singer, "No Right to Exclude," 1299, 1354. For an example, see Miss. Code Ann. § 97-23-17 ("right to choose customers").
11. For an overview of state public accommodations provisions, see Elizabeth Sepper, "The Role of Religion in State Public Accommodations Laws," *Saint Louis University Law Journal* 60 (forthcoming): 8–13. For example, New York's antidiscrimination law provides, in part, "It shall be an unlawful discriminatory practice for any person, being the owner, lessee, proprietor, manager, superintendent, agent or employee of any place of public accommodation, resort or amusement, because of the race, creed, color, national origin, sexual orientation, military status, sex, or disability or marital status of any person, directly or indirectly, to refuse, withhold from or deny to such person any of the accommodations, advantages, facilities or privileges thereof." N.Y. Exec. Law § 296 (McKinney). See also N.Y. Civil Rights Law § 40 (McKinney)

("All persons within the jurisdiction of this state shall be entitled to the full and equal accommodations, advantages, facilities and privileges of any places of public accommodations, resort or amusement, subject only to the conditions and limitations established by law and applicable alike to all persons.").

New York's human rights law defines "public accommodations" like this:

> The term "place of public accommodation, resort or amusement" shall include, except as hereinafter specified, all places included in the meaning of such terms as: inns, taverns, road houses, hotels, motels, whether conducted for the entertainment of transient guests or for the accommodation of those seeking health, recreation or rest, or restaurants, or eating houses, or any place where food is sold for consumption on the premises; buffets, saloons, barrooms, or any store, park or enclosure where spirituous or malt liquors are sold; ice cream parlors, confectionaries, soda fountains, and all stores where ice cream, ice and fruit preparations or their derivatives, or where beverages of any kind are retailed for consumption on the premises; wholesale and retail stores and establishments dealing with goods or services of any kind, dispensaries, clinics, hospitals, bath-houses, swimming pools, laundries and all other cleaning establishments, barber shops, beauty parlors, theatres, motion picture houses, airdromes, roof gardens, music halls, race courses, skating rinks, amusement and recreation parks, trailer camps, resort camps, fairs, bowling alleys, golf courses, gymnasiums, shooting galleries, billiard and pool parlors; garages, all public conveyances operated on land or water or in the air, as well as the stations and terminals thereof; travel or tour advisory services, agencies or bureaus; public halls and public elevators of buildings and structures occupied by two or more tenants, or by the owner and one or more tenants.

N.Y. Executive Law § 292(9) (McKinney). See also N.Y. Civil Rights Law § 40 (McKinney) (offering a similar definition, but explicitly including educational institutions and libraries).

12. Sepper describes these factors, as they appear in state laws, in "The Role of Religion," 16. For one example, see N.Y. City Administrative Code § 8-102 (1986) ("The term 'place or provider of public accommodation' . . . shall not include any club which proves that it is in its nature distinctly private. A club shall not be considered in its nature distinctly private if it has more than four hundred members, provides regular meal service and regularly receives payment for dues, fees, use of space, facilities, services, meals or beverages directly or indirectly from or on behalf of nonmembers for the furtherance of trade or business.").

13. Roberts v. U.S. Jaycees, 468 U.S. 609, 616 (1984). The court held that the group was expressive, but that the state's interests in prohibiting discrimination were compelling. Justice Sandra Day O'Connor concurred separately on the ground that the group was commercial in nature, not expressive, and therefore did not trigger First Amendment protection.
14. For details, see Nelson Tebbe, "Religion and Marriage Equality Statutes," *Harvard Law and Policy Review* 9 (2015): 47n101. Sepper surveys public accommodations statutes and finds that "public accommodations laws typically do not offer religious exemptions." Sepper, "The Role of Religion," 6.
15. Utah S.B. 296 (2015), codified in various provisions of the Utah Code, including § 34A-5-106 (employment) and § 57-21-5 (housing). The provision excluding religious organizations from the definition of employer is codified at § 34A-5-102(i)(ii). See also Sepper, "The Role of Religion," 28, which notes, "In the realm of state public accommodations laws, Utah stands out for its absolute exemption of religious organizations."
16. Bernstein v. Ocean Grove Camp Meeting Association, No. PN34XB-03008 (N.J. Dept. of Law and Pub. Safety, Dec. 29, 2008).
17. Benjamin Woodard, "Loyola University Limits Campus Weddings in Wake of Same-Sex Marriage Law," DNAinfo Chicago, February 26, 2014, https://www.dnainfo.com/chicago/20140226/rogers-park/loyola-university-limits-campus-weddings-wake-of-same-sex-marriage-law.
18. Haw. Revised Statutes § 572-12.2 (2013). For other examples, see Tebbe, "Religion and Marriage Equality Statutes," 26n3, 48–49. Mississippi H.B. 1523 (2016), § 4 ("The state government shall not take any discriminatory action against a religious organization wholly or partially on the basis that such organization: . . . provides or declines to provide services, accommodations, facilities, goods or privileges for a purpose related to the solemnization, formation, celebration or recognition of any marriage, based upon or in a manner consistent with a sincerely held religious belief or moral conviction . . . ."); ibid., § 5 (defining "discriminatory action" to include any government action to "[i]mpose, levy or assess a monetary fine, fee, penalty or injunction"). An exception is Delaware's marriage equality law, which contains no such exemption (for religious organizations that decline to provide services and the like for marriages because of theological objections). An Act to Amend Title 13 of the Delaware Code Relating to Domestic Relations to Provide for Same–Gender Civil Marriage and to Convert Existing Civil Unions to Civil Marriages, 79 Del. Laws ch. 19 (2013).
19. Patricia Wen, "Catholic Charities Stuns State, Ends Adoptions," *Boston Globe*, March 11, 2006; Ira C. Lupu and Robert W. Tuttle, "Same-Sex Family Equality and Religious Freedom," *Northwestern Journal of Law and Social Policy* 5 (2010): 302.

20. Cynthia Godsoe, "Adopting the Gay Family," *Tulane Law Review* 90 (2015): 318.
21. Nevertheless, adoption agencies may well be subject to public accommodations requirements, and some states already have found them to be covered by those civil rights laws. For a case holding that a gay couple could state a claim under a public accommodations law when a private adoption agency refused to serve unmarried couples, at a time when California excluded them from civil marriage, see Butler v. Adoption Media LLC, 486 F. Supp. 2d 1022, 1056–1057 (N.D. Cal. 2007). On pharmacy licensing, see Stormans v. Wiesman, 794 F.3d 1064, 1071–1072 (9th Cir. 2015), cert. denied, 136 S.Ct. 2433 (2016).
22. Mary Moore, "Accreditation Board Gives Gordon College a Year to Review Policy on Homosexuality," *Boston Business Journal*, September 25, 2014, http://www.bizjournals.com/boston/news/2014/09/25/accreditation-board-gives-gordon-college-a-year-to.html?ana=twt&page=all&r=full. A similar issue has arisen in Canada, where a bar association refused to accredit a religious law school because of its policy banning intimate sexual conduct outside of marriage, including all intimate relations between same-sex partners. The Supreme Court of British Columbia ruled for the school on religious freedom grounds, among other points. Trinity Western University v. The Law Society of British Columbia, 2015 BCSC 2326, para. 152 (Can. B.C.). The decision has been appealed.
23. Conn. Gen. Stat. Ann. § 46b-35b (2009) ("Nothing in public act 09-13 shall be deemed or construed to affect the manner in which a religious organization may provide adoption, foster care or social services if such religious organization does not receive state or federal funds for that specific program or purpose."). Mich. Comp. Laws Ann. § 400.5a (2015) ("[T]he department shall not take an adverse action against a child placing agency on the basis that the child placing agency has declined or will decline to provide services that conflict with, or provide services under circumstances that conflict with, the child placing agency's sincerely held religious beliefs contained in a written policy, statement of faith, or other document adhered to by the child placing agency."); John Riley, "Michigan Gov. Snyder Signs Bills Allowing Adoption Agencies to Discriminate: Conscience Clause–Style Law Allows Placement Agencies to Refuse Prospective Parents Based on Religious Objections," Metroweekly, June 11, 2015.
24. R.I. Gen. Laws Ann. § 15-3-6.1(c)(2) (2013). For a detailed analysis of these state provisions, see Tebbe, "Religion and Marriage Equality Statutes," 49–52.
25. Burwell v. Hobby Lobby Stores, Inc., 134 S.Ct. 2751 (2014). See for instance EEOC v. R.G. & G.R. Funeral Homes, Inc., __ F. Supp. 3d __, 2016 WL

4396083 (E.D. Mich. 2016) (ruling for a business under RFRA in an employment discrimination case).

26. Douglas Laycock, "The Campaign against Religious Liberty," in *The Rise of Corporate Religious Liberty:* Hobby Lobby *and the New Law of Religion in America,* ed. Micah Schwartzman, Chad Flanders, and Zöe Robinson (New York: Oxford University Press, 2016), 249; Shruti Chaganti, "Why the Religious Freedom Restoration Act Provides a Defense in Suits by Private Plaintiffs," *Virginia Law Review* 99 (2013): 343–344.
27. Monica Davey, Campbell Robertson, and Richard Pérez-Peña, "Indiana and Arkansas Revise Rights Bills, Seeking to Remove Divisive Parts," *New York Times,* April 2, 2015. However, the Indiana amendment exempted religious organizations, meaning they could continue to exclude LGBT people, even in localities with civil rights laws that protected against discrimination on the basis of sexual orientation and gender identity. Ind. Code § 34-13-9-7.5 (2015).
28. Miss. H.B. 1523 (2016), § 4(5).
29. Newman v. Piggie Park Enterprises, Inc., 390 U.S. 400, 402 n.5 (1968). But see Rasmussen v. Glass, 498 N.W.2d 508 (Minn. Ct. App. 1993) (ruling for a deli owner who refused to deliver to an abortion clinic on the ground that he was not discriminating on the basis of "creed" or any other protected category, and then finding that even if he could be deemed to have been discriminating on the basis of creed, the state religious freedom provision would protect him). For an argument that state public accommodations laws provide only limited religion exemptions, see Sepper, "The Role of Religion," 25. She also notes that these laws do not exempt small businesses. Ibid., 12.

    It could be argued that RFRAs and other state protections for religious freedom alter this analysis, because they provide some degree of latitude for religious groups that seek relief from public accommodations laws. So they might be thought to suggest that religion exemptions from antidiscrimination laws are somewhat wider than suggested here. Yet, again, religion exemptions from civil rights laws have not generally been granted, even under RFRAs, when the discrimination at issue involves race, gender, ethnicity, or marital status. Various rationales have been given for this, including that the state has a compelling interest in prohibiting discrimination on these grounds among commercial businesses and other public providers. So comparison to civil rights laws would not generally lead to exemptions when it comes to the ability to exclude LGBT people, either. Compare ibid., 43–45 (arguing that state public accommodations laws serve equality interests that would be hard to satisfy with narrower means).
30. For a general background, see Douglas NeJaime and Reva Siegel, "Conscience Wars: Complicity-Based Conscience Claims in Religion and Politics,"

Yale Law Journal 124 (2015): 2534–2542; see also Elizabeth Sepper, "Doctoring Discrimination in the Same-Sex Marriage Debates," *Indiana Law Journal* 89 (2014): 722–723.

31. For an example of a proposal that uses health care exemptions as a model, see Robin Fretwell Wilson, "Matters of Conscience: Lessons for Same-Sex Marriage from the Healthcare Context," in *Same-Sex Marriage and Religious Liberty: Emerging Conflicts*, ed. Douglas Laycock, Anthony R. Picarello Jr., and Robin Fretwell Wilson (Lanham, MD: Rowman and Littlefield, 2008), 77, 80–81.
32. As Riley, "Michigan Gov. Snyder Signs Bills," notes, this type of law is "often known as 'conscience clause' legislation." The provision can be found at Mich. Comp. Laws Ann. 400.5a (2015).
33. NeJaime and Siegel, "Conscience Wars," 2537 (noting that the Church Amendment "was concerned with those professionals directly involved in the procedures" and citing legislative history). For a description of the more recent clauses that are more expansive, see ibid., 2538–2541.
34. Sepper, "Doctoring Discrimination," 743, argues that religion exemptions in the context of same-sex marriage are distinct from conscience clauses in the medical context, mostly because "virtually all objections to marriage founder on the requirements of causal and proximate responsibility for the act of marriage."
35. 42 U.S.C. § 3603(b).
36. See, for instance, Stormans v. Wiesman, 794 F.3d 1064, 1071 (9th Cir. 2015) (upholding Washington state rules that "permit a religiously objecting individual pharmacist to deny delivery, so long as another pharmacist working for the pharmacy provides timely delivery," but "unless an enumerated exemption applies, the rules require a pharmacy to deliver all prescription medications, even if the owner of the pharmacy has a religious objection").
37. As Douglas NeJaime notes, "the analogy to conscience clauses reflects a lack of appreciation for the temporal difference between an abortion, which occurs at a specific moment in time, and a marriage, which endures over a significant period of time." Douglas NeJaime, "Marriage Inequality: Same-Sex Relationships, Religious Exemptions, and the Production of Sexual Orientation Discrimination," *California Law Review* 100 (2012): 1229.
38. An exception is the Mississippi FADA, which applies not only to "religious beliefs" that oppose same-sex marriage and gender fluidity but also to equivalent "moral convictions." Mississippi H.B. 1523 (2016). On the other hand, it is hard to gainsay that almost all familiar objections to marriage equality have been grounded in religion, as a matter of actual social practice in the United States at this historical moment.

39. Kent Greenawalt, "Religious Toleration and Claims of Conscience," *Journal of Law and Politics* 28 (2013): 113. On interracial marriages, see Loving v. Virginia, 388 U.S. 1, 7 (1967) (noting Virginia's rationales for prohibiting interracial marriage, including prevention of "corruption of blood" and creation of a "mongrel breed of citizens"); ibid., 3 (quoting the trial court as saying "Almighty God created the races white, black, yellow, malay and red. . . . The fact that he separated the races shows that he did not intend for the races to mix."). For a fuller treatment of the race analogy, see James M. Oleske Jr., "The Evolution of Accommodation: Comparing the Unequal Treatment of Religious Objections to Interracial and Same-Sex Marriages," *Harvard Civil Rights-Civil Liberties Law Review* 50 (2015): 117–118.
40. Koppelman, "Gay Rights, Religious Accommodations," 624; Sepper, "Gays in the Moralized Marketplace," 156. ("Ensuring a competitive market . . . hardly suffices to address the material harm of discrimination, let alone its long-accepted dignitary and expressive goals. Religious refusals raise economic costs for same-sex couples, most obviously in the form of search costs.")
41. Sepper, "Gays in the Moralized Marketplace," 158.
42. This could either be because they do not fall within the definition of public accommodations, because they are "bona fide" or "distinctly" private entities, or because they are protected by the First Amendment regardless of whether they qualify as public accommodations.
43. Erik Eckholm, "Boy Scouts End Ban on Gay Leaders, over Protests by Mormon Church," *New York Times,* July 27, 2015, A1.
44. Obergefell v. Hodges, 135 S.Ct. 2584, 2602 (2015).
45. Micah Schwartzman, Nelson Tebbe, and Robert Tuttle, "Indiana's New Law Allows Discrimination. That Was the Point," *Slate,* March 30, 2015, http://www.slate.com/blogs/outward/2015/03/30/gov_mike_pence_s_characterization_of_indiana_s_new_religion_law_is_wrong.html, addresses the original version of the Indiana RFRA, before it was amended. Although it did not accommodate religious actors specifically, North Carolina's 2016 law not only declined to extend state civil rights law to LGBT people, but it went further and prohibited local governments from providing that protection themselves. That law relegated LGBT citizens to a different status from other minority groups in violation of equal protection. North Carolina H.B. 2 (2016), § 2.1(c) (overriding local laws prohibiting discrimination in employment), § 3.3(b) (public accommodations). The Supreme Court struck down a similar prohibition in Romer v. Evans, 517 U.S. 620 (1996). One court ruled that a state exemption enclosed religious opposition to LGBT conduct. See Barber v. Bryant, __ F. Supp. 3d __, 2016 WL 3562647 (S.D. Miss. 2016).

46. Mich. Comp. Laws Ann. § 400.5a (2015); Miss. H.B. 1523, § 4(2) (2016). In another example, governor Sam Brownback of Kansas issued an executive order providing that the state would not take action "against a religious organization, including those providing social services" on the ground that it "declines . . . to provide services, accommodations, facilities, goods, or privileges for a purpose related to the . . . recognition of any marriage, based upon or consistent with a sincerely held religious belief or moral conviction." Kan. Exec. Order No. 15-05 (2015). That order seems to have been taken to protect religious adoption agencies (though it also covers the religious facilities just discussed). As Bryan Lowry reports, "Among other things, the order is intended to protect religious organizations that provide adoption services for the state from having to place children with gay couples if that conflicts with their beliefs." Bryan Lowry, "Gov. Sam Brownback Issues Executive Order on Religious Liberty after Same-Sex Marriage Ruling," *Wichita Eagle,* July 7, 2015, http://www.kansas.com/news/politics-government/article26668207.html. Though the order is largely symbolic, since Kansas does not prohibit discrimination on the basis of LGBT status in its public accommodations law, it could have some practical effect in cities and towns that extend greater protection.
47. Laurie Goodstein, "Bishops Say Rules on Gay Parents Limit Freedom of Religion," *New York Times,* December 29, 2011, A16; Cheryl Corley, "Illinois, Catholic Charities at Odds over Gay Adoptions," National Public Radio, July 5, 2011, http://www.npr.org/2011/07/05/137622143/illinois-catholic-agencies-at-odds-over-gay-adoptions.
48. Conn. Gen. Stat. Ann. § 46b–35b (2009).
49. Wooley v. Maynard, 430 U.S. 705 (1977); West Virginia State Board of Education v. Barnette, 319 U.S. 624, 642 (1943).
50. Elane Photography, LLC v. Willock, 309 P. 3d 53, 65 (N.M. 2013). The New Mexico Supreme Court noted that "unlike the laws at issue in *Wooley* and *Barnette,* the [civil rights law] does not require Elane Photography to recite or display any message. It does not even require Elane Photography to take photographs. The [law] only mandates that if Elane Photography operates a business as a public accommodation, it cannot discriminate against potential clients based on their sexual orientation." Ibid., 64.
51. David French, "Gordon College Keeps Its Faith and Its Accreditation," *National Review,* May 1, 2015, http://www.nationalreview.com/article/417788/gordon-college-keeps-its-faith-and-its-accreditation-david-french; "Joint Statement by Gordon College and the Commission on Institutions of Higher Education, NEASC," April 25, 2015, https://cihe.neasc.org/sites/cihe.neasc.org/files/downloads/Public_Statement/Joint_Statement_by_Gordon_College_and_CIHE.pdf.

8. Employment Discrimination

1. Adam Ragusea, "Gay Teacher Files Sex Discrimination Claim against Georgia School," National Public Radio, July 9, 2014, http://www.npr.org/2014/07/09/329235789/gay-teacher-files-sex-discrimination-claim-against-georgia-school; Barrett v. Fontbonne Academy, No. CIV2014-751 (Mass. Sup. Ct. Dec. 16, 2015); EEOC v. R.G. & G.R. Funeral Homes, Inc., __ F. Supp. 3d __, 2016 WL 4396083 (E.D. Mich. 2016). See also Alanna Durkin, "Virginia Man Says He Was Fired from Job at Catholic Assisted Living Home Because He's Gay," *US News and World Report,* October 13, 2015, http://www.usnews.com/news/us/articles/2015/10/13/man-claims-he-lost-job-at-catholic-home-because-hes-gay.
2. That theory depends on the ministerial exception to employment law, embraced by the court in Hosanna-Tabor Evangelical Lutheran Church and School v. Equal Employment Opportunity Commission, 132 S.Ct. 694 (2012). For background, see Carol Pogash, "Morals Clause in Catholic Schools Roils Bay Area: Archbishop Cordileone of San Francisco Defends Changes," *New York Times,* February 26, 2015, A13.
3. The contraception mandate cases are Burwell v. Hobby Lobby Stores, Inc., 134 S.Ct. 2751 (2014), and Zubik v. Burwell, 136 S.Ct. 1557 (2016). Herx's case was decided in Herx v. Diocese of Ft. Wayne–South Bend Inc., 48 F. Supp.3d 1168 (N.D. Ind. 2014), appeal dismissed, 772 F.3d 1085 (7th Cir. 2014). Helen M. Alvare questions the court's determination that Herx was fired because of sex, rather than on the basis of religion. Helen M. Alvare, "The Opposite of Anarchy and the Transmission of Faith: The Freedom to Teach after *Smith, Hosanna Tabor, Obergefell* and the Ascendancy of Sexual Expressionism," http://ssrn.com/abstract=2668677. For background on Coty Richardson's case, see Carrie Johnson, "Professor Sues Religious University after Allegedly Being Fired for Getting Pregnant," National Public Radio, August 12, 2015, http://www.npr.org/2015/08/12/431959372/professor-sues-religious-university-after-allegedly-being-fired-for-getting-preg.
4. Jon Herskovitz and Jim Forsyth, "Two Houston Daycare Workers File Complaint after Firing over Transgender Child," Reuters, November 11, 2015, http://www.reuters.com/article/2015/11/11/us-texas-transgender-idUSKCN0T02KP20151111#gLTI6qWbkvKd4OwS.97.
5. Howard Friedman, "Suit Alleges Discrimination against Same-Sex Spouse Constitutes 'Sex' Discrimination," http://religionclause.blogspot.com/2015/07/suit-alleges-discrimination-against.html. Obergefell v. Hodges, 135 S.Ct. 2584 (2015).

6. For reasons like these, Andrew Koppelman does not think government should exempt religious employers from antidiscrimination laws that protect same-sex spouses, even though he argues that it should show magnanimity in public accommodations law in the wake of marriage equality. Andrew Koppelman, "Gay Rights, Religious Accommodations, and the Purposes of Antidiscrimination Law," *Southern California Law Review* 88 (2015): 628 (arguing for magnanimity in public accommodations law), 620 (arguing that employers should still be required to adhere to civil rights laws).
7. Arkansas Act 975 of 2015. Notably, however, Walmart itself opposed an earlier, broader version of the Arkansas RFRA. Jeff M. Sellers, "Deliver Us from Wal-Mart?," *Christianity Today,* April 22, 2005, http://www.christianitytoday.com/ct/2005/may/17.40.html. The Mississippi employment provision can be found at Mississippi H.B. 1523 (2016), § 4(b).
8. Hosanna-Tabor v. EEOC; Christopher L. Eisgruber and Lawrence G. Sager, *Religious Freedom and the Constitution* (Cambridge, MA: Harvard University Press, 2007), 57.
9. 42 U.S.C. § 2000e-1.
10. Courts have generally not allowed religious employers to take adverse employment actions against employees who are members of protected classes, even where the actions are religiously motivated. U.S. Department of Justice, Memorandum for William P. Marshall, Deputy Counsel to the President, October 12, 2000, 31 (explaining that "the courts uniformly have concluded that Section 702 does not exempt qualifying employers from title VII's prohibitions on any form of discrimination other than preference for coreligionists, even where such discrimination is religiously motivated," and citing cases).
11. 42 U.S.C. § 2000e(b); N.Y. Exec. Law § 292(5).
12. For example, the solicitor general of the United States argued that the freedom of expressive association doctrine of *Dale* could (and should have) governed the ministerial exemption case. Hosanna-Tabor v. EEOC, 706 (describing the solicitor general's argument).
13. Notably, Shiffrin did not address employment in her seminal article on expressive association. See Seana Shiffrin, "What Is Really Wrong with Compelled Association?," *Northwestern Law Review* 99 (2005): 865–866.
14. Eisgruber and Sager, *Religious Freedom and the Constitution,* 124.
15. Douglas Laycock reports that although the Utah compromise was supported by both sides initially, some Utah Republicans are having second thoughts. He is quoted in Thomas Reese, "Bishops' Strategy Endangering Religious Freedom," *National Catholic Reporter Online,* July 16, 2015, http://ncronline.org/blogs/faith-and-justice/bishops-strategy-endangering-religious-freedom. See also Douglas Laycock, "The Campaign against Religious Lib-

erty," in *The Rise of Corporate Religious Liberty:* Hobby Lobby *and the New Law of Religion in America,* ed. Micah Schwartzman, Chad Flanders, and Zöe Robinson (New York: Oxford University Press, 2016), 252.

16. Utah Code Ann. § 34A-5-102(i)(ii) (2015).
17. It is true that the amendments made some changes to the definition of employer. Whereas the law had excluded only "religious organizations" from the category of employer before 2015, it now also excludes "a religious corporation sole, a religious association, a religious society, a religious educational institution, or a religious leader." Utah Code Ann. § 34A-5-102 (2015). Most likely, however, that change was simply meant to clarify that the term *religious organization* had always meant to cover not only houses of worship but a wider range of religious entities. So Utah's 2015 amendments are best seen as mostly just adding LGBT employees to the preexisting list of protected workers.
18. Nelson Tebbe, Richard Schragger, and Micah Schwartzman, "Utah 'Compromise' to Protect LGBT Citizens from Discrimination Is No Model for the Nation," *Slate,* March 18, 2015, http://www.slate.com/blogs/outward/2015/03/18/gay_rights_the_utah_compromise_is_no_model_for_the_nation.html.
19. Baldwin v. Foxx, EEOC DOC 0120133080, 2015 WL 4397641 (EEOC July 15, 2015). But see Hively v. Ivy Tech Comm. Coll., __ F. 3d __, 2016 WL 4039703, *3–*7 (7th Cir. 2016) (disagreeing with *Baldwin v. Foxx*). For the academic arguments, see for instance Nan D. Hunter, "The Sex Discrimination Argument in Gay Rights Cases," *Journal of Law and Policy* 9 (2001): 397–416, and sources cited there.
20. 42 U.S.C.A. § 2000e-2 (Title VII); 29 U.S.C.A. § 633a (ADEA); 42 U.S.C.A. § 12112 (ADA). For one version of ENDA, see H.R. 3017, 111th Cong. (2009).
21. S. 815, 113th Cong. (2013–2014). The proposed exemption would have read, "This Act shall not apply to a corporation, association, educational institution or institution of learning, or society that is exempt from the religious discrimination provisions of title VII of the Civil Rights Act of 1964 (42 U.S.C. 2000e et seq.) pursuant to section 702(a) or 703(e)(2) of such Act (42 U.S.C. 2000e-1(a), 2000e-2(e)(2)) (referred to in this section as a 'religious employer')."
22. 42 U.S.C. § 2000e-1.
23. Christi Parsons and Michael A. Memoli, "Obama to Sign Executive Order Curbing Discrimination against Gays," *Los Angeles Times,* June 16, 2014, http://www.latimes.com/nation/la-na-obama-discrimination-20140617-story.html.
24. Julie Hirschfeld Davis and Erik Eckholm, "Faith Groups Seek Exclusion from Bias Rule," *New York Times,* July 8, 2014, A1; National Association of Evangelicals, "Letter to the President on Executive Order on Hiring Decisions," http://nae.net/letter-to-the-president-on-executive-order-on-hiring-decisions/.

25. Davis and Eckholm, "Faith Groups Seek Exclusion from Bias Rule"; "Religious Groups' Letter to Obama," http://www.nytimes.com/interactive/2014/07/09/us/politics/enda-document.html?smid=pl-share&_r=0.
26. Antonia Blumburg, "Faith Leaders Sign Letter Opposing Religious Exemption for LGBT Hiring Non-Discrimination," *Huffington Post,* July 8, 2014, http://www.huffingtonpost.com/2014/07/08/religious-exemption-lgbt-discrimination_n_5567510.html; Letter to president Barack Obama, July 14, 2014, https://web.law.columbia.edu/sites/default/files/microsites/gender-sexuality/executive_order_letter_final_0.pdf (citing E.O. 11246, available at http://www.dol.gov/ofccp/regs/statutes/eo11246.htm). The letter from legal scholars included the present author.
27. They wrote:

> ENDA's discriminatory [religion] provision, unprecedented in federal laws prohibiting employment discrimination, could provide religiously affiliated organizations—including hospitals, nursing homes and universities—a blank check to engage in workplace discrimination against LGBT people. The provision essentially says that anti-LGBT discrimination is different—more acceptable and legitimate—than discrimination against individuals based on their race or sex. . . . All of this is unacceptable.
>
> The Supreme Court's decision in Hobby Lobby has made it all the more important that we not accept this inappropriate provision. Because opponents of LGBT equality are already misreading that decision as having broadly endorsed rights to discriminate against others, we cannot accept a bill that sanctions discrimination and declares that discrimination against LGBT people is more acceptable than other kinds of discrimination.

"Joint Statement on Withdrawal of Support for ENDA and Call for Equal Workplace Protections for LGBT People," July 8, 2014, http://www.nclrights.org/press-room/press-release/joint-statement-on-withdrawal-of-support-for-enda-and-call-for-equal-workplace-protections-for-lgbt-people/.
28. Exec. Order, 2014 WL 3569065 (July 21, 2014); Equality Act, H.R. 3185 (July 23, 2015), Section 1107.
29. Section 702 applies to any "religious corporation, association, educational institution, or society." 42 U.S.C.A. § 2000e-1. Courts use a multifactor test to determine whether an institution is religious or educational for purposes of the statutory exemption. Fike v. United Methodist Children's Home of Virginia, Inc., 547 F. Supp. 286, 290 (E.D. Va. 1982), aff'd, 709 F.2d 284 (4th Cir. 1983) (finding that the United Methodist Children's Home is a

secular organization, and "Methodist only in name"); Saeemodarae v. Mercy Health Services, 456 F. Supp. 2d 1021, 1036 (N.D. Iowa 2006) (explaining that "in determining whether an institution or entity is entitled to assert the exemption, the court must 'look at all the facts,' and in making this inquiry, it is appropriate to consider and weigh the religious and secular characteristics of the institution" and going on to hold that a hospital was religious in its operations, under the facts, and could invoke Section 702) (internal quotation marks and alterations omitted); Hall v. Baptist Memorial Health Care Corporation, 215 F.3d 618, 624 (6th Cir. 2000) (reiterating the multifactor test for whether the organization qualifies as a religious or educational institution for purposes of the statute); Equal Employment Opportunity Commission v. Townley Engineering and Manufacturing Co., 859 F.2d 610, 618 (9th Cir. 1988) ("Like the *Fike* court, we shall not attempt to outline section 702's precise scope. The effort to do so would fail. Rather, each case must turn on its own facts. All significant religious and secular characteristics must be weighed to determine whether the corporation's purpose and character are primarily religious. Only when that is the case will the corporation be able to avail itself of the exemption."). For a trenchant discussion, see Carlos A. Ball, *The First Amendment and LGBT Rights: A Contentious History* (Cambridge, MA: Harvard University Press, forthcoming), 228–229.

30. "Indeed, we conclude that sexual orientation is inherently a 'sex-based consideration,' and an allegation of discrimination based on sexual orientation is necessarily an allegation of sex discrimination under Title VII." Baldwin v. Foxx, 6.
31. Carol Pogash, "Morals Clause in Catholic Schools Roils Bay Area: Archbishop Cordileone of San Francisco Defends Changes," *New York Times*, February 26, 2015.
32. California Labor Code Section 96(k) (contemplating "[c]laims for loss of wages as the result of demotion, suspension, or discharge from employment for lawful conduct occurring during nonworking hours away from the employer's premises"); State of California, Department of Industrial Relations, "Filing a Retaliation/Discrimination Complaint," http://www.dir.ca.gov/dlse/FilingARetaliationComplaint1.pdf.
33. Hosanna-Tabor Evangelical Lutheran Church and School v. EEOC, 707.
34. But compare Fratello v. Roman Catholic Archdiocese of New York, __ F. Supp. 3d __, 2016 WL 1249609, *12 (S.D.N.Y. 2016) (holding that the principal of a parochial school was a minister for purposes of the ministerial exception, even though she was not ordained, and could not have been ordained under church law, because she helped to convey the teachings of the church, inter alia).

35. For a description of the solicitor general's argument, see Burwell v. Hobby Lobby Stores, Inc., 2783.
36. Pogash, "Morals Clause in Catholic Schools Roils Bay Area" (reporting that the archbishop knew that not all the teachers at local parochial schools were Catholic).
37. Shiffrin, "What Is Really Wrong with Compelled Association?," 880–888.
38. But see Fratello v. Roman Catholic Archdiocese of New York, *12 (holding that the principal of a parochial school was a minister and therefore could not bring a claim of sex discrimination, even though sex selectivity for non-clergy is not demanded by the church's theology).
39. 42 U.S.C.A. § 2000e-1.
40. The first provision reads, "An employee may express the employee's religious or moral beliefs and commitments in the workplace in a reasonable, non-disruptive, and non-harassing way on equal terms with similar types of expression of beliefs or commitments allowed by the employer in the workplace, unless the expression is in direct conflict with the essential business-related interests of the employer." Utah Code Ann. § 34A-5-112(1). This was passed as part of S.B. 296, the statute that extended workplace protections to LGBT people but exempted virtually all religious employers.
41. Utah Code Ann. § 34A-5-112(2).

9. Public Officials

1. Robin Fretwell Wilson noted in 2010, "Not a single state has shielded the government employee at the front line of same-sex marriage." Robin Fretwell Wilson, "Insubstantial Burdens: The Case for Government Employee Exemptions to Same-Sex Marriage Laws," *Northwestern Journal of Law and Social Policy* 5 (2010): 320. One arguable exception was Delaware, which exempted marriage celebrants without specifically excluding government officials. Del. Code Ann. tit. 13, § 106 (2013). For an example of an argument for a religion exemption for public officials, see the letter from Edward McGlynn Gaffney Jr., Valparaiso University School of Law, to Senator Rosalyn H. Baker, Hawaii State Capitol, October 17, 2013, http://mirrorofjustice.blogs.com/files/hawaii-special-session-letter-10-17-13-1.pdf, 4–5. Under that approach, clerks would be able to refuse to issue licenses to couples for religious reasons only if another clerk were available, but judges would have an absolute right to exempt themselves.
2. David French, "Justice Kennedy: The Rule of Law Requires You to Enforce the Laws I Made Up," *National Review*, October 30, 2015, http://www

.nationalreview.com/corner/426372/justice-kennedy-rule-law-requires-you-enforce-laws-i-made-david-french.

3. Ken Paxton, Attorney General of Texas, Opinion No. KP-0025, June 28, 2105, https://www.texasattorneygeneral.gov/opinions/opinions/51paxton/op/2015/kp0025.pdf.
4. "Governor McCrory Defends Constitution," press release, May 28, 2015, http://governor.nc.gov/press-release/governor-mccrory-defends-constitution.
5. N.C. Gen. Stat. § 51-5.5 (2015); Taylor Wofford, "Magistrates in a North Carolina County Refuse to Perform Same-Sex Marriages," *Newsweek,* September 10, 2015, http://www.newsweek.com/northcarolinajudgesrecusesamesexmarriage-370971. For a critical evaluation of the law, see Lydia E. Lavelle, "WWJD? What the Judiciary Should Do about North Carolina's Magistrate Recusal Bill," http://ssrn.com/abstract=2640692. The North Carolina law is now the subject of a court challenge. See Ansley v. Warren, 2016 WL 3647979 (W.D.N.C. 2016).
6. Utah S.B. 297 (2015), codified in pertinent part at Utah Code Ann. § 17-20-4 (2015).
7. Miller v. Davis, Civil Action No. 15-44-DLB, 2015 WL 9461520 (E.D.K.Y. Sept. 11, 2015) (order denying Davis's emergency motion for injunction pending appeal); Ky. Rev. Stat. Ann. § 402.100 (2016).
8. Bil Browning, "Fired Antigay Clerk in Indiana Sues for 'Religious Discrimination,'" *Advocate,* July 24, 2015, http://www.advocate.com/marriage-equality/2015/07/24/indiana-clerk-fired-refusing-same-sex-marriage-license-claims-biblical-; Complaint, Summers v. Whitis, Case 4:15-cv-00093-RLY-DML (S.D. Ind. filed July 17, 2015); Camila Domonoske, "Alabama Chief Justice Orders Judges to Enforce Ban on Same-Sex Marriage," National Public Radio, January 6, 2016, http://www.npr.org/sections/thetwo-way/2016/01/06/462161670/alabama-chief-justice-orders-state-to-enforce-ban-on-same-sex-marriage.
9. Model Code of Judicial Conduct Rule 2.07 comment [1] (2011). For general analyses of judicial obligations to serve impartially, drawing on rules of judicial conduct, oaths of office, the Constitution, and other sources, see Memorandum from Pamela Weaver Best, North Carolina Administrative Office of the Courts, to Superior Court Judges, Chief District Court Judges, District Court Judges, Clerks of Superior Court, and Magistrates, October 14, 2014, http://equalitync.org/assets/AOC_instructions_to_Magistrates.pdf; and Public Rights/Private Conscience Project, Columbia Law School, "Memorandum: Proposed Conscience or Religion-Based Exemption for Public Officials Authorized to Solemnize Marriages," June 30, 2015, http://web

.law.columbia.edu/sites/default/files/microsites/gender-sexuality/marriage_exemptions_memo_june_30.pdf.

For examples of state statutes embodying the norm of impartiality, see Arizona Code of Judicial Conduct, Rule 2.2 Comment 2 (2016) ("Although each judge comes to the bench with a unique background and personal philosophy, a judge must interpret and apply the law without regard to whether the judge approves or disapproves of the law in question."); Ibid., Rule 2.3 (A)–(B) ("A judge shall not, in the performance of judicial duties, by words or conduct manifest bias or prejudice, or engage in harassment, including . . . based upon . . . sexual orientation."); N.C. Gen. Stat. Ann. § 11-7 (2016) ("I, ____, do solemnly and sincerely swear that I will support the Constitution of the United States; that I will be faithful and bear true allegiance to the State of North Carolina, and to the constitutional powers and authorities which are or may be established for the government thereof; and that I will endeavor to support, maintain and defend the Constitution of said State, not inconsistent with the Constitution of the United States, to the best of my knowledge and ability; so help me God.").

10. Memorandum from Pamela Weaver Best: "If a valid marriage license issued . . . is presented, it is a statutory duty of the magistrate to conduct the marriage between the persons named in the license in the same manner as the magistrate would conduct any other marriage. A failure to do so would be a violation of the U.S. Constitution under the federal ruling, and would constitute a violation of the oath and a failure to perform a duty of the office." See also Katie Zezima, "Obey Same-Sex Marriage Law, Officials Told," *New York Times,* April 26, 2004, http://nyti.ms/2d6lo1Q, which reports on how officials were directed to follow the same-sex marriage ruling in Massachusetts regardless of any objections.
11. Rodriguez v. City of Chicago, 156 F.3d 771, 779 (7th Cir. 1998) (Posner, J., concurring).
12. Endres v. Indiana State Police, 349 F.3d 922, 927 (7th Cir. 2003) (Easterbrook, J.).
13. Miller v. Davis, 2015 WL 9461520; Lyle Denniston, "Same-Sex Marriage Issue Returns to the Court (Further Updated)," *SCOTUSblog,* August 29, 2015, http://www.scotusblog.com/2015/08/same-sex-marriage-issue-returning-to-the-court/; Inquiry Concerning a Judge: Honorable Vance D. Day, Oregon Commission on Judicial Fitness and Disability, Case No. 12-139 and 14-86, January 25, 2016, 39–40.
14. Nelson Tebbe, "Government Nonendorsement," *Minnesota Law Review* 98 (2013): 648–712.
15. Mississippi H.B. 1523, Section 4 (2016). Wilson similarly argues that the Mississippi law's "impede or delay" provision "doesn't address dignitary harms."

Robin Fretwell Wilson, "Laws Should Show 'Malice toward None, Charity to All,'" *Hattiesburg American*, April 6, 2016, http://www.hattiesburgamerican.com/story/opinion/2016/04/07/laws-reflect-malice-toward-none-charity-toward/82735254/.

16. For an explanation of the undue hardship standard and how it works with the constitutional principle against shifting harm to third parties, see Chapter 3.
17. Oklahoma proposed one version of a law that would leave marriage to private actors. Cheryl Wetzstein, "Oklahoma Bill Abolishes State Marriage Licenses," *Washington Times*, March 11, 2015, http://www.washingtontimes.com/news/2015/mar/11/oklahoma-bill-abolishes-state-marriage-licenses/?page=all.
18. Palmer v. Thompson, 403 U.S. 217 (1971).
19. For discussion of the hypothetical white supremacist town, see Chapter 6.
20. Here I differ from Wilson, "Insubstantial Burdens," 359n258, which posits that expressive harm cannot disable an accommodation if it does not affect the direct experience of a couple seeking to marry:

> A harder question is whether a same-sex couple, who experiences no delay but is in fact aware that a shift was made from one clerk to another, will nonetheless suffer a hardship. I think this is a difficult question. But I do believe that it goes too far to say that a member of the public is harmed simply because an exemption is granted to religious objectors if the member of the public has no personal experience of a shift being made from one government employee to another. In such a case, it is the idea of an exemption that gives offense, not the experience of it. If the abstract idea of a legislative exemption for one person can by itself invalidate an exemption, there would be no room for exemptions in any context.

On the one hand, it is possible for "the idea of an exemption" to communicate opposition to same-sex marriage in violation of a constitutional right, as argued here. On the other hand, not every accommodation sends that kind of message—some simply communicate government regard for the intense and sincere convictions of religious officials.

21. Caroline A. Placey, "Of Judicial Bypass Procedures, Moral Recusal, and Protected Political Speech: Throwing Pregnant Minors under the Campaign Bus," *Emory Law Journal* 56 (2006): 693–740. Placey points out that recusals in the abortion context can be particularly concerning where the judges are elected and may be seeking to bolster their chances of reelection in conservative areas. Ibid., 711, 715. The statute accommodating government

employees with moral or religious objections to the death penalty is 18 U.S.C. § 3597(b).

22. 42 U.S.C. 2000e(f) ("the term 'employee' shall not include any person elected to public office in any State or political subdivision of any State by the qualified voters thereof, or any person chosen by such officer to be on such officer's personal staff, or an appointee on the policy making level or an immediate adviser with respect to the exercise of the constitutional or legal powers of the office"). The Supreme Court held that parallel language in the Age Discrimination in Employment Act meant that Title VII did not apply to appointed state judges. Gregory v. Ashcroft, 501 U.S. 452 (1991). For the accommodation of officials with moral or religious objections to the death penalty, see 18 U.S.C. § 3597(b).
23. Wilson, "Insubstantial Burdens," 322, 328.
24. Davis v. Miller, No. 15-5880, 2015 WL 10692640 (6th Cir. August 26, 2015), 2–3 (order denying Davis's motion for a stay of the preliminary injunction).
25. Ibid., 2.
26. Miller v. Davis, Civil Action No. 15-44-DLB (E.D.K.Y. Sept. 8, 2015), 1–2 (order releasing Davis from custody).
27. Plaintiffs' Motion to Enforce Sept. 3 and Sept. 8 Orders, Exhibit 1, Miller v. Davis (E.D.K.Y. Sept. 21, 2015) (Civil Action No. 15-44-DLB), https://www.aclu.org/sites/default/files/field_document/motion_to_enforce_final_filed.pdf (reproducing Davis's altered marriage license form); Ky. Rev. Stat. Ann. § 402.100 (2016).
28. As Michael Muskal notes, "According to Douglas Laycock, a law professor at the University of Virginia who specializes in religious freedom cases, the Kentucky case seems clear given federal laws on when a person can claim a religious exemption. 'Her office cannot claim a religious exemption,' Laycock said. 'The county has no religion so it is not allowed to claim an exemption. She doesn't have to do it personally, but someone in her office has to issue the license.'" Michael Muskal, "She Did It Again: Kentucky Clerk Refuses Marriage License to Gay Couple," *Los Angeles Times,* September 2, 2015, http://www.latimes.com/nation/la-na-same-sex-marriage-kentucky-20150902-story.html.
29. The Sixth Circuit similarly distinguished between Davis's role as a government official and Davis's status as a private citizen, writing, "The injunction operates not against Davis personally, but against the holder of her office of Rowan County Clerk. In light of the binding holding of *Obergefell,* it cannot be defensibly argued that the holder of the Rowan County Clerk's office, apart from who personally occupies that office, may decline to act in conformity with the United States Constitution as interpreted by a dispositive

holding of the United States Supreme Court. There is thus little or no likelihood that the Clerk in her official capacity will prevail on appeal." Miller v. Davis (6th Cir. Aug. 26, 2015), 2.

It is possible to imagine situations in which a religion accommodation of one marriage official does impose undue hardship on other officials. In North Carolina, for example, magistrates are the only state officials authorized to perform marriages. See Lavelle, "WWJD?," 1 (citing N.C. Gen. Stat. § 7A-292[9]). Moreover, many counties have a limited number of magistrates, only one of whom is on duty at any given time. See the letter from Judge John W. Smith, director of the North Carolina Office of the Administration of Courts, to Senator Phil Berger, November 5, 2014, http://www.nccourts.org/News/Documents/Marriage/Response-on-Marriages-by-Magistrates.pdf, 2, noting that "forty-nine counties now staffed with only three or four magistrates" and that "[a]ll of these counties have only one magistrate on duty for extended periods of time." Already, all magistrates in one county have ceased performing marriages, requiring officials from other counties to travel there. Wofford, "Magistrates in a North Carolina County." Under these circumstances, it may well be the case that accommodating one magistrate shifts undue hardship onto others, and onto the court system.

30. Plaintiffs' Motion to Enforce, 8; Marty Lederman, "Responses of Kim Davis and Judge Bunning to Plaintiffs' Motion to Require Issuance of Unadulterated Marriage Licenses," October 15, 2015, *Balkinization*, http://balkin.blogspot.com/2015/10/responses-of-kim-davis-and-judge.html.
31. For an analysis of the possibility of accommodating Davis, and the accompanying danger of "demeaning" same-sex couples, see Ruth Colker, "Religious Accommodations for County Clerks?," *Ohio State Law Journal Furthermore* 76 (2015): 99–100. On death penalty cases, see John H. Garvey and Amy V. Coney, "Catholic Judges in Capital Cases," *Marquette Law Review* 81 (1998), stating that the legal system "allows (indeed it requires) the recusal of judges whose convictions keep them from doing their job" (ibid., 303), and that "the moral impossibility of enforcing capital punishment . . . is a sufficient reason for recusal under federal law" (ibid., 306). Garvey and Coney believe that recusal is appropriate (and religiously mandated) when the judge has a conscience-based objection to enforcing the death penalty, even in situations where bias is not relevant, such as where the judge simply must enforce the ruling of the jury (ibid., 334). They make some connection to the possibility of discretionary rulings by the judge, which might open the door to bias, but their analysis seems to hold even in the absence of such opportunities for judgment (ibid., 335). See also Michelle Jones, "Religiously Devout Judges: A Decision-Making Framework for Judicial Disqualification," *Indiana Law Journal* 88 (2013):

1089–1112. The two federal recusal statutes are 28 U.S.C. § 455 and 28 U.S.C. § 144.

32. 42 U.S.C. 2000e(f).
33. Endres v. Indiana State Police, 349 F.3d 922, 925 (7th Cir. 2003) (Easterbrook, J.).
34. Rodriguez v. City of Chicago, 156 F.3d 771, 779 (7th Cir. 1998) (Posner, J. concurring).
35. Rodriguez was offered a patrol area that did not include abortion clinics. Rodriguez v. City of Chicago, 775–776. Endres was offered an accommodation that was not acceptable to him, and the appellate court treated his case as one in which no accommodation had been offered, ruling ultimately that any accommodation would have been unreasonable given the circumstances. Wilson, "Insubstantial Burdens," 351 (citing Endres v. Indiana State Police, 1092).
36. See, for instance, Haring v. Blumenthal, 471 F. Supp. 1172, 1183 (D.D.C. 1979) (explaining that an IRS official opposed to abortion could be exempted from handling persons or organizations involved in terminating pregnancies without undermining public confidence).
37. The few officials who have objected to presiding at interracial marriages have not been accommodated. See, for example, Shawn Nottingham, "Louisiana Justice Who Refused Interracial Marriage Resigns," CNN, November 3, 2009, http://perma.cc/WX9H-N53Y; and Wilson, "Insubstantial Burdens," 335n80 (citing a 1994 news report that officials in Chester County, Tennessee, had refused to marry an interracial couple). One state marriage equality law did seem to exempt government officials with religion objections to any sort of marriage, although the provision was not without ambiguity. Del. Code Ann. tit. 13, § 106 (2013): "[N]othing in this section shall be construed to require any person, including any clergyperson or minister of any religion, authorized to solemnize a marriage to solemnize any marriage, and no such authorized person who fails or refuses for any reason to solemnize a marriage shall be subject to any fine or other penalty for such failure or refusal."

10. Government Subsidy and Support

1. The decision upholding school vouchers, a form of indirect aid that flows through parents, is Zelman v. Simmons-Harris, 536 U.S. 639 (2002). The cases allowing forms of direct aid to schools, overruling older decisions, are Mitchell v. Helms, 530 U.S. 793, 835 (2000) (plurality opinion, overruling Meek v. Pittenger, 421 U.S. 349 [1975] and Wolman v. Walter, 433 U.S. 229 [1977]); Agostini v. Felton, 521 U.S. 203 (1997) (overruling Aguilar v. Felton, 473 U.S. 402 [1985], and partially overruling School District of Grand Rapids

v. Ball, 473 U.S. 373 [1985]). On FBOs, see Hein v. Freedom from Religion Foundation, 551 U.S. 587 (2007) (turning away an Establishment Clause challenge on standing grounds). On local development programs, see American Atheists, Inc. v. City of Detroit Downtown Development Authority, 567 F.3d 278 (6th Cir. 2009). Justice O'Connor, writing the controlling opinion in *Mitchell*, reiterated the ban on cash aid, citing concerns that the aid could be diverted to core religious uses. Mitchell v. Helms, 890, 891n12 (O'Connor, J., concurring in the judgment). Her ruling is still binding law.

2. Nelson Tebbe, "Excluding Religion," *University of Pennsylvania Law Review* 156 (2008): 1263–1339. The pending Supreme Court case presents the question of whether a state can deny funding for playgrounds to religious schools, even where the denial is not required by the federal Establishment Clause. Trinity Lutheran Church of Columbia v. Pauley, 788 F.3d 779 (8th Cir. 2015), cert. granted, 2016 WL 205949 (2016). Because it concerns direct cash aid, it could have bearing on the continued validity of Justice O'Connor's rule against that form of support.
3. Bob Jones University v. United States, 461 U.S. 574 (1983).
4. For example, soon after Roe v. Wade, 410 U.S. 113 (1973), the state of Connecticut denied Medicaid coverage for all first-trimester abortions except those that were medically necessary. Connecticut Welfare Department, Public Assistance Program Manual, Vol. 3, c. III, s 275 (1975). And in 1976 Congress passed the first Hyde Amendment, which prohibited the use of any federal funds appropriated under the Medicaid program from supporting abortions. Congress regularly passed such provisions thereafter. Harris v. McRae, 448 U.S. 297, 302–303 (1980) (recounting this legislative history).
5. Transcript of oral argument, Obergefell v. Hodges, 135 S.Ct. 2584 (2015), 38.
6. Obergefell v. Hodges, 2626 (Roberts, C. J., dissenting).
7. See, for instance, Mark Oppenheimer, "Now's the Time to End Tax Exemptions for Religious Institutions," *Time*, June 28, 2015, http://time.com/3939143/nows-the-time-to-end-tax-exemptions-for-religious-institutions/.
8. John Inazu, for example, has argued that although the decision may have made sense in the context of its particular moment in the civil rights struggle, its outcome could not be supported today. His argument, in essence, is that government should not be able to use its significant leverage over funding to flatten out pluralism among private groups, including religious organizations. John D. Inazu, *Confident Pluralism: Surviving and Thriving through Deep Difference* (Chicago: University of Chicago Press, 2016), 74–80. See also Richard Epstein, *The Classical Liberal Constitution* (Cambridge, MA: Harvard University Press, 2014), 469–470.
9. Douglas Laycock makes this point, noting that "*Bob Jones* has not been extended beyond race in the thirty years since it was decided, and it is

politically unimaginable that an administration of either party in the foreseeable future would extend *Bob Jones* to religious resistance to same-sex marriage. If such an extension ever happens, it will happen only when open resistance to marriage equality has become as rare and disreputable as open resistance to racial equality is today." Douglas Laycock, "The Campaign against Religious Liberty," in *The Rise of Corporate Religious Liberty:* Hobby Lobby *and the New Law of Religion in America,* ed. Micah Schwartzman, Chad Flanders, and Zöe Robinson (New York: Oxford University Press, 2016), 244–245. Laurie Goodstein and Adam Liptak quote Ira Lupu: "'*Bob Jones* has never been extended to any context other than race.' . . . That includes sex discrimination, [Lupu] said, to say nothing of sexual-orientation discrimination. Loss of tax exemptions on that last ground, Mr. Lupu said, 'would never happen until the religiously affiliated schools still doing that were complete outliers.'" Laurie Goodstein and Adam Liptak, "Schools Fear Gay Marriage Ruling Could End Tax Exemptions," *New York Times,* June 24, 2015, A13.

10. Laycock puts it this way: "[R]eligious conservatives are understandably not reassured by such political predictions [that government denials of tax-exempt status will be limited to organizations that discriminate on the basis of race]; public opinion on these issues has already moved astonishingly far at astonishing speed. And we have to assume that one of the Solicitor General's clients—some federal agency—insisted that he not give any such conciliatory answer." Laycock, "The Campaign against Religious Liberty," 245. Goodstein and Liptak, "Gay Marriage Ruling," quote Richard Garnett: "'Although many people insist that this will not happen . . . they tend to rely on political predictions—which are probably accurate, in the short term—and not on in-principle arguments or distinctions.'" They also cite the letter from colleges.

11. For one version of the federal FADA, see H.R. 2802, 114th Congress, June 17, 2015, https://www.congress.gov/114/bills/hr2802/BILLS-114hr2802ih.pdf; Senator Mike Lee, "Religious Freedom Bill," letter to the editor, *New York Times,* September 22, 2015, http://www.nytimes.com/2015/09/22/opinion/religious-freedom-bill.html?_r=0 (citing the solicitor general's remarks as a motivation for FADA). The first FADA to be enacted into law is Mississippi H.B. 1523 (2016).

    Three prominent academics wrote an op-ed piece in support of the federal FADA's core aims, but they argued that the bill should be limited to religious nonprofits. They said it goes too far in protecting government employees, regardless of their duties, and business corporations, whatever their structure and size. But they proposed that the bill should continue to protect religious universities and social service organizations against defunding because of opposition to same-sex marriage. Richard W. Garnett,

John D. Inazu, and Michael W. McConnell, "How to Protect Endangered Religious Groups You Admire," *Christianity Today,* August 4, 2015, http://www.christianitytoday.com/ct/2015/august-web-only/how-to-protect-endangered-religious-groups-you-admire.html?start=1.

12. Jack Healy, "To Keep Free of Federal Reins, Wyoming Catholic College Rejects Student Aid," *New York Times,* April 11, 2015, A14.
13. See, for instance, the statutes upheld in Maher v. Roe, 432 U.S. 464 (1977); Harris v. McRae, 448 U.S. 297 (1980); and Rust v. Sullivan, 500 U.S. 173 (1991).
14. Maher v. Roe; Harris v. McRae; and Rust v. Sullivan. See also Planned Parenthood v. Casey, 505 U.S. 833, 878 (1992).
15. Recall, for instance, the decision from the civil rights era, Palmer v. Thompson, 403 U.S. 217 (1971). There the city of Jackson, Mississippi, faced a court order to desegregate its public swimming pools, which had not been open to racial minorities. Rather than comply, the city closed all of its public swimming pools, which it was not required to offer in the first place. The Supreme Court upheld that decision. Whether its ruling was correct, given that the city's motive in closing the pools appeared to be discriminatory, remains a question. Regardless, it is bedrock constitutional law that the city could not operate swimming pools in a discriminatory fashion, even though it need not provide them at all.
16. Locke v. Davey, 540 U.S. 712, 721 (2004).
17. Ibid., 726 (Scalia, J., dissenting) ("[T]he minimum requirement of neutrality [toward religion] is that a law not discriminate on its face.").
18. Rosenberger v. Rector and Visitors of the University of Virginia, 515 U.S. 819, 828–831 (1995). It also ruled that providing the funds to religious publications on the same terms as other publications would not violate the Establishment Clause. Ibid., 845–846.
19. Tebbe, "Excluding Religion," 1304–1305. Distinguishing between defunding of religion and viewpoint discrimination also helps to justify *Christian Legal Society v. Martinez,* a decision that has been criticized alongside the Bob Jones University case. There a public law school had a policy that required recognized student groups to accept "all comers" for membership and leadership positions. Under that policy, the school refused to recognize the Christian Legal Society (CLS) because that group excluded members and leaders who could not agree to the group's theological tenets, including a prohibition on same-sex intimate relationships. The school found that the group's policy violated the school's antidiscrimination rules. Without official recognition, the group could not receive student activity funds and certain other benefits, though it could continue to use school meeting rooms and bulletin boards to announce its events. Upholding the school's decision, the court emphasized

that it was withholding support to CLS, not preventing it from meeting. In other words, the government was acting as funder, not regulator, and that left the organization free to operate using its own resources. Moreover, because the school denied support to *all* groups that refused to accept all comers, not just religious ones, it was not discriminating on the basis of viewpoint. Christian Legal Society Chapter of the University of California, Hastings College of the Law v. Martinez, 561 U.S. 661, 672–673 (2010) ("CLS's bylaws, Hastings explained, did not comply with the Nondiscrimination Policy because CLS barred students based on religion and sexual orientation."); ibid., 682, 682n13 (distinguishing between regulation and defunding). There was a factual dispute about whether the school really did require student groups to accept all comers or whether it only prohibited discrimination against certain protected classes of students. The court held CLS to its factual stipulation in a lower court that the school had an all-comers policy. Ibid., 678. So *Christian Legal Society v. Martinez* confirms the ability of officials to deny support for protected activity without infringing constitutional rights.

20. Tebbe, "Excluding Religion," 1327–1331.
21. Ibid.
22. H.R. 2802, 114th Congress (June 17, 2015) (one version of FADA); Letter from Religious Leaders to Senator Mitch McConnell and Speaker John Boehner, June 3, 2015, http://downloads.frc.org/EF/EF15F04.pdf; Kan. Exec. Order 15-05 (2015), "Preservation and Protection of Religious Freedom," https://governor.ks.gov/media-room/executive-orders/2015/07/07/executive-order-15-05; Mississippi H.B. 1523 (2016).
23. As Laycock comments, "If you want to see social conflict, try stripping the tax exemption from every Catholic institution in the United States, every evangelical institution, many Orthodox Jewish institutions—every religious institution in the country that does not perform same-sex weddings or recognize same-sex marriages. Of course that is not going to happen." Laycock, "The Campaign against Religious Liberty," 244.
24. Lawrence G. Sager, *Justice in Plainclothes: A Theory of American Constitutional Practice* (New Haven, CT: Yale University Press, 2004) (explaining and defending underenforcement of certain constitutional rights).
25. Conn. Gen. Stat. Ann. § 46b-35b (2016); Minn. Stat. Ann. § 517.201(b) (2016).
26. Personal Responsibility and Work Opportunity Reconciliation Act of 1996, Pub. L. No. 104-93 § 104, codified at 42 U.S.C. § 604A. For helpful background and a general characterization of the legislation, see Ira C. Lupu and Robert W. Tuttle, "The Faith-Based Initiative and the Constitution," *DePaul Law Review* 55 (2005): 6–7.

27. 42 U.S.C. §§ 5601–5792a (JJDPA); 42 U.S.C. § 3789d(c)(1) (Safe Streets Act) ("No person in any State shall on the ground of . . . religion . . . be subjected to discrimination under or denied employment in connection with any programs or activity funded in whole or in part with funds made available under this chapter."). As Ira C. Lupu and Robert W. Tuttle explain, "Several federal statutes contain broad non-discrimination provisions [that seem to prohibit religious discrimination in hiring]. . . . For example, the Workforce Investment Act—designed to provide employment opportunity as a service benefit itself—prohibits religious discrimination against participants. Similarly, various substance abuse programs administered by the Substance Abuse and Mental Health Administration (SAMHSA) contain non-discrimination provisions which forbid religious selectivity and appear to cover employment practices by providers." Ira C. Lupu and Robert W. Tuttle, *The State of the Law 2008: A Cumulative Report on Legal Developments Affecting Government Partnerships with Faith-Based Organizations*, http://www.rockinst.org/pdf/faith-based_social_services/2008-12-state_of_the_law.pdf, 30.
28. Office of Legal Counsel, "Application of the Religious Freedom Restoration Act to the Award of a Grant Pursuant to the Juvenile Justice and Delinquency Prevention Act," June 29, 2007, https://www.justice.gov/sites/default/files/olc/opinions/attachments/2015/06/01/op-olc-v031-p0162.pdf, 20–23.
29. "Request for Review and Reconsideration of June 29, 2007 Office of Legal Counsel Memorandum Re: RFRA," August 20, 2015, https://www.au.org/files/2015-08-20%20-%20OLC%20Memo%20Letter%20to%20President-FINAL_2.pdf. A variation on this argument is Lupu and Tuttle's contention that loss of federal funding cannot constitute a substantial burden under RFRA. Lupu and Tuttle, *The State of the Law 2008*, 34, 36.
30. "Comments on Interim Final Rule on Unaccompanied Children," February 20, 2015, http://www.usccb.org/about/general-counsel/rulemaking/upload/02-20-15-comments-UM.pdf. The Obama administration promulgated a rule that prohibits FBOs from excluding beneficiaries because of their religion or "refusal to hold a religious belief," but it does not appear to address FBOs that exclude beneficiaries because of the FBOs' religious opposition to beneficiaries' behavior, such as use of contraception. "Federal Agency Final Regulations Implementing Executive Order 13559: Fundamental Principles and Policymaking Criteria for Partnerships with Faith-Based and Other Neighborhood Organizations," *Federal Register* 81 (2016): 19355, 19358.
31. For more on excluding religion in government speech, see Tebbe, "Excluding Religion," 1296–1318.

INDEX